nebraska symposium or
1973
James K. Cole and Richard Dienstbier, Editors

Alan P. Bell

Senior Research Psychologist
Institute for Sex Research, Indiana University

John H. Gagnon

Professor of Sociology
State University of New York at Stony Brook

William Simon

Program Supervisor, Sociology and
Anthropology
Institute for Juvenile Research, Chicago

Henry B. Biller

Associate Professor of Psychology
University of Rhode Island

Alfred B. Heilbrun, Jr.

Professor of Psychology
Emory University

Benjamin G. Rosenberg

Professor of Psychology
Bowling Green State University

Brian Sutton-Smith

Professor of Psychology
Teachers College, Columbia University

John Money

Professor of Medical Psychology and
Associate Professor of Pediatrics
Johns Hopkins University School of Medicine

university of nebraska press
lincoln
1973

Copyright © 1974 by the University of Nebraska Press
International Standard Book Number 0-8032-0615-1 (Clothbound)
International Standard Book Number 0-8032-5621-3 (Paperback)
Library of Congress Catalog Card Number 53–11655
Manufactured in the United States of America

Contents

Introduction

As was the case in the 1972 volume, the current *Nebraska Symposium on Motivation* is devoted to a single common theme, sexuality. Following last year's topic of aggression with this topic might seem suggestive of a psychoanalytic bent on the part of the symposium editors; Freud would certainly have agreed that we had examined two of the most important motivational concepts. Our intent was not, however, to examine sexuality from one or even very few particular theoretical positions, but rather to bring together researchers and theorists representing a variety of approaches to some of the broad areas subsumed under the rubric of sexuality. Altogether, eight contributors participated in the two sessions of the symposium, delivering seven papers. Although they represent several different theoretical approaches and topical areas, some similarity in theme and approach gives a sense of coordination and consistency through the seven papers.

In approach, all authors discuss sexuality at least partially from a developmental perspective. The papers of Professor Henry B. Biller, Professor Alfred B. Heilbrun, Jr., Professor Benjamin G. Rosenberg and Professor Brian Sutton-Smith, and Professor John Money clearly reflect that developmental emphasis, even in their titles. Although it is not as immediately obvious, the papers of Professor Alan P. Bell, Professor John H. Gagnon, and Professor William Simon have a similar developmental perspective, considering adult sexuality as a function of childhood and adolescent experiences.

A common theme present through all the papers is the complexity and diversity of human experience. This theme often finds expression in the idea that although past theorizing and research had searched for simple relationships between obvious, single causal factors and the development of different gender or sexual role behaviors, far greater understanding and prediction is gained from considering the interaction of a number of predictor variables.

This focus on the greater complexity of predictors necessary in the areas of sex and gender reflects, we believe, a major and healthy trend in the whole of psychology—a trend away from simple, single-factor explanations of complex psychological patterns and toward an appreciation of inherent complexities. It is evident from these papers that there can be more order in this "second order" complexity than in the unmanageable complexity of unsystematized observation which originally inspired the search for unitary causes.

The primary theme presented in Professor Alan Bell's paper on homosexuality is implied by his use of the plural noun *homosexualities*, used in his title, "Homosexualities: Their Range and Character." Professor Bell refers to data from a current study by the Institute for Sex Research (the "Kinsey Institute") to point out that the tendency to view homosexuality as a unity phenomenon, or homosexuals as a homogeneous class of people, is grossly misleading. It is apparent that the behavior, relationships, and perceptions of homosexuals vary widely, and more importantly, the experiences that are important include far more than the type or nature of sexual activity alone. As Professor Bell points out, they include "a variety of life styles and interpersonal transactions as well as the potential for both favorable and unfavorable social consequences."

Furthermore, in considering psychological adjustment and behavioral management dimensions, the data suggest greater differences *within* homosexual and heterosexual samples than between them. The individual's developmental experiences, the management of each person's sexuality, and the nature of personal and social adjustments are more important in understanding individuals than the ability to classify an individual as either homosexual or heterosexual. Professor Bell's data presentation, the percentages and statistics, clearly imply vast differences within homosexual samples. Indeed, as Professor Bell states, "Where a person stands on the so-called Kinsey scale is not the most important indicator of where one is sexually." The researcher needs to view human sexuality within the context of the total personality and social characteristics of individuals. Clearly, the homosexual-heterosexual dichotomy alone does not provide us with very much understanding into the reality of individual sexuality.

It is not surprising, therefore, that Professor Bell does not find support for past theories which suggest a unitary, etiological route which leads to a homosexual orientation. Just as there are many homosexualities that can be identified in meaningful ways, there are likely multiple routes into these orientations.

One of the most important characteristics of the data samples which Professor Bell attempts to interpret in this paper is the fact that the homosexual samples he analyzes were not drawn from clinical populations. Although the samples used are not representative of all homosexual populations, efforts were made to ensure a wide variety of life styles and adjustments. Drawn from the San Francisco area, the samples can be compared with other Kinsey Institute samples from Chicago, New York, Amsterdam, and Copenhagen. The importance of these samples is clear when the data are compared to other studies which have attempted to generalize about homosexuality primarily by referring to homosexuals who have been or are in treatment. Although Professor Bell is not the first to make this point (e.g., Schofield, 1965), his paper clearly indicates that homosexuals and heterosexuals in treatment are more like each other than they are like their counterparts not in treatment.

In his paper "Scripts and the coordination of sexual conduct," Professor Gagnon introduces the concept of *scripts*, which he regards as similar to the concepts of *plans* or *schemas*. Scripts are described as highly symbolic, with nonverbal elements in organized sequence, used to project into the future as well as to check on the ongoing present. Thus scripts are coordinators of behavior, but they are separable from concrete behavior and therefore modifiable without concrete experience. Professor Gagnon illustrates the application of sexual scripts by using the model of a first heterosexual encounter for a pair of young people. Making their transition from an intruding public world into a private coital encounter with different and limited scripts, Professor Gagnon's pair move toward both success and failure as they attempt to coordinate their individual scripts.

The application of the script concept is also seen as useful in accounting for the differential labeling of early sensual activity as sexual or nonsexual, and the change in sexual labeling and scripting as the ability of women to experience orgasm changed in the face of historical and cultural variations. The early masturbation fantasy is seen as becoming (in part) the basis for the male's scripting of sexual behavior, a basis that requires certain modifications in later nonmasturbatory sexual encounters. The lesser frequency of female masturbation to orgasm and the more common association of fantasy with romantic rather than sexual themes account in part for the different content of sexual scripts for the female. These different male and female scripts require some coordination in the early petting of teenagers, with the female script becoming modified to include more of a sense of the physical aspects of sexuality. As the scripts change and earlier versions are discarded, the early prototype scripts are easily forgotten, making it easier to adopt a "simple reproductive or drive-based sexual teleology" for the past complexity.

In his paper, Professor William Simon disagrees with the concept of universal man maintaining a basic similarity across social-cultural history, especially as these assumed similarities are applied to sexual patterns. Notions of a simple continuity in sexual patterns are supported by the model of comparative psychology, which leads to a mistaken view of sexual behavior as organized solely around its reproductive functions. Through this limiting approach it is impossible to explain the variety of complex purposes actually served by sexual experience.

Professor Simon explores three areas of sexual experience—the sensual (bodily responses and their meanings), the erotic (the changing images of our personal sexual cultures), and the social (the nonsexual motivational inputs for sexually relevant decisions). Although it is the sensual that has attracted the most attention in research and theory in the past in explaining our sexual behavior, with sexual motivation being seen as representing physiological demand, this characteristic of sexual behavior cannot account for the vast differences in the quantity or quality of sexual behavior between otherwise normal people. The erotic component of human sexuality is the least understood in acquisition and influence, and may become involved with other needs, particularly the power need.

Until the erotic component is understood, our understanding of our sexuality must remain incomplete.

With respect to the social component, Professor Simon suggests that sexuality, usually thought of in "id function" terms, may provide "ego satisfactions" through fulfillment of a variety of complex social needs, and that the quantity and quality of association of sexual functions with social functions differs between the two sexes. These differences in the degree and quality of integration of the sexual and social are illustrated by Professor Simon in the differences between male and female homosexual behavior.

Professor Biller's paper, "Paternal and Sex-Role Factors in Cognitive and Academic Functioning," deals with the issue of the relationship of the father and the child's sex-role development in cognitive and academic functioning. The data suggest that underachieving boys have inadequate relationships with their fathers, and that often such underachievement is related to fathers insecure in their masculinity and to mothers who perceive their husbands and sons as inadequate. Achievement, quality of child-paternal relationships, and absence or presence of fathers are functionally related. High-achieving boys see themselves as closer to and more similar to their fathers, but middle-class children (both boys and girls) are not as handicapped by father absence as are lower-class children. Actually, with middle-class children, higher scores in verbal ability appear more with father absence than with father presence, but father surrogates, male peers, or siblings all help in this higher ability.

The length of time and the age of onset of father absence, and the quality of interactions with the father, are not usually considered in this area of research, nor are nonclinical populations usually studied. When matched groups of children with varying degrees of father interaction are compared, those who get a high degree of interaction with their fathers are clearly superior in achievement test scores. In comparison with father presence or late onset of father absence, early departure of the father has the greatest detrimental effect on the child's cognitive development and on the development of the boy's emerging masculine self-concept. These paternal influences show up even in college-age males, as indicated by personality inventory data.

Different children suffer differentially from father absence. While girls are less affected than boys, black children, particularly boys, seem most adversely affected. It is suggested that among lower-class boys, the absence of the father may leave the child with greater insecurity in gender identity, leading to a greater dependence on peers and a greater rejection of school activities which may appear particularly feminine in the eyes of the lower-class boy.

Professor Biller concludes with some suggestions pertaining to the role of the school in making school work and situations more acceptable and compatible with the gender role needs of the child.

The initial theme of Professor Heilbrun's paper, "Parent Identification and Filial Sex-Role Behavior: The Importance of Biological Context," is that the understanding of human sex-role behavior has been hampered by the oversimplifying theories of the past. He argues, for example, that the biological gender and gender role behavior of parents may or may not coincide. He suggests that imitative learning is the only form of learning systematically related to parental identification, and that the most important form of reinforcement involved is a vicarious reinforcement. He sees the identification process continuing as long as the child has active contact with the parent—probably often to about age 18.

In his research, Professor Heilbrun measures identification from the child's standpoint. His concern is the degree to which the child perceives he has imitated the parent. The major issues of Professor Heilbrun's investigations center upon the differential impact of identification with mothers or fathers who represent typical masculine or feminine qualities as compared with parents with incongruous biological sex and sex-role behavior. Early studies are reviewed which indicate a tendency for poor identification with fathers on the part of male college students with psychiatric problems, although a similar relationship was not found for females. Later data suggest that for males, only identification with a highly masculine father is related to psychological health. For females, though identification with a masculine father is associated with adjustment, identification with masculine mothers is associated with maladjustment. For males, identification with a feminine mother is associated with maladjustment.

The second major issue in Professor Heilbrun's paper deals with the question of the degree to which the meaning of masculinity and femininity depend upon the biological context—the actual sex of the parent. Although the fit or congruity of the biological identity of parent and the parent's sex role influences the son systematically, this is not the case for the daughter. Areas explored include personality traits, sex-role behavior, the level of adjustment, attitudes toward the women's role, and susceptibility to vicarious experience. Professor Heilbrun introduces and evaluates several hypotheses on the reasons for the differential findings between sons and daughters.

In "Family Structure and Sex-Role Variations," Professors Rosenberg and Sutton-Smith discuss data from three major sources —the Berkeley Guidance and Oakland Growth Studies, data incorporated into their book *The Sibling*, and data from a study of 1,000 students at Bowling Green State University. All these data illustrate the importance of the influence of the family structure on the development of gender role. The relationships between roles chosen by the maturing child and early family background are presented to assess whether the emerging roles offer evidence of a counteraction of earlier family influence or a replication of those early roles. When the number of offspring, characteristics of spouse, and various personality and sex-role characteristics of the subjects are examined, trends generally suggest that the dominant tendency is to replicate the original family structure, a replication seen by the authors as seeking an emotional climate similar to that provided by the original family. But the data are complex. For example, knowing only the ordinal position of the individual provides little predictive power, while the interaction of position with sex of siblings, size of family, etc., yields greater predictive power. Emphasizing this complexity, the authors suggest that if a "multisignificant trait" such as sex role is to be understood, it is "inconceivable that it is the product of one causal system or variable."

Finally, the authors find so few even moderately consistent differences between sexes and so much overlap in personality characteristics between the sexes that they suggest that sex-role researchers have been victimized by a greater belief in the consistency and simplicity of sex-role stereotypes than the facts warrant.

Professor Money, in "Prenatal Hormones and Postnatal Socialization in Gender Identity Differentiation," deals with the chain of events leading to the differentiation of gender dimorphic identity, including the genetic message, the development of the gonads, the gonadal hormones, particularly as they influence genital development and brain pathways, and the social-familial influences. Particular attention is paid to the role of the male prenatal hormones in differentiating the male from the female. It is primarily the resulting genital appearance of the child and the identification of the child as boy or girl which have a major impact on the development of gender identification in the child, for vast quantities of behavior toward the child are guided by that initial labeling of its sex. But Professor Money asserts that the androgen hormones also appear to influence the neural pathways which lead to a "tomboyism" syndrome in the genetic female. This syndrome is characterized by dominance assertion, rough-and-tumble play, career orientation of an extra-domestic nature, a delay of entrance into the "romantic age," and possibly more susceptibility to visual erotic imagery. The prenatal component of gender dimorphic behavior resulting from prenatal androgens can be incorporated into later gender identity, since these components do not automatically dictate the totality of gender identity.

Through the presentation of matched pairs of hermaphroditic children with identical diagnoses but where one is raised as a male and the other female, Professor Money illustrates the interaction of the physical and social, and the impact of similar rearing despite the differing genetic and gonadal configurations. The learning of gender identity can result from the direct modeling of the parent (identification) and from the parent playing an appropriate reciprocal or complementary role toward the child (complementation). It is important that the boundaries that define gender-appropriate behavior be clearly demonstrated to the child and that both parents agree on what is masculine and feminine. When these boundaries are indefinite, problems in children's sex identity are encountered, and children may want to change sex.

With adolescence, the activation of the gender identity, already influenced by the pubertal hormones, takes place, though the specific qualities which get activated have already been laid down in the development of the juvenile gender identity. Thus, when sadistic or homosexual trends or those relating to transvestism or transsexualism appear in adolescence, they are not the result of hormonal differences per se. Professor Money discusses the transvestite and transsexual syndromes in this context.

Once again, a substantial portion of the cost for the symposium was provided by the Clinical Psychology Training Grant provided by the National Institute of Mental Health. The University of Nebraska has also continued to support the symposium. The faculty and students associated with the symposium wish to express their gratitude for this support.

JAMES K. COLE
Professor of Psychology

RICHARD DIENSTBIER
Associate Professor of Psychology

Homosexualities: Their Range and Character[1]

ALAN P. BELL

Institute for Sex Research, Indiana University

INTRODUCTION

Probably the outstanding characteristic of most of the research pertaining to the development and management of homosexuality, at least as reported in the literature since 1940, is the tendency to view homosexuality as a unitary phenomenon. Generally defined as "a definite preferential erotic attraction to members of the same sex" (Marmor, 1965), whether or not sexual relations with members of the same sex even occur, homosexuality has been viewed as a condition with but a single parameter, one's standing on the so-called Kinsey Scale. In most studies, the homosexual group is composed of males or females who have been rated (by the subjects themselves or by the experimenters) 6, 5, or 4 on the 7-point scale, indicating that they are more or less exclusively homosexual in their sexual behaviors and interests. When the study includes a control group of heterosexual men or women, this group is presumably made up of those who have received ratings of 0, 1, or 2 on the scale, which denote more or less exclusive heterosexual sexual behaviors and interests. Almost without exception, the researcher will proceed to collapse the categories which indicate subjects' standings on the homosexual-heterosexual continuum and to make comparisons between the dichotomized groups. The contention of this paper is that the failure of researchers to delineate their homosexual and heterosexual samples more precisely, even with regard to the one parameter used as the basis for assigning subjects to a given group,

1. This report is based on research funded by NIMH Grant RO1MH15527.

1

has tended to hide the nature and consequences of psychosexual development. To put it another way, before between-group differences are ever to emerge in ways that are truly enlightening, much more attention must be given to within-group differences than has been true of the past. If homosexuality (or heterosexuality) is to be understood, a more complete assessment of its range and character must be made (Hooker, 1959).

In order to make the kind of assessment I have in mind, special attention must be given to the two types of sampling issues which are basic to research in this and other areas. The first involves *people samples* and the extent to which a study sample includes, even if it does not exactly represent, the broad range of experience which can be found in the larger population of interest. The second issue pertains to what could be termed *item samples*, or the degree to which the measurements we use are not only valid but sufficiently comprehensive. It is the contention of this paper that most investigations of homosexuality have involved serious truncations with respect to both types of samples, and with predictable results. Homosexuality has been too narrowly defined by person samples offering too narrow a range of experience and who, in turn, have been investigated within too narrow a scope of inquiry. The paper will address itself to these issues with reference to some of the methodology employed in a current study of the development and management of human sexuality by the Institute for Sex Research and will include certain findings from that study which indicate the range and variation of homosexual experience as well as the importance of construing that experience more broadly.

People Samples

While it is unrealistic to suppose that in a "homoerotophobic" society such as ours (Churchill, 1967) a representative sample of persons whose sexual behaviors and/or feelings are homosexual could be obtained, this particular sense of the matter should hardly make us content with the fact that most of the samples so far obtained have been composed of people seeking psychological treatment or who have been incarcerated or who are members of homophile organizations. Relatively easy access to such groups has led to sometimes competing and equally erroneous impressions of homosexuality. While it has been pointed out to psychoanalysts frequently enough that it is a mistake to make generalizations about homosexuality on the basis of what they see in the life of a single patient, perhaps social scientists have not been warned sufficiently enough that larger numbers of subjects do little more than compound misimpressions if their findings are based upon an idiosyncratic sample. The importance of the nature of the homosexual sample in determining our view of the developmental or psychological correlates of homosexuality is illustrated by Schofield's findings (Schofield, 1965). Comparisons made between homosexuals and heterosexuals in prison, under psychiatric treatment and not under psychiatric treatment, indicated few differences between homosexuals and heterosexuals within a given group but large differences between homosexuals and heterosexuals across groups. For example, it was found that homosexuals and heterosexuals in treatment were more like each other developmentally and psychologically than they were like their counterparts not in treatment. Even if a majority of homosexuals seek psychiatric treatment, much smaller numbers do so in order to change their sexual orientation, and those who do apparently experience themselves as well as their homosexuality quite differently from those who do not. The even smaller numbers of homosexuals incarcerated for sexual offenses or belonging to homophile organizations make these kinds of samples even less representative of homosexuals in general.

The representativeness of a given sample is, of course, extremely important when one is attempting to estimate the incidence of a particular characteristic in the population. For example, if the interest is in determining the extent to which homosexuals in general display a given psychological characteristic or prefer one sexual technique over another, one would have to demonstrate the degree to which the sample represents homosexuals in general. Since all researchers in this area have failed to obtain such samples, any research which has the estimation of "incidence" as its aim must present its findings with extreme caution. Usually this is not what is done, or when the reader is warned not to generalize findings to the entire population of homosexuals, the words of caution appear more like a ritualistic gesture, a bone tossed in the direction of potential critics who are often more wary of others' findings than they are of their own.

When the primary aim of research is that of viewing relationships between various measures, the representativeness of a given (analytic) sample may be less crucial (Riley, 1963). For example, estimating the degree to which homosexuals are psychologically adjusted (i.e., an "incidence" study) is quite a different matter from estimating the degree to which psychological adjustment is related to various sociosexual life styles. It could be said, of course, that with a different sample, different indices of psychological adjustment might emerge, or that different sociosexual life styles would be represented, and even that relationships between the two measures might change; and yet, if the relationships which appear within a given sample make sense theoretically, the researcher's confidence in such findings can perhaps be more certain than those of the epidemiologist, despite the absence of a representative sample.

Finally, there is another related kind of research which does not rely at all upon representative samples, in which subjects are chosen beforehand or later classified on the basis of a given characteristic and then compared with other subjects who have been similarly chosen. This type of research, for example, can address itself to certain theoretical assumptions regarding homosexuality and go on to explore additional areas that are theoretically relevant. Hooker's work (1957, 1958) is of this kind. She deliberately chose for her homosexual sample those homosexuals who were not in therapy and who gave every evidence of "normal" adjustment, comparing their responses to various projective measures with those of a heterosexual sample chosen on the basis of the same criteria. Her studies did not demonstrate the extent to which homosexuals in general are better or worse adjusted than heterosexuals in general. What they did demonstrate, at least to her satisfaction, was that not all homosexuals are psychologically maladjusted and that, therefore, the theoretical assumption that homosexuality is ipso facto pathological could not be upheld. Williams and Weinberg (1971) did a similar thing. In their exploration of the relationship between "stigmatization" and various social and psychological consequences, they compared homosexuals who had received an honorable discharge from the military with those who had received a less-than-honorable discharge.

Despite the fact that they did not have a representative sample of homosexuals who had served in the military, at the very least they were able to demonstrate that (a) not all homosexuals serving in the military receive a less-than-honorable discharge and (b) not all homosexuals who receive such a discharge and are stigmatized on that account suffer severe social or psychological consequences. The first point has implications for those who assume that a homosexual cannot function satisfactorily in the military. The second finding has important implications for labeling theory. Neither relies upon the representativeness of their particular sample.

Keenly aware of the sampling issues which I have just enumerated, we considered several sampling strategies for the institute's study of the development and management of human sexuality. The first possibility, involving a random sample of 10,000 to 20,000 persons from which both the homosexual and heterosexual samples would be drawn, was rejected because the cost of such an operation was prohibitive. Another, less costly, procedure would have involved generating homosexual and heterosexual "pools" of prospective interviewees through extensive publicity, limiting them to telephone volunteers. This plan was also rejected, in the belief that samples generated in this way would not have included the variety of persons which our study required. Still another plan would have involved recruiting homosexuals and heterosexuals from "equivalent" locales. It was decided not to proceed in this way, inasmuch as homosexuals and heterosexuals drawn from comparable locales are hardly equivalent. For example, the type of homosexual found attending church is not like the typical heterosexual churchgoer. The gay bar has a different place and purpose in the gay community than the neighborhood, or even "singles," bar has in a straight setting.

It was finally decided that we would generate stratified random samples of heterosexuals from the general population of San Francisco and Alameda counties by means of block-sampling techniques. Homosexuals—male and female, black and white—were to be recruited from as many different sources as possible: through public advertising, in public and private bars, steam baths, and other public places, through personal contacts, and by means of various mailing lists which were made available to us. Approximately two dozen recruiters, many of them homosexuals who could function comfortably in the role, were assigned to various locales with which they were familiar and were allowed the amount of time which we believed would be necessary to produce an adequate number of potential subjects. Over one entire summer, 4,639 individuals were recruited as potential respondents.

SAMPLE SOURCES

Public advertising consisted of paid advertising and feature articles in major newspapers, appeals made on radio and television, and strategically placed posters and matchbooks describing our study and the need for volunteers. Approximately 1,000 hours were spent recruiting persons in a total of 82 gay bars and restaurants in the San Francisco Bay Area. Although no bar was visited the same time and day every week, recruiters generally geared their activities to the times when the largest number of people could be informed of the study and recruited as potential respondents. The same was true of the three private bars where recruiting took place. Probably the most covert individuals were obtained by means of personal contacts, at small gatherings in private homes or contacts made on a one-to-one basis by persons who had been interviewed themselves or who, for whatever reason, had a special interest in the study. Using the mailing lists of various homophile organizations, bars, and bookstores, information about the study together with mailback cards were sent to almost 6,000 individuals. Posters and recruitment cards were placed on the premises of eight different steam baths, and eventually recruiting was done face to face in the hallways, steam rooms, and individual cubicles. The 23 homophile organizations in the Bay Area invited our recruiters to their meetings and to other social activities. Although we were accused of being "exploitative" or "establishment" by some of the more radical groups, our field work was supported by the vast majority of the homophile leadership. Probably the most difficult recruiting took place in what we termed "public places": men's rooms, theater lobbies and balconies, parks and beaches, and streets and public squares. Despite the fact that our recruiters made contact with several thousand males in these places, only 137 white males and 24 black males were recruited from these sources.

After much of the recruiting had been done, we determined what percentage of each homosexual sample (the white males, white females, black males, and black females) should come from each of the nine sources. This determination was based upon our estimate of the percentages of homosexuals likely to be found in a given locale and upon the actual number of persons recruited from each source. We also wanted each source to be sufficiently represented so that we could determine the influence of source upon our subsequent data, anticipating the possibility that it might be necessary to hold "source" constant in our multivariate analyses.

After determining the approximate percentage of persons we wanted derived from a given source for a particular sample, we then determined how many persons in a particular sample had been recruited from a given source and how many fell into a particular age and education cell. Interviewees were then selected at random from each of these mini-pools. On this basis, for example, of the 575 white male homosexuals who were eventually interviewed, approximately 20% had been recruited from bars, 14% each from personal contacts, steam baths, and public advertising, and 9% each from private bars, homophile organizations, public places, and mailing lists. Much larger percentages of the white females and the black samples were obtained from personal contacts. No females were obtained from steam baths or public places. While the sample is not representative of homosexuals in general nor even of homosexuals living in the Bay Area, we did make every effort to include persons from even the most difficult sources in order to ensure a variety of life styles and adjustments, all too often lacking in others' research.

Although we have no particular epidemiological interest, we are in a position to compare many of our subjects' responses with those of other institute samples interviewed in Chicago, New York, Amsterdam, and Copenhagen, thus increasing our confidence in estimating various incidences of homosexual experience on the part of those homosexuals most accessible to research of this kind. More important than the degree to which our sample may represent such a population is that it enables us to look at the relationship between homosexuality and a wide range of psychological processes and social characteristics, the next issue to which I would direct your attention.

An important question involves how homosexuality is to be defined, how broadly it should be construed, and what sexual, social, or psychological parameters it should include. Gagnon and Simon (1967), in reviewing the research that has been done in this area, quite correctly observe that homosexuality cannot be summed up by specifically sexual variables, that the erotic aspects of homosexuals' lives are but one, and perhaps the least important, of the reinforcing agents in their lives, and that if more is to be learned about this phenomenon, attention must be given to the social context in which it occurs. Before commenting on the extent to which the homosexual is more than a sexual creature, I would first like to underline the importance of delineating the homosexual's experience of his homosexuality and of sexuality in general more precisely than has been done in the past. I shall list some of the ways in which the homosexual's (or heterosexual's) experience of his sexuality can be delineated and then point out, on the basis of our data, the extent to which homosexuals differ with regard to that experience.

SEXUAL VARIABLES

As I have indicated elsewhere (1972), where a person stands on the so-called Kinsey Scale is probably not the most important indicator of where one is sexually. And if more is to be learned about the development and management of human sexuality, within-group differences with respect to other parameters of the sexual experience must be taken into account before between-group differences (homosexuals versus heterosexuals) on any other dimension can be properly reported. These other sexual parameters include: level of sexual interest (how important is sex vis-à-vis other areas of a person's life?); the conditions under which we become aroused sexually and the secondary feelings associated with that arousal; the extensiveness of sexual experience (how often does sexual activity occur and what is the range of one's sexual repertoire?); the number and type of sexual problems (does guilt or inferiority predominate?); the number of sexual partners; and the nature of our temporal and emotional involvement with them. Further important differentiations which can be made among homosexuals (and in comparable ways among heterosexuals as well) include the amount and kind of

cruising they do, their feelings about and attitudes toward homosexuality in themselves and others, and the extent to which they are
covert. Regardless of a person's sexual orientation, certainly the
conscious and unconscious motivations underlying sexual behavior
are another parameter with regard to which people can be differentiated. And until comparisons made between homosexuals and
heterosexuals include controlling for one or another of these parameters, the exact size or nature of the between-group differences will
never be known. For example, it might be that whatever differences
one finds between homosexuals and heterosexuals with regard to a
certain psychological characteristic will be increased or else "wash
out" completely when the comparisons include controlling for
"sexual inhibition" or "extensiveness of sexual experience."

THE HOMOSEXUAL-HETEROSEXUAL CONTINUUM

In our own study, a person's homosexual-heterosexual classifica-
tion was based on ratings with regard to sexual behavior as well as to
sexual feelings on the so-called Kinsey Scale, on the degree to which
a person considered himself more homosexually than heterosexually
responsive, on the proportion of dreams and masturbatory fantasies
involving sexual encounters with members of the opposite sex, and
on the number and frequency of various homosexual and heterosexual experiences which occurred during the past year. My general
impression is that the white males tended to be more exclusively
homosexual than the white females or either of the black samples.
Among the white samples, 21% of the females and 28% of the males
had never experienced heterosexual arousal; larger percentages of
the black samples had. It seems that a person's standing on the
homosexual-heterosexual continuum, shifts which occur in that
standing over the course of a person's life, the ages at which these
shifts have occurred, as well as the degree to which behavior and
certain sexual feeling states have been incongruent, are crucial
variables in the consideration of psychosexual development. And up
until now, most of the researchers in this area have failed to report
the nature of their samples with respect to these important dimensions. Developmentally and psychologically, it is not unreasonable
to suppose that a person who has been exclusively homosexual

throughout his or her life is quite different from one whose behaviors and feelings have varied. And it goes without saying that the implications of this variable for therapeutic goals and outcomes are enormous (Hatterer, 1970).

Levels of Sexual Interest

Despite persisting notions that homosexuality involves primarily a sexual preoccupation, my impression of the data is that heterosexuals have *higher* levels of sexual interest and that among the homosexual samples the white males have the highest and white females the lowest levels of sexual interest. This latter fact is but further evidence that most people's impressions of homosexuality are based on the white males, whose characteristics cannot be generalized to either females or to blacks. Even among our white males we found differences in the levels of sexual interest. While 40% reported that sex was a very important aspect of their lives, 13% considered sex relatively unimportant. Thirty-seven percent thought quite a bit about sexual things during the course of a day, while 18% hardly did at all.

Sexual Stimuli

When asked what aspects of another person they found attractive or which they desired in a sexual partner, our white male homosexual sample tended to stress the less explicitly sexual stimuli. For example, the largest number (67%) reported that they would be very much attracted by a good-looking male stranger in a social situation, a smaller number (42%) by the naked chest of a male in real life, and even smaller numbers by seeing the buttocks of a male (37%) or male genitals in photos (36%). While the largest number (42%) specified 3 or 4 physical characteristics which they liked in a sexual partner, the number of characteristics specified ranged from none to 19. And again, the nature of those characteristics varied. In descending order of frequency were references made to weight or body frame (42%), a masculine appearance (26%), an athletic-type build (22%), a lack of baldness or a certain color hair (21%), a muscular body (15%), a pleasant face (13%), a tall stature (13%), and a large penis (12%). Less frequently specified preferences were for a lot of body hair on the part of the partner (8%), a lack of body hair (7%), eyes of a certain color (7%), a large scrotum (7%), and youthfulness or a younger age (9%). When asked if there were some special person from the past who possessed the preferred physical characteristics they had mentioned, approximately one-half (51%) could recall such a person, most often a past lover (37%).

SEXUAL REPERTOIRE

Although some homosexuals are locked into sociosexual roles, most simply prefer one technique over another and, depending on the circumstances, will engage in a variety of sexual activities. The largest number of our white male homosexuals preferred performing fellatio on their partners, followed by a slightly smaller number who preferred performing anal intercourse. The vast majority had never engaged in sadomasochistic activity. In addition to differences in technical preferences are the degrees of their sexual activity. For example, 16% of our white males reported that they had engaged in sexual activity of some kind with a partner four or more times a week; the same percentage reported having had sex once a month or less during the past year. I would guess that the range of a person's sexual repertoire as well as the frequency of sexual activity is related to age, the length of the homosexual career, and the extent to which he has been exposed to various sexual techniques and is involved with persons who represent a wide range of sexual life styles. Much would depend upon the extent to which the person has broken through stereotypical roles and behaviors, so often found in the more naive homosexual, and has managed to fashion a more realistic and viable identity.

SEXUAL PROBLEMS

Between 20 and 50% of our white male homosexual sample reported that nine different aspects of their sexual lives were problematic for them. In descending order of frequency, we find that difficulties associated with finding a suitable sexual partner are the most problematic, followed by a lack of frequency, coming too fast, the partner's failure to respond to his sexual requests, maintaining affection for his partner, concerns about his sexual adequacy, maintaining an erection, responding to his partner's sexual requests, and feeling that his sexual needs are exorbitant. In comparison with the white male heterosexuals, not only do we find more homosexuals reporting sexual problems, but also a difference in the nature of those problems. More heterosexuals are concerned about their partner's failure to reach orgasm and about coming too fast, while fewer report difficulties in finding a suitable sexual partner or are concerned with their sexual adequacy. Differences within the homosexual sample or between them and the heterosexual respondents are probably related to differences in the management of their sexuality. In a homoerotophobic culture such as ours which discourages anything more than surreptitious sociosexual encounters between homosexual males, we would expect to find the kinds of differences I have just reported. On the other hand, I would suspect that homosexuals whose sexual lives are lived out in less stressful circumstances, who are enjoying a relatively permanent relationship with a sexual partner, and who are generally relaxed about their homosexuality would report far fewer difficulties than those not in such circumstances.

Sexual Partnerships

Differences between the male homosexual and heterosexual sample, and related to the same issue which I have just commented on, are most apparent when one looks at the number and nature of their sexual partnerships. A modal view of the white male homosexual, based on our findings, would be that of a person reporting 1,000 or more sexual partners throughout his lifetime, most of whom were strangers prior to their sexual meeting and with whom sexual activity occurred only once. Only a few of these partners were persons for whom there was much care or affection, and few were ever seen socially again. During the past year, 28% reported having had more than 50 partners; however, 31% claimed to have had 10 partners or less. A modal view of the white male heterosexual, on the other hand, would be that of a person who reports having had between 5 and 9 partners during his lifetime, only a few of whom were strangers but most of whom were cared about—people with whom sexual activity occurred more than once. While there has been much speculation about those factors responsible for such differences —the dynamics of homosexuality per se which reflect or result in an inability to integrate one's affectional and sexual needs—one must be ever mindful of the different set of social circumstances under which male homosexuals and heterosexuals pursue their sexual interests. One must also be aware of the differences in sexual trans-actions which occur between males as opposed to those between males and females. Female homosexuals present quite a different picture. And I would expect that the degree to which a homosexual community provides more than a gay bar or a public rest room for meetings would have an important bearing on the sociosexual encounters which take place.

Among our white homosexual males 17% reported that having a permanent living arrangement with a sexual partner is the most important thing in life and 20% did not consider it important at all. Nine percent reported never having had a relatively steady relationship (the "affair") with another male, while 57% were currently involved in such a relationship at the time they were interviewed, most of whom were living together with the partner. Only 39% were currently living with a roommate, and of these, two-thirds were having sex with him.

CRUISING

An important variable in this regard, and one in which we find considerable differences between homosexuals, is how often and where they "cruise," a term used to denote going out to look for a sexual partner. The most significant differences are found between the males and the females. Over 80% of the latter reported that they had not cruised at all during the last year, and those who do are apt to seek a prospective sexual partner in more private settings than the males. However, even among the males we find more than one-third reporting that they had gone out looking for a sexual partner once a month or less. Forty-three percent reported cruising once a week or more. In addition to differences in the amount of cruising reported are the locales in which it is done. The greatest number reported having cruised at least once in a gay bar, followed in decreasing order of frequency by steam baths, streets, private parties, parks and beaches, public toilets, and movie theaters. Needless to say, where one cruises has a bearing on the extent to which a sexual encounter is casual and anonymous as well as the kinds of social consequences which may be experienced. There may be an inverse relationship between the extent to which partners make themselves known to each other and the potential for exposure to the public authorities. Other aspects of those settings and circumstances under which sexual partners are pursued include the ease (or lack of it) with which a person can interact socially with others, the extent to which one is involved in the gay community, and, of course, the degree to which a person's homosexuality is covert. For example, it has been found (Humphreys, 1970) that many of those who frequent public toilets for sex are predominantly heterosexual, married males whose homosexual proclivities are unknown to others. Yet another factor which can account for differences between homosexuals with regard to their cruising practices is the age of those involved. An older male may avoid the bar scene altogether, either because he has settled into a relationship with another male or because his age has made him a less desirable commodity than the younger, more attractive male who is apt to frequent the bars. And finally, even the cruising behaviors employed may tell us a great deal about differences between male homosexuals in their psychological and social characteristics. Forty-one percent of our white males reported that they usually waited for the partner to approach them first; 28% reported that they more often made the first approach. And the reasons they give for the way in which they operate are also varied. Some indicate simply that they use a particular cruising technique because it works. Others describe themselves as too shy or passive, concerned about their personal safety, unwilling to take responsibility for what happens, wanting the partner to be more aggressive than they, or wishing to be sure the feeling is mutual.

ACCEPTANCE OF HOMOSEXUALITY

Another important way in which homosexuals differ is in the feelings and attitudes they have toward their own and others' homosexuality. Males tend to view their own homosexuality more negatively than females, but even among males there is a large variation. Twenty-seven percent of our white males tended to view homosexuality as an emotional disorder. Similar percentages tended to regret being homosexual and wished they had been entirely heterosexual from birth. A smaller percentage reported that if there were a magic pill that could make them completely and permanently heterosexual, they would take it. Twenty-nine percent had seriously considered discontinuing their homosexuality at one time or other, and of these, 63% had made at least one serious attempt to stop. Differing views of their homosexuality may be related to the extent to which they have experienced severe social consequences as a result of their homosexual status or behaviors, the degree to which their own personal moral value system departs from parental and various institutional evaluations of sexual behavior, and the degree of their acculturation in the homosexual community. In some persons, negative feelings about their homosexuality may represent phobic reactions to sex in general and/or a more pervasive lack of self-esteem. Needless to say, the extent to which homosexuality is ego-alien to a homosexual will powerfully affect the core feeling state he brings to his sexual encounters.

OVERTNESS AND COVERTNESS

Finally, an important dimension to the management of homosexuality has to do with the extent to which it is overt (or covert). Of some interest in this regard are the differences we found between males and females. More females reported that one or both parents knew about their homosexuality, but *fewer* females reported that their homosexuality was known or suspected by their heterosexual friends, neighbors, employers, or fellow employees. In both groups, mothers were more likely to know than fathers. Probably a variety of psychological and social correlates are to be found with respect to "known-aboutness." There is probably an inverse relationship between the degree to which one's homosexuality is known about and the size of the community in which a homosexual lives (Weinberg & Williams, 1974, in press). A positive relationship would be expected between "knownaboutness" and self-employment or employment in occupations associated with homosexual employees, the extent to which one's homosexuality is not ego-alien, and the degree to which one associates socially with other homosexuals or is apt to have a relatively enduring homosexual partnership. It would certainly be related to the way in which one has managed his homosexuality and whether or not his behaviors have resulted in an arrest or conviction. One's social status would also be expected to have a bearing on whether or not a person remains "in the closet"; lower-status individuals have less to lose if their homosexuality is made known by choice or by accident (Leznoff & Westley, 1956, Weinberg & Williams, 1974, in press). This last dichotomy may be an even more significant variable in differentiating homosexuals than simply the number or kinds of persons who know about their homosexuality. By way of summary, our study has probably delineated the experience and management of homosexuality more precisely than the evidence we find in others' work. Our interest is in developing a typology which includes far more than such simple dichotomies as inserter versus insertee. We are in a position to move beyond the trichotomous motivations for homosexuality posited by Ovesey (1963): homosexuality, dependency, and power. Homosexuality, in our work, is not viewed as narrowly, and the range of motivations which are thought to originate and/or maintain the homosexual experience is considerably broader than what has been conceptualized by him and others. It is our intention to determine the ways in which homosexuality serves a variety of psychological and social needs, to sort out the psychological and social correlates of various experiences of homosexuality, and to trace the origins of these experiences with reference to a variety of developmental variables.

It cannot be stressed too often that there are many different ways of being homosexual and that the experience includes far more than a series of sexual events. At the very least, it includes a variety of life styles and interpersonal transactions as well as the potential for both favorable and unfavorable social consequences. A careful delineation of homosexuality must therefore include a variety of social and psychological dimensions.

PSYCHOLOGICAL ADJUSTMENT

The questionnaire which we designed for our study incorporated, sometimes with modifications, items from others' psychological instruments which tapped a number of psychological dimensions. These include such feeling states as loneliness, depression, boredom, worry, anxiety, well-being, and suspiciousness, as well as level of self-esteem and various psychosomatic complaints. In addition, subjects were given the Dynamic Personality Inventory (Grygier, 1956) to fill out on their own at the conclusion of the interview. Following the general framework of the psychoanalytic approach to the study of personality, the inventory includes 325 items and 33 scales such as orality, anal dependence, narcissism, masculinity, femininity, phallic interests, ego strength, and compulsivity. A good deal of attention was also given to their experience with psychotherapy and to the nature of subjects' past suicidal ideation.

Unlike what the medical model of homosexuality might have predicted, our data reveal much greater differences within the homosexual and heterosexual samples than between them. For example, while 58% of the white male homosexuals had gone to a professional because of what they or others had construed as an emotional problem, 42% had not. Twenty-six percent had never imagined committing suicide; 37% had thought about it but had never considered it seriously; 19% did consider it seriously but never attempted it, while 18% reported that they had actually attempted suicide one or more times. Similar differences are found with regard to their current feeling states. During the year preceding the interview, 37% reported that they often felt on top of the world; 24%, that they rarely or never felt this way; 15%, that they often felt depressed; and 13%, that they never felt depressed. Twenty-eight percent described themselves as very happy, while 17% considered themselves either not too happy or very unhappy.

Although such data may do little to change the views of those who argue that the only valid data are those generated on the psychoanalytic couch (Socarides, 1970), and although even I am impatient with a methodology which does not include a more extensive clinical interview, the very least that can be said is that homosexuals differ from each other in their self-reports quite as much as heterosexuals do and that it may be possible to account for this variation on the basis of their developmental experiences, the management of their sexuality, and/or the nature of their social adjustments.

Social Adjustments

Our data indicate a broad range of social characteristics and adjustments on the part of our homosexual samples. Occupationally we find few differences between the white male homosexual and heterosexual groups. These include more white male homosexuals employed in the field of organization than technology, fewer at the professional and managerial occupational levels, and a smaller percentage employed by government. We do not find large numbers employed in what are thought to be gay occupations. In terms of their religious involvement, we find 50% of the white male homosexuals describing themselves as not at all religious, but 22% as moderately to very religious. More than two-thirds (69%) do not attend church at all, while 18% attend at least once a month. Differences also appear with regard to their political involvement. Most (72%) vote regularly in local elections, and 27% describe themselves as active in politics. The largest number (42%) consider themselves Independent, 36% Democratic, and 17% Republican.

Even greater differences between the white male homosexuals can be found with regard to their social involvement. While 15% say that they spend almost every night at home, 17% go out almost every night. Twenty-three percent claim that more than half their leisure time is spent alone, while 38% spend almost none of their leisure time by themselves.

Homosexuals differ with respect to the number of close friends or acquaintances they have and the proportion of those friends, male or female, who are predominantly homosexual. Some associate only with homosexuals, others with equal numbers of homosexuals and heterosexuals—and in this last group some associate with their homosexual and heterosexual friends on separate occasions, while others report a more integrated friendship structure. Differences in this regard are related to other ways in which homosexuals can be categorized, having to do chiefly with how one copes with one's homosexuality in a predominantly heterosexual culture. Some leave the field entirely, becoming ghettoized occupationally, residentially, and emotionally. Such persons may live in one of the "lavender" ghettoes which can be found in any large urban center, seek employment in various enterprises where most of their fellow workers are known to be homosexual, frequent gay-owned business establishments, and limit their social contacts to those provided by various gay settings. At the other end of the continuum are those who are relatively uninvolved in, if not rejecting of, the gay subculture. How the disparity between the two worlds is experienced and managed would appear to reflect a variety of motivations and to be reflected in a variety of social postures, such as the nature of one's political or religious involvement.

Another more general set of categories which are useful in differentiating homosexuals in the social sphere has to do with the social consequences of their homosexuality. For some, the consequences may be so severely negative that it is possible to view their homosexuality as but one of many masochistic features in their personality. They may be rolled or robbed or arrested repeatedly. They may be fired from their jobs on more than one occasion. This experience of homosexuality may reflect and promote a growing sense of social isolation. At the other end of the continuum will be found perhaps even larger numbers of homosexuals whose experience of homosexuality does not even remotely resemble a masochistic enterprise. They may report that their homosexual, minority status has developed in themselves very useful and important capacities for social criticism, enhanced their creative abilities, or made them more sensitive to the needs of others. Many experience personal growth through a variety of social and sexual contacts. Others report a kind of freedom which they feel is seldom found by heterosexuals. Still others may report that their educational and occupational pursuits have benefited from their experience of homosexuality. Many describe a way of life replete with positive reinforcements quite apart from whatever sexual satisfactions they enjoy.

ETIOLOGIES

Although sociologists tend to emphasize the importance of current social circumstances in the maintenance of homosexuality, and while certain kinds of psychologists, at least, tend to view the maintenance of homosexuality as a reflection of ongoing oedipal issues in a person's life, I suppose I prefer to view homosexuality (like heterosexuality) as all of one piece, and in which temporal distinctions are acknowledged as arbitrary, artificial, and not always useful. We must always remind ourselves of the fact that our data are usually obtained from subjects at a single point in time and that what we choose to call antecedent variables are a function of our subjects' current needs and perceptions. In other words, the difference between reporting that the parents of N number of subjects possessed this or that characteristic and reporting that the parents of N number of subjects were *described* as possessing this or that characteristic must be clearly understood. We may never know the degree to which subjects' perceptions of persons or events in the past are distorted, but this uncertainty is of little consequence as long as it is understood that our data amount to no more than our subjects' current perceptions. This understanding also renders meaningless the debate over whether research conducted in the area of homosexuality should be concerned chiefly with the present or past circumstances of the subjects involved. A detailed description of the past is, in fact, a present circumstance. And whatever perceptions of the past have been filtered by more current life experiences (or vice versa) are quite beside the point.

Since homosexuality is most often viewed in the literature as a relatively undifferentiated (usually pathological) condition, the tendency has been to seek a single set of etiological factors to account for its development. Most, though not all, are thought to involve the original experiences of parents which are interpreted with reference to the psychoanalytic conception of the oedipal conflict. An over-intense relationship with the mother together with an indifferent or hostile relationship with the father is thought by many to be the predominant, if not exclusive, etiological factor in male homosexuality. Some suppose that an opposite set of circumstances accounts for homosexuality in the female. Subsequent homosexual behaviors are then interpreted, often in different ways, as the result of these parental fixations. For example, male homosexual behaviors may be understood as the desire to be loved by the father or sometimes as a reaction formation designed to disguise a fear of or hostility toward all male figures (Bieber, 1965), beginning with the father. Others emphasize an exaggerated fear of the paternal phallic figure which results in an abandonment of females as sexual objects. Still others tend to emphasize the prehomosexual's guilt over his successful competition with an inadequate father for the mother's affections (Bell, 1969).

The mother-son relationship has been interpreted in as many different ways. A mother's dependency upon her relationship with the son may lead the son to avoid whatever contacts with females would disrupt that relationship, out of guilt over abandoning the mother. Some view a male's disinclination to become sexually or emotionally involved with females as reflecting fears of the kind of engulfment which was first experienced with the mother.

Hatterer (1970) lists 15 different etiologies stemming from the maternal relationship, 12 from the paternal relationship, 10 from the nature of the interparental relationship, and 6 which are a function of sibling relationships. He indicates 7 different aspects of the American culture and 5 characteristics of early peer relationships which increase the likelihood of a homosexual commitment. In addition, he gives 10 different motivations for a homosexuality associated with the search for a viable male identity.

Another, more behavioral, emphasis has concerned itself with the nature of a person's sexual conditioning. Early punishments of heterosexual behaviors or an early trauma resulting from a premature introduction to heterosexuality, especially when it has been unwillingly imposed, are thought to provide the original habit of avoidance of the opposite sex. Others, like Kinsey (1948), tend to understand homosexuality primarily as the result of positive reinforcement. They seek evidence of early satisfactions associated with a homosexual outlet as a sufficient condition for the maintenance of homosexual behaviors.

Finally, one sociological perspective on the development of homosexuality stresses the impact of labeling on the formation of a homosexual identity. It traces the experience of being sexually different through the process of being defined by others as sexually different to an outcome which usually involves a more or less exclusive association with others who have been labeled similarly.

A preliminary view of our own data which were gathered with reference to more than one theoretical perspective leads me to suppose that just as there is such a diversity of adult homosexuality (sufficient to speak, instead, of "homosexualities"), so there are multiple routes into this orientation, routes which may well account for differences in the way a particular person experiences and expresses his homosexuality as well as the nature of his psychological makeup and of his social adjustment.

For example, there is a considerable range of experiences and perceptions of parents reported by our white male homosexual sample, sometimes tending in a direction which contradicts previously held assumptions about homosexuals' parental relationships. Twenty-nine percent perceived their mothers as having been extremely involved with them during the time they were growing up, 25% as having been relatively uninvolved. Twenty-four percent described them as extremely overprotective, 21% as more nonprotective. While fathers tended to be viewed as less involved than mothers, 23% viewed their fathers as more involved than detached. Twenty-five percent described their fathers as not at all hostile toward them, and 14% as not at all rejecting. Mothers tended to be viewed as more feminine than masculine and fathers as more masculine than feminine. Only 39% reported that their mothers tended to dominate their fathers. Slightly less than half of the sample (46%) said they were very little or not at all afraid of their fathers; 78% stated that their mothers did not tend to be seductive. Since so many believe that homosexuality inevitably involves an impaired gender identity, often understood as the result of an identification made with a parent of the opposite sex, it is interesting to note that I was able to identify 17 white male subjects who reported that during the time they were growing up they did not feel similar to their mothers, did feel similar to their fathers, did not want to be the kind of person their mother was, but did want to be the kind of person their father was, and who described themselves as more masculine than feminine during childhood and adolescence, enjoyed boys' activities and did not enjoy girls' activities, and never engaged in cross-sex dressing.

While a larger number, 37 of our white male subjects, had an opposite experience which conforms to a widely held view of homosexuality, it is clear that for a large number of our white male subjects there are varying degrees to which their homosexuality may involve an uncertain gender identification. Further evidence of this can be found in our subjects' responses to additional questions related to gender development. Seventy-three percent report having had a close same-sex friend during elementary school; the majority (55%) palled around with a group of boys during that period. Thirty-two percent reported having enjoyed boys' activities; only a minority (37%) ever engaged in cross sex dressing. Nineteen percent had only sisters, 23%, only brothers.

In terms of their social relations during grade school, 38% described themselves as being very much loners, 30% as having felt very much different from their peers. Even if larger numbers of homosexuals than heterosexuals report a greater degree of social isolation during childhood and adolescence, what must be remembered is that large numbers do not. Again, differences between homosexuals become evident in their reports of sexual arousal and activity before, at, and after puberty. The majority (56%) report having had a prepubertal heterosexual experience; 28% report that they have never experienced heterosexual arousal. Thirty-eight percent experienced homosexual arousal by the age of 11, another 38% between the ages of 12 and 14, and 24% at age 15 or later. We find some reporting extensive prepubertal homosexual activity, many describing themselves as exclusively homosexual for as long as they can remember. On the other hand, there are those who begin their homosexual activity at later ages, who have engaged in a great deal of heterosexual experimentation, particularly during adolescence, and whose ratings on the Kinsey Scale, beginning at age 12, show considerable variation into young adulthood.

When we asked our subjects to enumerate the factors *they* thought were responsible for their homosexuality, the majority of the white males did not mention parental influence at all. Of those who did, the largest numbers mentioned an absent or distant father and/or a dominating or suffocating and overprotective mother. Of those who mentioned nonparental factors, 16% thought that their early homosexual experiences were responsible for their becoming homosexual,

15% said that they had simply been born that way, and 10% spoke of factors which resulted in an opposite-sex gender identification. Differences in these perceptions, regardless of their relationship to reality, may prompt or reflect an abiding sense of what one thinks one's homosexuality amounts to and the degree to which a person's perceptions correspond to conventional notions of what homosexuality involves.

SUMMARY

By way of summary, our data appear to indicate that homosexuality involves a large number of widely divergent experiences, developmental, sexual, social, and psychological, and that even after a person has been labeled "homosexual" on the basis of his or her preferred sexual object there is little that can be predicted about the person on the basis of that label. One's experience of homosexuality differs according to one's age, social status, sex, race, and geographical residence. It differs according to the time and culture in which it is expressed. In addition, the homosexual experience must be delineated much more precisely than has been done in the past and on the basis of parameters shared in common with heterosexuals.

Perhaps it is not sufficient even to explore relationships between a much larger number of variables than are found in past investigations or to develop a typology of homosexual experience based upon a variety of commonly held experiences on the part of one type versus another. It may be that an additional differentiation must be made on the basis of what is figure and what is ground for a given homosexual. For example, it is possible that for some homosexuals the most prominent feature of their homosexuality is their attempt to deal with the guilt which they experience over their behaviors; for others it may be the management of the tension they experience between the gay and straight worlds; for still others it might become experienced primarily as a social protest, as the search for a long-lasting relationship, or as an attempt to overcome sexual inhibitions. What is figure for some is ground for others; and for all, what is figure at one point in their lives may become ground at another. Clearly, where one is, homosexually, reflects and is accounted for by a wide range of experiences and motivations, none of which justifies a differentiation between a so-called real versus a pseudo homosexuality (Bergler, 1954). No homosexuality can be considered simply a function of sexual motivations nor of interests or conflicts arising either from the present or the past. Each expresses exactly where a given homosexual is, has been, and wants to go in his life— experiential strands involving discontinuities as well as continuities. And it is this wider view of the matter which, hopefully, will come to characterize whatever research addresses itself to the incredible variety of human sexual experience.

REFERENCES

Bell, A. P. The Scylla and Charybdis of psychosexual development. *Journal of Sex Research*, 1969, **5**, 86–89.

Bell, A. P. Human sexuality—a response. *International Journal of Psychiatry*, 1972, **10**, 99–102.

Bergler, E. Spurious homosexuality. *Psychiatric Quarterly*, 1954, **128**, 68–77.

Bieber, I. Clinical aspects of male homosexuality. In J. Marmor (Ed.), *Sexual inversion: The multiple roots of homosexuality*. New York: Basic Books, 1965.

Churchill, W. *Homosexual behavior among males: A cross-cultural and cross-species investigation*. New York: Hawthorn Books, 1967.

Gagnon, J. H., & Simon, W. The sociological perspective on homosexuality. *Dublin Review*, 1967, **512**, 96–114.

Grygier, T. G. *Dynamic personality inventory*. London: National Foundation for Educational Research, 1956.

Hatterer, L. J. *Changing homosexuality in the male*. New York: McGraw-Hill, 1970.

Hooker, E. The adjustment of the male overt homosexual. *Journal of Projective Techniques*, 1957, **21**, 18–31.

Hooker, E. Male homosexuality in the Rorschach. *Journal of Projective Techniques*, 1958, **22**, 33–54.

Hooker, E. What is a criterion? *Journal of Projective Techniques*, 1959, **23**, 278–281.

Humphreys, R. A. L. *Tearoom trade*. Chicago: Aldine, 1970.

Kinsey, A. C.; Pomeroy, W. B.; & Martin, C. E. *Sexual behavior in the human male*. Philadelphia: W. B. Saunders, 1948.

Leznoff, M., & Westley, W. A. The homosexual community. *Social Problems*, 1956, **3** (4), 257–263.

Marmor, J. (Ed.) *Sexual inversion: The multiple roots of homosexuality*. New York: Basic Books, 1965.

Ovesey, L.; Gaylin, W. M.; & Hendin, H. Psychotherapy of male homosexuality: Psychodynamic formulation. *Archives of General Psychiatry*, 1963, **9** (1), 19–31.

Riley, M. W. *Sociological research*. New York: Harcourt, Brace & World, 1963.

Schofield, M. G. *Sociological aspects of homosexuality : A comparative study of three types of homosexuals.* Boston: Little, Brown, & Co., 1965.

Socarides, C. W. Homosexuality and medicine. *Journal of the American Medical Association,* 1970, **212** (7), 1,199–1,202.

Weinberg, M. S., & Williams, C. J. *Male homosexuals : Their problems and adaptations in three societies.* New York: Oxford University Press, 1974, in press.

Williams, C. J., & Weinberg, M. S. *Homosexuals and the military.* New York: Harper & Row, 1971.

Scripts and the Coordination of Sexual Conduct[1]

JOHN H. GAGNON

State University of New York at Stony Brook

Most sociologists are poorly equipped to deal with the problems of motivation as they are discussed among psychologists. I must confess at the outset that I share in this disciplinary deficiency. In part the difficulty arises from a certain barrier that exists between the two fields: the complex debate in psychology about the utility of the concept of motivation in explaining the genesis and maintenance of behavior—a debate that antedates the earliest of the Nebraska Symposia on Motivation—is largely unknown to sociologists. Part of the problem, both in terms of data and theory, is a consequence of the magnitude of the information involved, but perhaps more importantly, it stems from the different styles of imagining that have evolved in the actual activities of the two disciplines. Such styles of imagining which are central to a discipline's problem sense and its canons of credibility emerge from the daily practice of reading, teaching, and research, and it is through these practices that the intellectual and moral boundaries of the discipline are defined. Regardless of the formal similarities of the condensates of a field's activities as represented in journal articles, it is the shared life of *doing* psychology or *doing* sociology that creates both the tacit understandings which allow work within a field to go forward as well as the communicative gulf between fields.

When first invited to this symposium I felt a considerable strain to examine the points of convergence and divergence that exist

1. This research was supported by USPHS grants from the National Institute of Child Health and Human Development (HD 4156) and a special postdoctoral fellowship from the National Institute of Mental Health (MH54372).

27

between the sociological and psychological approaches to motivational theory, but upon a cursory examination of both literatures it struck me that the outcome of that effort would be entirely too casual to bear much palatable fruit, and the prospect tended to be somewhat paralyzing as well. As a consequence my tactic has been to use that portion of the relevant psychological literature over which I have some command, but in general to stay within the intellectual styles with which I am comfortable, hoping that the result will be clear enough to be intelligible and perhaps useful to those outside the field of sociology.

Conventionally the starting point in a discussion of sexual conduct is at the beginning of life. This is a strategy which draws largely upon the psychoanalytic tradition and its double emphases: first, the centrality of sexual forces in ultimate character formation and, second, the primary significance of the earliest experiences of infancy and childhood in setting the limits and possibilities of future development. For those concerned with the complexities of adulthood, this perspective poses a dilemma in that it views adult life, in both its sexual and nonsexual dimensions, as schematized and over-specified by developmental constraints. In some psychoanalytic formulations adulthood seems only a reenactment of an individual's childhood history. Even the Freudian revisionists' attempts to recognize the significance of cultural and social life in human development, such as those of Erik Erikson, are both partial and limited, focusing primarily on the constancies and continuities in development rather than the changeable and discontinuous qualities observable over the total life cycle (Erikson, 1963). While the processes of socialization do have a narrowing and limiting function in any cultural-historical context by increasingly specifying outcomes—that is, by eliciting and creating what is an acceptable adult in a given society—to see these processes as fixed by an inescapable human nature or by some ordained sequence of human needs is to satisfy what might be called a conceptual "rage for order" at the expense of the observable disorder. While it is not my intention to posit an alternative rage for chaos, it is important to take account of the flexibility and discontinuity in human development and to recognize the remarkable adaptive capacities of human beings as they face and create novel circumstances throughout the life cycle.

It is these adaptive capacities in dealing with novel conditions that I would like to emphasize in this paper. Changing environmental demands, both in terms of cultural-historical change and in terms of the changing demands on a person during his life cycle in any culture, require the coordination and management of a wide variety of skills learned previously in a variety of contexts, as well as the creation of novel responses through the recombination of older skills. These novel activities themselves become more effortlessly managed and become parts of other goals and plans later in the life cycle. This process of discontinuous and continuous combination and recombination of cultural and psychological resources to meet adaptive exigencies consists, in part, of ways in which the culturally provided plans and goals of persons contain the motives for behavior, and of the role that these plans have in shaping and coordinating both the verbal and nonverbal activities that are involved in sexual conduct.

In another context William Simon and I have called these plans *sexual scripts*, which we meant to be a subclass of the general category of scripted social behavior (Simon & Gagnon, 1969). The concept *script* shares certain similarities with the concepts of plans or schemes in that it is a unit large enough to comprehend symbolic and nonverbal elements in an organized and time-bound sequence of conduct through which persons both envisage future behavior and check on the quality of ongoing conduct. Such scripts name the actors, describe their qualities, indicate the motives for the behavior of the participants, and set the sequence of appropriate activities, both verbal and nonverbal, that should take place to conclude behavior successfully and allow transitions into new activities. The relation of such scripts to concrete behavior is quite complex and indirect; they are neither direct reflections of any concrete situation nor are they surprise-free in their capacity to control any concrete situation. They are often relatively incomplete, that is, they do not specify every act and the order in which it is to occur; indeed, as I will note later, the incompleteness of specification is required, since in any concrete situation many of the subelements of the script must be carried out without the actor noticing that he or she is performing them. They have a major advantage over concrete behavior, however, in that they are manipulable in terms of their content, sequence, and symbolic valuations, often without reference to any concrete situation. We commonly call this process of symbolic reorganization a fantasy when it appears that there is no situation in which a script in its reorganized form may be tested or performed, but in fact, such apparently inapplicable scripts have significant value even in situations which do not contain all or even any of the concrete elements which exist in the symbolic map offered by the script.

Clearly, scripts vary in their flexibility and the details that are specified (the coronations of monarchs are planned in detail, as are the plays of Molière as played by the Comédie Française) both in terms of different kinds of scripts as well as varying performances by different individuals. Scripts are manipulable, but not without limits. While the rules for manipulating symbolic versions of the world are more flexible than those for dealing with concrete situations, these rules and the scripts to which they relate arise from the cultural circumstances in the same fashion as do the concrete situations for which they serve as a map or format. The flexibility of scripts in terms of their internal order and their capacity to be assembled or disassembled in creative or adaptive responses to new circumstances is a critical element in our capacity to manage a changing internal and external environment. The history of an individual's socialization is in part the record of the creation, reorganization, and destruction of script materials, both as a response to the innovative capacities of the scripts themselves as well as to the exigencies of concrete situations. The capacity to use responses learned in one concrete situation in another, together with other responses learned in still other situations at other moments in the life cycle, is central to the process of human adaptation.

The view that personal motives are embedded in these scripts— that is, that our explanatory assertions are deeply associated with our behavioral plans—suggests that motives, in this context, might be called practical motivation or practical explanation. My concern is with that class of explanatory statements that persons make about themselves or to external interlocutors, including the inquiring or experimenting scientist, about why they have done something. As one moves further from infancy, the significance of these acquired theories or ad hoc reasons for behavior becomes more evident, and they become more powerful in their capacity to constrain and shape human conduct. In this sense individual actors are what might be called practical psychologists or practical sociologists; they possess and exploit culturally received sets of explanations for their own and others' behavior. The existence of these culturally provided explanations has been noted by Albert Baldwin (1969) in his discussion of the socialization of children when he raises the hypothesis that "the socialization practices of a society reflect the culture's implicit or explicit hypotheses about how children function and what influences will modify that function [p. 343]." Baldwin describes these theories as being "naive," perhaps in contrast to fashionable scientific explanatory assertions; yet from certain points of view, especially when removed from the body of activity that generated them, it is difficult to recognize superiority between naive and sophisticated psychologies. Our tendency is to degrade the explanatory assertions that persons make about their behavior, often to the status of rationalizations, as we seek to see through or replace these explanations with assertions about people's "real" motives.

It must be noted here that there is no impenetrable barrier between the social science community and the larger society and that the explanatory statements that members of the academy create to account for human behavior can quickly become part of the motivational accounts of members of the larger community. As part of the sociologizing and psychologizing of the larger society, various alternative academic theories of behavior are now generally available to large segments of society. There is a certain reticence among members of the academy about this process, since it commonly is referred to as a process of vulgarization. The tendency to convert all introductory courses in the social sciences into undergraduate versions of graduate courses—all students must come to understand what we do in the form that we do it—is an example of a countereffort to "devulgarize" our course offerings at the expense of their intelligibility. However, in spite of our most powerful attempts to deemphasize the application of the social sciences, nonacademics manage to take what we offer and turn it to their own devices. Indeed, there is a reverse process through which the larger community challenges our academic versions and explanations of the world, both by refusing to conform to our predictions and often by offering more promising versions of their own motives than we can conceive.

Given that my intent is to emphasize complexity, novelty, and discontinuity in psychosexual development, perhaps the best strategy is to begin in the middle of the life cycle and read backward in time, rather than forward from infancy. A description of an adult sexual performance cannot only begin to suggest an alternative way of examining the problem of scripts, the coordination of concrete behavior, and the coordination that their relation implies—a coordination of physiological processes, psychological processes, cultural resources, and social events—but it can also shed some light on the manner in which prior experiences in the socialization process are relevant to current activities. I will try to describe, in some modest detail and with some marginal comment, a heterosexual act occurring for the first time between a young couple in their late teens, tracing the ways in which scripts elicit behavior and the flexibility of scripts in their relation to concrete social arrangements. I have chosen a heterosexual act because it reflects the differential socialization process of women and men, although I could have chosen a homosexual act as easily and it would have illustrated common processes. However, there would have been sufficient differences in detail and potential for raising anxieties that I might have obscured the argument by linking it to the unconventional.

The following, then, is a description of a common social event which contains the conventional cultural materials that allow us to identify it as sexual. I make this complex introductory statement because it is not always obvious, for reasons that I will consider later, that the majority of the elements in the situation which I am going to describe are cultural conventions and are the outcome of a complex of sociohistorical processes, only limited parts of which are related to the necessities of biological reproduction. Let us consider a young man and a young woman who are in a social relationship that is going to result in intercourse. It is voluntary and it involves no direct exchange of money. It is the culmination of a larger series of experiences with each other that they mutually recognize as being likely to lead to intercourse at their stage in the life cycle. Let me further specify that neither of them is very experienced in completing sexual activity in intercourse, but that they are the modal conventional outcomes of middle-class and working-class socialization for sexual performance in United States society. This implies that they both possess at least a fragmentary version of the sequence of activities that they are going to perform, even though they may have had little practice.

As the couple move beyond that tipping point when the conventionally sexual becomes salient, they are very likely to be alone together, in a private place, screened from the public—perhaps his abode or hers, or a friend's if they are still living at home. They are somewhat old for the couch in the living room of one of their parents or the back seat of a car. They will begin touching each other while still clothed, and that clothing will be appropriate to the public contexts in which they have been prior to finding their way to a sheltered place. In these other contexts the couple will commonly conceal that they might be thinking of intercourse, even though they might be defined as in love or engaged, for in these other contexts sexual modesty needs to be preserved. The time could be afternoon or evening, much to the disgust of those who enforce or prescribe the times when young people should be in bed, alone. (Such constraints are only enforceable through a belief on the part of the young that sexual activity is only proper at night.) The light in the room is more likely to be dim or even dark rather than bright, offering a certain privacy in the midst of mutual intimacy.

As they begin they are likely to talk in a slightly desultory manner, probably a little anxiously, given the danger, novelty, and transgressive nature of the behavior in which they are going to participate. The shyness of their talk and its unspecific reference demonstrate the difficulty of moving easily from a public world in which the physical aspects of the sexual largely do not exist and in which sexual talk between women and men is only obliquely referential to that physical activity. The achievement of an easy transition between the worlds of the public and the private may well never be achieved—in part because we lack a legitimate speech in which we can disclose this aspect of our sexuality, even to this very small audience.

No matter how often they have made physical love short of intercourse, which is so inexactly described as petting (perhaps to indicate that something more serious is yet to happen), this moment is seen to be different. It is, to use one colloquialism, "going all the way"; it is a rite of passage, a moment of particular significance that is linked to historically specific ideas about what a critical sexual transition is. After coitus the couple will change, with reference to themselves, to each other, and to their surrounding social world. Some young women have reported an uneasy sense that after their first intercourse other people could see a change in their faces—that the private moment was somehow turned into a visible stigma.

The couple will begin by kissing, and if they have had some physical contact before, they will perhaps move quickly to tongue kissing. His hands will touch her body outside of her clothing, tentatively or more directly, depending on the history of their relationship. She may resist, at first more and then less, perhaps only because she has resisted such gestures so often before, but she indicates in her permission her own desire. They will kiss almost continuously, maintaining a sense of intimate contact and in some degree avoiding direct attention on what their hands may be doing. They will begin to undress, or rather, parts of their clothing will be loosened, unbuttoned, unzipped, conventionally hers first and then his. There will be fumblings, slightly inept gestures; he may never have undressed anyone but himself before, she has rarely been undressed by others since childhood and perhaps never by a man. The initiative is still largely his; buttons turn out to be stubborn, removing her bra turns into a slightly tense ballet. Each of these moments represents a momentary stumble, a deflection of attention from the sense of passion and a break into the inattentions or differential inattentions that are part of managing the concrete activity. As their clothing is finally completely removed, usually hers first and then his (from some obscure origin there is a convention that allows her to be nude before he is), there will be a slight clammy chill as the cool air of the room touches the bare, perhaps perspiring, bodies. To master these interruptions and transitions they may kiss more fiercely. She may straddle his leg or he may intrude it between hers and they will make movements which simulate coitis, giving the act both a genital focus and predicting its conclusion.

There will continue to be distractions, both internal and external. Footsteps in the hallway, the turning of keys in locks, the sounds of passing traffic—the external world continues to make its presence felt. There is also a lingering double presence, a sense of anticipation and risk. He wonders whether he will stay erect, whether she is enjoying what he is doing; she wonders how to keep him doing things that do feel good and how to stop him from doing other things that don't, whether she will have an orgasm, whether there is any danger of getting pregnant. There will be gentle grunts and moans and whispers of affectionate fragments, words, and sentences, which they can mutually interpret to be signs of pleasure and permission.

After some time the distractions lessen and focus is held (except for nagging doubts): they test each other's readiness (more commonly he tests hers) and she opens her legs to let him enter. He may or may not have difficulty, for there is a tense moment as the erect penis begins to enter the vagina. The mechanics intrude; there may be pain for her and sometimes for him. If it is too difficult he may lose his erection; if he is too excited he may ejaculate too soon, sometimes before entry or at the moment when his penis touches her. If she feels too much pain she may close herself to him and simply endure the wanted and unwanted intrusion. And in these moments when what was subliminally coordinated fails, there is a sense of sadness, a resonance of personal failure, a hoped-for and often given, but necessarily inadequate, commiseration. He is apologetic, she is disheartened. Can the failure be repaired? Should they try again? They will talk, sometimes too much, seeking to heal the damage, to make sense of the failure, and perhaps to try again, if not now, then later.

But failure only sometimes occurs. The couple is joined together, there is a set of physical sensations on parts of their bodies that have been imagined, but never experienced. It may be fumbling, to be sure—are the limbs quite coordinated, does it hurt, is the rhythm of movement correct—there may return the double presence as she compares what is happening with literary or cinematic models while he tries to recall whatever sexological advice he has heard or read or picked up from his other sexual experiences about the arousability of women. They may, in a moment of inattention, become uncoupled, and this results in a spasm of activity—his hand, perhaps hers; there is an eruption of the physical into their dreaming life; the genital fluids make their undeodorized presence known. The romance in the head is confronted with a transient reminder of the reality of the regions below. They continue, he more often active but also passive, she more often passive and sometimes active, as they move, largely apart, but seeking to be together, toward orgasm. It is a dumb show in which their private passions and excitements are coordinated through quickening movements, sounds, and vague tensions which anticipate culmination. Such inarticulate pleasures contain their own anxieties: if he has climax too soon he may lose his erection, she may remain unsatisfied. But in the best of circumstances, given our current cultural blueprint, they move relatively closely to climax, or at least they both will have orgasm. At this moment there may be vocalizations (perhaps calling upon the Deity), requests for activity, assurances of affection. The external world is largely gone—the movement of the bed, the floor perhaps creaking, the sounds of a passing and disinterested world— but even at this moment there can be that instant of double consciousness: What if the neighbors are listening? What if a roommate returns?

When they are done—and the moment and quality of doneness is often difficult to define—there is the moment of separation and awareness. The coolness of the room, the stickiness of the flesh—the world intrudes, only to be held at bay by expressions of mutual affection, talking, touching, assurances of trust, gentle reminders of the social relationship that bounds and allows the sexual moment. There is a problem of reentry into that other world, even between themselves. There is mutual nudity, his body and hers without that protecting cloak of the erotic by which they have modified the boundaries of modesty. They must clean up, remove the evidence of physical intimacy, and dress in their cold and rumpled clothing, perhaps untangling hers from his; they must share or sequentially use the toilet, washbasin, or shower. They may smoke, have a cup of coffee, talk, sit across a table and look at each other. In the end they must admit the claims of the external world, when they are together and when they are alone, when she is with her friends and he with his. There are the dilemmas of partial and total disclosure, to what audiences. For him there may be the crudities of adolescent male judgments and braggadocio about his conquest that will exist ambivalently with his sense of a betrayal of intimacy. For her there may be worries (more virtuous girls quietly moralizing) and justifications (she was in love, why else would she have done it?). For both of them the outcomes are ambiguous, and their scripts will be reordered and transformed to provide plans for the future and justifications for the past.

It is possible to create many such scenes which involve the sexual. This cryptic and incomplete description contains only a part of the reality of the specific act and suggests only one of a variety of circumstances under which first coitus can take place in this society at a specific historical-social moment. One can vary the ages, the personal histories, the degrees of skill, the quality of assent, the legal circumstances, and the social status of the participants and produce differences in what might be called the conventional social situation for first coitus. But even in this simple form, the extraordinary complexity of the situation and the levels of coordination necessary for finding a successful conclusion are most apparent. Within the social and psychological fields of the two young people are a wide range of subplans or script elements, in the sense that the word *plan* is used by Miller, Galanter, and Pribram (1960), that must be integrated, organized, and reassessed. These are plans that have relevance at the physiological, psychological, and social and cultural levels. When sexual conduct (of which the physical aspects are only a small part) is viewed in this manner, its explanation is not simply a matter of determining a sequence through which a kind of biological mandate is expressed. Rather, the emphasis is on psychosocial processes and cultural-historical situations which provide meaning for behavior, allow for the integration and reorganization of information and skills learned at earlier stages in the life cycle, and indeed elicit from an underspecified organism the culturally appropriate responses to novel situations.

From the point of view of socialization, little of this complexity can be predicted with any ease from the versions of developing psychosexuality which exist in the original or revised Freudian paradigm. That version of the socialization process is excessively linear and suggests a very rapid closure to the possibilities and requirements of adaptation later in the life cycle. It is likely that the majority of cultural resources that are ultimately brought to bear on sexual conduct are learned in contexts which, at the time they are learned, are irrelevant to the ultimate outcomes or circumstances in which they are used. Human beings in response to novel or only vaguely anticipated circumstances bring to bear upon them only loosely the adaptive resources learned in other situations; the outcomes are not random, but they are also not fixed by the creaking machinery of the laws of development which are the individual equivalent of Newton's clockwork universe.

Not only sexual socialization, but many other aspects of the socialization process which are currently described in the literature, suffer from a largely restricted historical and cultural framework. Lives of individuals not only have a sequential character (the usual pattern is infancy, childhood, adolescence, adulthood, old age), but they also exist in a wide range of sociocultural and historical contexts which serve as the local sources for learning the content of these various stages of development. Further it must be noted that even these stages of the life cycle have been notoriously flexible in their beginnings and endings, and some of them clearly are cultural inventions that have appeared at recent points in human history (Aries, 1962). We are at this very moment trying to solve at the sociocultural level the emerging disjuncture between the moment when one is allowed or can gain occupational independence and when one has legitimate access to sexual activity. The problem concerns the existence of a historical assumption that occupational maturity and sexual maturity, the access to money and the access to sexual pleasure, require an orderly and sequential relationship. The fact that sexual activity, if not pleasure, is now both possible and practicable prior to apprenticeship in the occupational order, especially among college students, raises the specter of unearned pleasure prior to labor, a peculiarly irritating thought to those of a puritan bent.

The developmental process in various cultural and historical contexts contains a very wide set of expectations of appropriate learning and activities for persons of various age grades. Not only are overt activities learned (some taught, some observed, others inferred —the mechanisms are varied and differ over the life cycle), but they are associated and interactive with the acquisition of scripts that contain classes of assertions about the causes, sources, and meanings of these activities. The scripts and their embedded practical assertions about the meaning of concrete activities are learned not only in the context of the life cycle, but in particular cultural-historical circumstances. The elements in the scripts do not exist in any one-to-one relation to elements in the concrete activities, and in this sense they are not a direct map of the concrete situation. It is this loose relationship between scripts and concrete behavior that makes inferences about the meaning of concrete behavior so problematic and invalidates much of cross-cultural and historical psychologizing. However, this same flexible relation between scripts and concrete behavior is critical to the processes of development as well as to individual and social change. To be sure, scripts and their associated practical motives are directly linked to the contexts in which they were learned and to the activities that they related to at that time. The meaning of development, however, is that what appear to be similar behaviors viewed at various points in the life cycle (as well as in various cultural contexts) actually have differing scripts, and what makes change over the life cycle possible is the detachment of scripts and activities from each other to be available as resources in new combinations of scripts and activities with changed motivational assertions at later points in the life cycle.

This adaptive capacity of human beings to separate scripts from concrete situations and independently operate with scripts, script elements, and explanatory assertions outside of their contextual origins is a well recognized and often highly rewarded skill in other areas of human endeavor. In scientific research we constantly seek new assertions about the meaning of behavior, often substituting a new explanatory model for data the gathering of which was guided by opposed or differing models. In the study of history this process of revision is constantly with us, as the events of the past, about which there may be little dispute regarding the "facts," are reinterpreted in novel and intriguing patterns. History as the record of kings and princes yields to Marxist, Freudian, or sociocultural explanation as new movements in the culture and the historical academy seek new standards for the interpretation of the past. Lest such revisionism be recognized only in the self-serving practices of Soviet encyclopedists, the every-decade revisions of the history of the Civil War in the United States may be offered as counterevidence. Carrying such a view of significant and useful revisions to issues of individual development, including the psychosexual, follows from an existentialist tradition. The past is not a fixed quantity in current interaction, but is rather a resource, for individuals are free within certain cultural specifications to edit, rewrite, anthologize, and bring to bear new explanations upon it; they make novel plans containing what were disparate elements, learned at different points in the life cycle, as they seek to adapt and design their current environment.

This process of anticipatory and retrospective "fictionalizing of the self" has been described by the novelist John Fowles in the following manner (Fowles, 1970):

> You do not think of your own past as quite real; you dress it up, you gild it or blacken it, censor it, tinker with it, . . . fictionalize it in a word, and put it away on a shelf—your book, your romanced biography. [P. 84]

> So we are all novelists, that is, we have a habit of writing fictional futures for ourselves, although today we incline more to put ourselves into a film. We screen in our mind hypotheses about how we might behave, about what might happen to us; and these novelistic or cinematic hypotheses often have very much more effect on how we actually do behave, when the real future becomes the present than we generally allow. [P. 295]

This process of fictionalization has to do not only with plans for the future, but with the rearrangement of the past and the present. Just as the novelist takes the past and present, both in the real world and in fiction, as part of his resources and then creates a new work—within the cultural specifications and formal requirements of what such a work should be—so the individual takes his own past and the cultural resources of the society that are available to him to create a present self in line with his plans for the future.

Perhaps a nonsexual example might suggest the power of this process. It is generally believed (or was, some years ago) that the rates of social mobility between blue- and white-collar occupations were vastly lower in England than in the United States. The extreme myth was that they were close to zero in England and unlimited in the United States. Research has suggested that this discrepancy is not the case, and as a matter of fact, rates of social mobility of this kind have been fairly similar in this century in the two countries because of similarities in their industrial and occupational structures. Where did our beliefs, then, come from? In part, at least, they arose from differences in culturally received styles of utilizing the past in current circumstances. In the United States it is still culturally appropriate to describe oneself as a self-made person; Horatio Alger lives, at least in the ways in which we distort our pasts to make our current accomplishments the function of our own efforts, desires, and accomplishments. We may tip our hat to our parents, but the tendency to see ourselves as poorer or less advantaged than we actually were and to expand the gap between then and now is a distorting mirror, if only a minor vice. In England, until the recent present, the tendency to obscure one's social origins was quite prevalent, being in part an aspect of a larger cultural reticence about one's private matters, but also expressing a sense of cultural disassociation with working-class origins. Such cultural differences are significant, for they are some of the basic factors in potentiality for change or stability, both at the individual and social levels. The processes of cultural change in England evidenced by the decline of the Oxbridge accent and the old school tie are more than simply an honest facing up to social reality, but are part of a change in the day-to-day character of social life. In contrast, Horatio Alger, or at least his bureaucratic equivalent, still seems firmly entrenched in the United States.

A recognition of this loose and flexible relation between social scripts, the explanatory assertions that they contain, and concrete social situations is necessary to an understanding of the limitations and confusions that exist in conventional theories of psychosexual development. Hence, the observation of children in what appears to be sexual activity from the point of view of adults fails to account seriously for the differences between adults' scripts and motives and those of children. Indeed, it is only as the child becomes adult and shares both the activities and the culturally prescribed motivations of an adult that it is sensible to describe his behavior as sexual, except in the most abstract sense.

The strategy that I would like to adopt for the remainder of the paper is to trace out a series of influences on one aspect of the sexual situation, not exhaustively, but suggestively, noting the shifting relationship between scripts, practical motives, and concrete activities as these are assembled into what is culturally acceptable heterosexual conduct in early adulthood. In this process it is possible to observe our own cultural specifications rather more clearly and perhaps to examine their origins in the interaction between individual development and psychological and cultural circumstances.

One of the problematic aspects of the fictitious young couple's sexual situation was their coordination of mutual sexual excitement and, particularly, the processes by which the timing of the movement toward orgasm could be managed satisfactorily. What is at issue is the way in which two young people attempt, through mutual stimulation and internal self-monitoring, to alter and adapt their prior experiences to enact what Masters and Johnson (1966) have called the orgasmic cycle (composed of four stages: excitement, plateau, orgasm, and resolution) in order to produce orgasm in some satisfactory sequence. There is considerable evidence from the clinical literature that the coordination of these events in coitus is not at all obvious, and even the experience of orgasm among many women is erratic or nonexistent in coitus. It seems profitable to examine the relationships between scripts and the orgasm experience as they develop over the life cycle as an uneven process of adaptation to an ambiguous cultural and personal environment.

There is some evidence that, at the physiological level, the capacity for orgasm, in the sense that there is some kind of biological competence, occurs relatively early in the life cycle. Kinsey reports observational data, from a variety of sources of mixed quality, regarding what appears to be orgasm in male and female children under 1 and 2 years (Kinsey, 1948, 1953). The external bodily signs, noted without any physiological instrumentation, include rapid breathing, vascularization, increasing body tension, and sudden release of tension, followed by resting. It is presently unclear what meaning this behavior has for the infant and whether infants who are so experienced have been set on an alternative path of development. It is also unclear whether the experience, which an external observer is describing as similar to adult orgasm, has any specifically sexual meaning (in an adult sense) or whether this experience would continually be sought, in the absence of any meaningful script. What evidence there is suggests that early childhood orgasm is relatively sporadic and, from what some parents report, is largely a sedative or self-soothing practice without any script materials that would connect with similar events among adults. There is also some evidence that orgasm occurs in later childhood before puberty, but this evidence, too, is fragmentary. There are reports from some adults who have had sexual contact with children of 7 to 11 years that these contacts have resulted in the same kinds of observable excitement and what appears to be orgasm. There is also some evidence of prepubertal orgasm as recalled by adults whose experiences seem to them in memory to be similar to those which they have had after puberty. What evidence does exist suggests that there is some possibility of a biological competence for orgasm existing before puberty, but that this competence does not quickly or easily translate into social orgasm performance in the absence of specific learning conditions to give it a sought-after character. The word *competence* is used here differently than it is by either effectance theorists or as it was by Robert White in his very useful and original description of psychosexual development in 1960 (White, 1960). It is used here in the sense that Chomsky distinguishes language competence, a tendency toward a specific organization of the biological substrate that makes possible what Chomsky describes as language perform- ance. However, in this case I would assign an overwhelming weight to the role that social and psychological factors have in converting orgasm competence into orgasm performance.

It is important to note here that the conversion of orgasm competence into orgasm performance is especially complex in women. From sociohistorical evidence it is apparent that orgasm performance among women was largely unnoticed or discounted in the eighteenth- and nineteenth-century literatures on sexuality, except, of course, in pornography, where women were not only granted an inexhaustible orgasm capacity, but an ejaculation paral- leling that of males as well. It has been conventional to argue that this lack of orgasm on the part of women was a simple function of the positive repression of a natural psychosexual function; but what seems more likely, viewed from the cultural perspective of the mid– nineteenth century, is that the sociosexual definitions of women, especially those women who became the models for twentieth-century respectability, existed without any elements that could have provided the basis for learning that orgasm was part of women's adaptive physiological equipment. The sense of refinement, passivity, general submission to male standards of modesty, and, at least in some part, resistance to male sexual exploitation left a large blank space in the gender socialization process of women. Such a general exclusion of the sexual from social life, especially those gender and sexual scripts that we have inherited from the nineteenth century as part of our received cultural repertoire of conduct, not only existed for women but also shaped the sexuality of many men as well. The problem was not the repression of an inborn drive, but the lack of a set of eliciting circumstances, including gender and sexual scripts, primarily for women, but also for men, that would convert orgasm competence into adequate orgasm performance.

Such a cultural inheritance still serves to differentiate the gender socialization patterns of men and women out of which our sexual patterns take many of their meanings. Thus, very young children are taught the appropriate modes of initiation, control, and dominance that should exist between girls and boys, women and men. They learn social scripts about gender—how boys should behave, how girls should behave, how they should behave together, and what are the shared and differing practical motivations for conduct. Such gender scripts contain conceptions of moral value, a sense of the appropriate explanations for behavior, and some understanding of how these may be used and changed from situation to situation. What is strikingly apparent regarding the sexuality of children is how few of the elements of the adult sexual script, except in the form of constraining gender scripts, are possessed by our children. Even when young children of 7 to 9 years engage in what we call sex play, even that which imitates coitus from an adult's point of view, it must be seen through the scripts and motivational resources of the children themselves. They are not practicing adult coitus in most western societies—the behavior is not an intrusion of the sexual impulse into childhood or the prologue to adult sexuality. The motives are embedded in the scripts and plans that are available to 7-to-9-year-olds in this culture. Perhaps even more rare than the experience of orgasm in this children's play is their engaging in the behavior with the goal of having orgasm. What is lacking during this period is any set of scripts that might include the learning of orgasm or its inclusion in any sequence of behavior. Even if general excitement occurs, involving erection in males and perhaps even random orgasm from this generalized arousal, organized scripts do not exist which would name the reasons for continuing the behavior. It is possible, however, to create a culture in which orgasm performance would be highly rewarded and in which there were educational processes to create orgasm-seeking behavior among young children and perhaps even to cast the behavior in terms of scripts which were available to adults in the society. To do so in western societies with their current cultural organization would not only require a radical shift in our sexual conduct, but the effects of such change would likely extend to the farthest reaches of occupational, familial, and religious life as well.

In terms of orgasm performance, the best evidence suggests that for this culture it emerges as a routine form of behavior among a majority of males and a less frequent and more intermittent behavior among females in conjunction with masturbation in early adolescence (from 12 to 14 years). There are some alternative patterns, varying by gender and social class, but the modal experience seems to be through masturbation. The significance of masturbation for males is not only that it produces an orgasm cycle of generalized excitement, intense arousal, and resolution, but that the behavior is accompanied by a series of more or less complex sexual narratives, the elements of which can be independently capable of eliciting and maintaining the sexual activity itself. What are called masturbatory fantasies are in fact rudimentary sexual scripts which include selected elements of gender scripts learned previously, combined with novel sexual elements that are screened in the head in coordination with genital or other self-stimulation. It is through this process that orgasm competence is beginning to be converted into orgasm performance for many males in this culture. The young male has begun to develop a protoadult male sexual script which contains a cast of characters (himself, young women, and, less often, other males), a rough imagery of the physical activities that might be going on in the scene, measures of the moral worth of the persons involved, and an ordered sequence of the nonsexual activities and symbolic materials that are needed to produce the desired effect. It is easy to miss the nonsexual elements in these fantasies, but a more-than-casual reading of Philip Roth's *Portnoy's Complaint* suggests the necessity of combining nonsexual attributes with sexual materials in order to create an erotic ambiance. The anxiety and considerable uneasiness about the risk and dangers of masturbation arise in part from the ambivalent combination of conventional elements into unconventional conduct as well as its largely unspecified character, since both its content and practice are learned sub rosa. These two processes are perhaps more anxiety-producing than any specific prohibitions about masturbation. Indeed, most of the descriptions of the behavior embedded in prohibitory statements are so vague that they may increase anxiety without reducing interest.

The interesting problem in terms of the developmental role of emergent scripts in the coordination of physical behavior is that in the earliest stages of masturbation, this coordination is relatively poor and males tend to have problems of maintaining focus on the fantasy or getting the manually induced orgasm to coordinate with the appropriate moment of sexual culmination in the fantasy itself. It is only through practice of the script and the self-stimulation that a certain level of skill emerges, a level of skill that accounts for elaboration in the script elements as well as the maintenance of excitement for longer periods of time prior to orgasm. Figure 1 below roughly suggests this coordination, using Masters and Johnson's graphic image for the orgasm cycle (Masters & Johnson, 1966, p. 5).[2] There are no quantitative measures on either axis (either for time or for excitement) and the trace line itself is clearly a convenient image rather than a true depiction of either any single or combined measure of physiological events or psychological excitement. The intent is to suggest the levels of coordination involved, and that in early masturbation excitement is rapid, the plateau stage is relatively short, and the young man comes relatively quickly to climax. What is important is that a patterned relationship emerges between scripted materials and the physical activities that must be modified in nonmasturbatory sexual activities and that even the subjective experience of orgasm itself may be modified in these transitions.

The present cultural-historical conditions with reference to female sexuality during this period is more complex, and the evidence

<hr />

2. The trace line used by Masters and Johnson is a very useful pictorial device and is largely in accord with the subjective sense of the orgasmic cycle, but does not describe any specific physiological process. See Masters and Johnson, 1966, p. 5, Fig. 1–1.

is far more fragmentary. In addition, since there is some evidence, at least at the ideological level, that changes are desired, if not already occurring, in female sexual and gender socialization, the current versions of early adolescence in the female may well be of a transient character. At this moment the evidence is that fewer females than males masturbate in early adolescence and that they masturbate less frequently. There is some evidence that the script content which accompanies, permits, and elicits the masturbation may contain little material that is "sexual" from the male point of view—content such as meeting "Mr. Right," falling in love, or getting married. How-

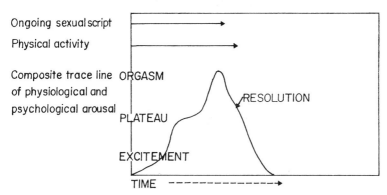

FIG. 1. An example of levels of coordination and possible durations of segments of the orgasmic cycle in early male adolescent masturbation (conventionally performed in private, manually, with a concurrent sociosexual narrative).

ever, such events contain a romantic and anticipatory excitement for young women that may parallel the excitement produced by thinking about coitus among young men. Further, a recent study by Ruth Clifford of the Department of Psychology at the State University of New York at Stony Brook suggests that some young women masturbate to orgasm without knowing either the labels for masturbation or for orgasm. They have the experience but do not know its sexual content. It might be possible to speculate that this activity is similar to and perhaps follows upon prepubertal self-stimulation that is tension-reducing or soothing without a sexual component in associated cognitive material. All of the evidence at this time points to the conclusion that self-stimulation with and without orgasm and the possession of a script with explicit sexual content are more sporadic among women during this period, and this behavior, when it occurs, is less well linked with the kinds of overt physical sexual activities that women will need to coordinate, under current cultural conditions, later in their life cycle.

It must be pointed out that masturbation is not a necessary element in the emergence of orgasm performance or ultimate coital success in either gender. There are some cultures in which masturbation is relatively rare in incidence and/or frequency. The Kinsey data, as well as that of other researchers, indicate that in the United States about 10% of males never masturbate and many working-class males do so only rarely (Kinsey, 1948). This suggests the multiple pathways and the different scripts and experiences that can be sequentially assembled to produce acceptable adult sexual performances. Adolescent masturbation is given its meaning and connectivity by the cultural context in which it occurs. In this culture, with the very few practice situations in which orgasm performance can be learned and with the differential experience of the two genders in masturbation, it attains a peculiar salience. In cultural situations in which coital activity is generally legitimate for both genders, either in early adolescence or even in later marriage, orgasm performance is likely to be easily attained.

It is largely in patterns of sociosexual interaction in middle adolescence that women begin to formulate and build into their romantic scripts about male-female interaction elements that contain a specifically sexual component. Most males by this point have at least a theoretical knowledge of the sequence of behaviors that are presumed necessary to get through a coital act. In this sociosexual interaction males begin to initiate at least some of these behaviors, and in such interaction young women begin to learn a reactive version of the young male's primitive sexual version of women. Women learn a pattern of responses not only to men, but to themselves (he is turned on by touching my breasts, I must be turned on by being touched on the breasts).[3] In this fashion, generalized

3. This is, of course, only one of a variety of learning circumstances in which a special character can be given the breasts in the sexual response cycle. A sense of the significance of breasts as an indicator of maturity or personal worth is also provided by the mass media, as well as by female peers (Kinsey, et al. 1948).

excitement is specified to body parts, and the local cultural sequence of physical intimacy and heightening excitement begins to be formed. But there are constraining elements in this process. The masturbatory script as well as the content of adolescence male-male interaction contains a cast of personae in which the women are commonly marked by their bad character, evidence of which can be found in their sexual accessibility. There are parallel beliefs among young women who are perfectly aware of this moral division between the sexually accessible and sexually inaccessible. A conception of the good-girl-bad-girl distinction comes long before any specifically sexual content is built into it. Rules about nudity and cross-gender touching and vague images of male and female virtues have already been set in place, even for the girl who has no idea of what the act of coitus might entail in any direct or concrete sense.

In middle and late adolescence, falling in love serves as a novel mechanism through which this constraint on sexual experimentation may be overcome. A new script element is added which serves to allow many forms of cross-gender intimacy, including the sexual. At the beginning of adolescent petting, a beginning marked by social and sexual ineptitude, anxiety, and fears about general masculinity and femininity as well as peer-group standing, there is a relatively wide separation between the genders. The young males have a relatively advanced sexual script, reinforced by peer-group values, relatively coordinated with the experience of masturbatory orgasm, and integrated with general cultural prescriptions, now linked to the sexual, about male initiation and dominance. The young females have a relatively more restricted sexual script, constrained by the female gate-keeper role, less likely to have autonomously sought orgasm in masturbation, and bound closely to a commitment to wifedom and motherhood as the fundamental female goal, but with the script of falling in love as a potent and facilitating basis for sexual experimentation.

If we recall adolescent petting in any detail, we remember that it is a rhythm of increasing general intimacy between pairs which peaks at various kinds of sexual activities linked to age grades, the possibility of falling in love, and marriage. It is an activity of extraordinary subjective excitement, with each performance often extended over long periods of time and commonly completed without orgasm. This pattern is suggested in Figure 2, with the dotted trace line suggesting the possibility of declines in excitement and the rare possibility of orgasm. The plateau is long sustained, and in the absence of orgasm, the resolution is long drawn out, often with males and females feeling some pain or discomfort in the groin or genitals. Once again, there are no quantities involved; what is important is a recognition of the differences in cycles of excitement and the conditions under which sexual learning goes forward, as well as the difference between durations of various parts of the orgasmic cycle when compared with prior orgasmic practice on the part of the male.

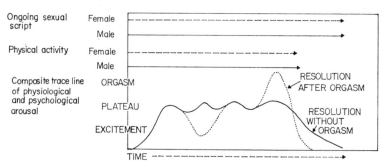

Fig. 2. An example of levels of coordination and possible durations of segments of the orgasmic cycle in middle adolescent petting (similar trace line for both genders) (conventionally performed in private or semipublic locations, with separate gender-specific scripts and motives and a division of labor in patterns of mutual physical stimulation).

This physical cycle is repeated over and over again, and only as couples get older and closer to marriage is it likely to result in the scene of first coitus that I described above. In these situations of petting, young people learn an enormous facility in kissing and a reasonable repertoire of noncoital skills. Both males and females learn to tolerate relatively high levels of psychological excitement and physiological tumescence without orgasm. Such petting that does not terminate in orgasm is quite worrisome to adults, but both young men and young women find it a remarkably pleasant activity in itself, even though it may not terminate in orgasm or coitus. Such restraint is sometimes difficult for males in that they had experience of orgasm as an appropriate culmination in masturbation, but there is no easy translation of the solitary, autonomous, fantasy-impregnated experience of orgasm to the dyadic, dependent, exploratory situation of petting. By contrast, females—whose bodies are now increasingly invested with erotic meaning derived from the males with whom they pet—learn that arousal is possible and pleasurable through the sequence of activities that males attempt and in which they ultimately cooperate. They learn in the context of love a sense of the physicality of sexuality and its role in sexual gratification.

What must be obvious is the infrequency of the dyadic practice of the complete orgasmic cycle. The young male is involved in sexual excitement that does not end in orgasm while engaged in concurrent masturbatory behavior which does result in orgasm. At the same time the scripts for these masturbatory performances are being modified by the concrete content of the experiences of petting as well as by materials from other sources, such as the media. The young woman retains a generally inexperienced role as far as the completion of the orgasmic cycle is concerned, but possesses an increasing awareness of its potentiality. It is in the late teens or early twenties that first premarital coitus usually occurs, a description of which I essayed earlier. It is no wonder that its performance seems so error ridden. The event has rarely been practiced, its subelements are badly integrated, the couple are anxious, and they are unsure of each other's and their own responses. At the moment they attempt coitus they have very little concrete experience to go on—what they do possess are scripts that are quite imprecise and badly articulated. As in the relation between masturbation and petting, the mastery of the sexual excitement cycle and the attendant scripting in petting does not translate directly into the mastery of the same processes in coitus, and the practice of the sexual excitement cycle without orgasm in petting only in part anticipates the general complexities of the coital situation. Petting does provide, however, a direct practice ground for some aspects of the coital situation: there is some practice in mutual disrobing, learning the social skills to secure privacy, developing the ability to focus on the body of the opposite gender, and the like.

While I am in some disagreement with the generality of Erving Goffman's (1971) description of the problematic nature of first trials for many kinds of behavior, especially those for which there has been substantial support or rehearsal, his words do apply to sexual experimentation:

> It should be . . . evident that almost every activity that any individual easily performs now was at some time for him something that required anxious mobilization of effort. To walk, to cross a road, to utter a complete sentence, to wear long pants, to tie one's own shoes, to add a column of figures—all these routines that allow the individual unthinking competent performance were attained through an acquisition process whose early stages were negotiated in cold sweat. A series of formal tests is likely to have been involved and solo trials, that is, distantly supervised practice under real, and hence fateful conditions. [P. 248]

Goffman overstates the case (how many people feel anxiety at a cold-sweat level and in how many activities is, of course, variable), but he points to a valuable lesson: ultimately competent performances conceal the processes of learning not only from observers, but from the person who went through the process. In part, the possession of a sufficiently powerful goal embedded in a script gives a person the capacity to overwhelm the cold sweat, to submerge error, and to forgive incompetence. Indeed, the tenacity of young people in continuing to engage in premarital sexual activity, given its problems of logistics and coordination and the low level of social support, suggests the power of learned social goals and the capacity of scripts, with their associated motives, to overcome the friction of brute reality.

In figure 3 there is an example of the two orgasmic cycles of the young couple I described, suggesting the differences between the two genders in the duration of the various elements of their response to the sexual situation. One may compare these with the figures for masturbation and petting to get some inkling of the commonalities and differences involved. The trace lines again do not stand for quantitative measures, although there is some evidence that the male will become excited more rapidly than the female, and there is some evidence of a rising and falling subjective sense of arousal in both partners. Where one puts the moments of disrobing, intromission, and other contingencies on this trace line, is dependent on the concrete situation. The durations of the various phases of the orgasmic cycle will vary across individuals and in the lifetime of a single individual. If one looks forward in time for this young couple, it is possible to predict that the quality of the coordination of the phases of the orgasmic cycle will become better, that is, it will meet the culturally specified definitions of good performance. Part of this improvement will result from practice together, in greater assurance about the sequence and order of pleasing each other. It will be possible to achieve a certain lack of attention to many aspects of the behavior: the risk of losing an erection will be less problematic; if she wishes something to be done she can indicate it by signs or words; the subelements of the final behavior will be integrated as

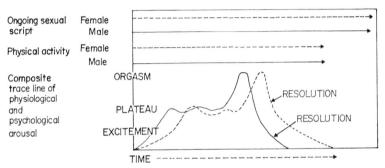

FIG. 3. An example of levels of coordination and possible durations of segments of the orgasmic cycle in late adolescent and early adult coitus (separate trace lines for each gender) (conventionally performed in private, with differing anticipatory and concurrent gender-specific scripts and a division of labor in patterns of mutual physical stimulation).

routine sequences. Such sequences of concrete behavior will become largely conventionalized, having a normal order and character between any couple.

Since there is a reasonable level of cultural agreement and specification in the learned order of sexual conduct, it will be possible for the members of any pair to move to new partners and behave with a fair level of accomplishment. This transition is rarely without minor crises or problematic elements regarding both physical coordination and changes in the social situation which require changes or additions to the script elements that are brought to bear on the situation. Thus, intercourse under conditions that do not involve love or which arise out of a summer affair requires the addition of a new set of script elements including practical motives for the performance of behavior. Intercourse with persons between marriages or, more complexly, with extramarital partners also requires additional script materials to allow for a successful performance in the concrete situation.

Few persons manage these transitions without some concern or disruption in concrete performance, but even so, the possession of the script and the capacity to manipulate script elements allows one to move from one concrete situation to another with (hopefully) a minimum of distress and error. This relationship between mental scripts and their role in organizing behavior—especially the loose relationship between script specifications and each subelement in the concrete situation, such as the duration of the plateau phase in the sexual excitement cycle—has been usefully explored by Michael Polanyi (1964):

> A mental effort has a heuristic effect: it tends to incorporate any available elements of the situation which are helpful for its purpose. . . . These actions are experienced only subsidiarily, in terms of an achievement to which they contribute. . . . This is how you invent a method of swimming without knowing that it consists of regulating your breath in a particular manner, or discover the principle of cycling without realizing that it consists in the adjustment of your momentary direction and velocity, so as to counteract your momentary accidental unbalance. Hence the practical discovery of a wide range of not consciously known skills and connoisseurship which comprise important technical processes that can rarely be specified. [P. 62]

The emergence of new scripts to coordinate behavior in new circumstances, a process that Polanyi describes in its polished form as connoisseurship, has a series of interesting adaptive consequences. In the process of transforming and performing previously learned skills (in my example, the coordination of the sexual excitement cycle in differing circumstances), the skills themselves must have the possibility of being removed from the contexts in which they were originally learned, to be put to use in novel concrete circumstances often far removed from the contexts of original learning. Hence, the coordination of fantasy, sexual excitement, and orgasm that occurs among male adolescents is not directly applicable to the coital situation, in which there is another person and sometimes a concern for the sexual pleasure of the partner. The relatively rapid movement from excitement to orgasm on the part of the male in masturbation is not initially coordinated with the behavior of many women who are just learning in coitus to identify and develop skills which were not learned earlier in the life cycle. From the point of view of the relation between sexual scripts and concrete sexual behavior, the beginning of coitus involves a male possessing a developed script and set of coordinated concrete behaviors, who interacts with a female with a differing and less well-developed script and a relative absence of subsidiary concrete skills. The problem for females is not so much one of direct repression as it is a lack of circumstances in conventional socialization which would provide content and connection between mental scripts and concrete action. For males, the issue may be the overdetermined relation between scripts and concrete activities.

This forgetting of the past which is involved in the dynamic process of the behavioral coordination of scripts and behavior at various moments in the life cycle has contributed to our dependence on linear and/or biological models of sexual development. In the process of editing, rewriting, and reorganizing our scripts to meet new concrete exigencies, we not only lose the older scripts that were linked to prior circumstances, but we also lose the relationship between these older scripts and the skills that were being learned or coordinated through the existence of such scripts. The capacity to coordinate and elicit the sexual excitement cycle in adolescence was dependent on the existence of the scripts that existed in that period of life. The skills that emerged, both directly and subsidiarily, which were of direct interest at that time are now either deleted or become subsidiary, often unnoticed, elements, especially if the coital performance is to succeed at all in the present situation.

This adaptive capacity—indeed, this adaptive necessity—for scripts and concrete skills to be detached from the original contexts in which they were learned and then to contribute flexibility to the new situation conceals from us the conditions of learning that existed before. This leads to two kinds of problems. First, since our own pasts are hidden from us and we now organize the world through our new scripts, in which are embedded our assertions about motivation, we begin to impose on persons at other moments in the developmental cycle our versions of the world. Second, since we lose the older connections and contexts in which the scripts and skills coexisted, we tend to simplify the processes by which our current stage of development came to be. In the absence of a clear-cut contact with our earlier experiences, a simple reproductive or drive-based sexual teleology is substituted for the complexity of learning situations, making adult sexual experience the outcome of biological imperatives, independent of historical and cultural contexts. As the historical and cultural situation changes, the inputs from that portion of the world also become lost, and we impose upon the past our current explanations, thinking that they have some universal applicability. At the same time we constrain the future by imposing the present upon it, reducing the potential variability of behavior as individuals encounter novel circumstances and engage in symbolic manipulations in order to adapt to them.

An example of this changing learned relationship between sexual scripts and concrete sexual performances may be found in the recent therapeutic work with various forms of sexual dysfunctions carried out first by Masters and Johnson (Masters & Johnson, 1970). In their work (and more recently in the work of other clinicians), the problems of secondary impotence, premature ejaculation, and lack of orgasm are being treated quite successfully through a combination of behavior modification techniques in a general context of individual security and permission for sexual conduct. An outstanding feature of these therapeutic endeavors is that they offer situations in which both scripts about sexual conduct and specific skills and errors in sexual performance may be changed. In some of the clinical cases, the success or failure of certain subsidiary concrete elements in the sexual performance is given a great deal of attention: the female worries about whether she is going to have an orgasm, the male worries about whether he is going to stay erect. In other cases there are problems regarding the kinds of sexual scripts that the patient may possess. The scripts may contain elements that the patient thinks are discordant with the behavior to be performed (I would note that most of the patients, at least from the Masters and Johnson case histories, suffer problems that would be familiar to Freud in their symbolic content), or there may be a failure in the coordination of the sexual excitement cycle between the couple. It should be noted that all of these problems were present in the experience of first coitus that I described earlier in the paper and that they are ordinarily solved or mastered in nontherapeutic circumstances. The quality of these solutions is clearly variable, but there are at least some persons who move through this inchoate and disordered socialization process to achieve what they, at least, view as satisfaction. In part, this level of satisfaction may well be the council of despair—the couple covertly agreeing that what they have attained is the best they can hope for in the circumstances. It is evident that most western cultures have very low standards for sexual connoisseurship—indeed, connoisseurship in sexuality is commonly defined as either nymphomania or Don Juanism.

While the specific treatment for the dysfunctions varies in this clinical approach, there is a common core of general permissiveness (sexual conduct is not dirty or wrong); therapists teach specific sexual skills, simultaneously allowing attention on elements that will become subsidiary while not directly attending to the performance element that is dysfunctional. Couples are instructed not to attempt to complete the entire sexual excitement cycle, but to attend to elements of general eroticism or specific skill learning. At the same time there is a revision of specific script elements if they interfere with performance—those inhibited about their own bodies are taught massage and those who are unable to deal with the concreteness of the body are given a learning situation in which bodily exploration is allowed. There is a studied inattention to a completion of the entire sequence of sexual excitement—often even a prohibition—in order to bring into focus the failure of coordination.

What is important about this emphasis on skill learning and symbolic change is that it highlights the significance of learned materials in the coordination of sexual scripts and the performance of concrete sexual acts. Masters and Johnson have largely interpreted their results as being the consequence of releasing natural processes by a decrease in anxiety and self-censoring brought about by conditions of sexual repression and inhibition. I prefer to argue that what they are doing is not releasing a natural process, but rather engaging in sexual reeducation, an additive rather than a revelatory process. This preference is based on the prior argument that successful performance of the sexual excitement process is an elicited and learned social-psychological process shaped by cultural and historical conditions. This emphasis on learning now needs to be carried beyond the domain of whose who are willing to be treated for what they experience as sexual difficulties; the approach is also necessary for an examination of the processes by which competent sexual performances occur, independent of therapeutic interventions, in ordinary situations (that is, in the artificial circumstances of a specific culture and at a moment in history, which is only transiently something that we can call "natural").

From the point of view of motives, it is important to note another problem. Sexual conduct shares with other aspects of human conduct the dilemma of the divergences in the scripts and the practical motives between parties involved in the most successful concrete performances. Women and men may come together sexually for goals and for practical motives that involve love or lust, exploitation or commiseration, self-aggrandizement or self-loathing, and even with the widest differences in scripts, they may manage to engage in what both experience as extremely successful activity. The practical motives are a variable part of the script, but once the subsidiary skills are learned, it is possible for persons to perform a concrete conventional sexual repertoire with all of the thoughtless grace of dancing a minuet. But this success should not blind us to the importance of sexual scripts, for they exist as a bridge, as sustaining heuristic devices to promote novel conduct and to solve problems of uncoordination. Their flexibility allows us to move from situation to situation and to recognize why one situation is the same as another or why another situation is different. The script is crucial, since it is through using or changing it that gaps in concrete life are managed and levels of connoisseurship are attained. This is implied in graffiti I found on a toilet-room wall (attributed there to John Barth): "Technique in art is like that in lovemaking, heartfelt ineptitude has its appeal, as does heartless skill, but what is wanted is passionate virtuosity." All of these are possible in the relationship between our sexual scripts and our concrete sexual acts. The fictional couple I described were characterized by the first, we have deep cultural reservations about the second, and the last may represent the limits of our present personal and cultural vision.

REFERENCES

Aries, Philippe. *Centuries of childhood: A social history of family life.* New York: Vintage Books, 1962.

Baldwin, A. L. A cognitive theory of socialization. In D. A. Goslin (Ed.), *Handbook of socialization theory and research.* Chicago: Rand McNally, 1969. Pp. 325–345.

Erikson, Erik. *Childhood and society.* (2d ed.) New York: Norton, 1963.

Fowles, John. *The French lieutenant's woman.* London: Panther Books, 1970.

Goffman, Erving. *Relations in public.* New York: Basic Books, 1971.

Kinsey, A. C., et al. *Sexual behavior in the human male.* Philadelphia: Saunders, 1948.

Kinsey, A. C., et al. *Sexual behavior in the human female.* Philadelphia: Saunders, 1953.

Masters, W. H., & Johnson, V. E. *Human sexual response.* Boston: Little, Brown & Co., 1966.

Masters, W. H., & Johnson, V. E. *Human sexual inadequacy.* Boston: Little, Brown & Co., 1970.

Miller, G. A.; Galanter, E.; & Pribram, K. H. *Plans and the structure of behavior.* New York: Holt, 1960.

Polanyi, Michael. *Personal knowledge: Towards a post-critical philosophy.* New York: Harper Torchbooks, 1964.

Simon, W., & Gagnon, J. H. On psychosexual development. In D. A. Goslin (Ed.), *Handbook of socialization theory and research.* Chicago: Rand McNally, 1969. Pp. 733–752.

White, Robert W. Competence and psychosexual stages of development. In M. R. Jones (Ed.), *Nebraska symposium on motivation, 1960.* Lincoln: University of Nebraska Press, 1960.

The Social, the Erotic, and the Sensual: The Complexities of Sexual Scripts[1]

WILLIAM SIMON

Institute for Juvenile Research, Chicago, Illinois

If the major task of motivational psychology is the explanation of the *why* of human behavior, its most critical tasks and opportunities must center upon that part of human behavior which is most problematic, or where the relationship between the actor, the environment, and the act or action is both complex and uncertain. This focus upon action, for our present purposes, serves two important and interrelated functions. First, it helps to narrow considerably our responsibility to motivational psychology (which often ranges with sufficient scope to make it a near synonym for psychology per se), and second, it constrains us to adopt a perspective that makes it difficult to escape into levels of abstraction where oversimplified labels for categories of actors (e.g., homosexual) and categories of behavior (e.g., gratification seeking, dissonance reduction, etc.) replace real people engaged in concrete, though complex, behaviors within an environment that may be mapped in numerous ways.

As one surveys the current literature on motivation, dominated as it appears to be by a heavy commitment to the experimental, one cannot help but be struck by a curious combination of the concrete and the abstract: behaviors, human and nonhuman, that appear without any sense of context, with meaning being derived from the labels that name the bits of behavior, providing us, more often than not, with parables rather than data (Berkowitz, 1969). It is a world in which the human experience becomes difficult to recognize and,

1. Research for this paper was carried out under NICHD grant HD 04156.

61

to the degree that it is expressive of the human experience, where that experience stands almost totally denuded of any sense of the historical—personal, social, or cultural. This occurs partly because in our immediate situation we are compelled to confront scientific ideologies that stand apart, or appear to stand apart, from our substantive activities (the master image being the relationship of the physicist and the atomic bomb) and partly because of a more long-standing commitment of the behavioral sciences to the assumption of a universal model of man. It is the latter, the commitment to a universal model of man, in terms of which all sociocultural moments or particular locations within the sociocultural moment are special adaptations, that allows us to play at meeting the "independent" norms of science and justifying our activities in terms of a "permanent" accumulation of wisdom that appear "transhistorical" in character. At the same time, it allows us to apply simplifying and homogenizing labels to what by that act—and possibly that act alone —become meaningfully comparable acts or attributes. (It has often been observed that one of the limitations of the historical record is that it disproportionately represents the perspectives of the victors. Similarly, the science of an era belongs disproportionately to the living, though students in social science classes will frequently dispute that. An Erikson can describe a Luther in terms which, while not necessarily making him a contemporary, make him under-standable in contemporary terms; in a highly deceptive way, this becomes an act of celebrating the illusion of the transhistorical nature of our own assumed natures. What is missing is the opportunity for a Reformation-Age counterpart to a behavioral scientist to explain a Billy Graham, a Pope John or Pope Paul, or an Alan Watts. Were this to become possible, we might then have to face an immense abyss separating the distinct sixteenth-century sense of the human from our own—an outcome that would threaten not only the permanence and meaning of the "truths" we labor so long and hard to produce, but also the very significance of our lives [Fischer, 1970].)

Nowhere, for the moment, does the concept of universal man (and woman) take on greater seeming validity than in the area of the sexual. Over millennia the body itself appears to have changed very little; the finite number of concave and convex surfaces of the body have generally combined in ways that appear to transcend historical and cultural variability. On the level of "organ grinding" (Marcus, 1966), very little changes; little that is new is left to be invented. All of this contributes to the illusion that the sexual remains a common thread running through the human record, and we are encouraged to apply identical or nearly identical language (with a substantial weighting of assumptions about motivation) to what appear to be identical or nearly identical behaviors (Freud, 1953; Kinsey, et al., 1948, 1953).

Reinforcing, and being reinforced by, the idea that the sexual man is the universal man (or man at his most universal level) is the conception of the sexual as being expressive of man's very rootedness in the natural order of things. Supported not only by the seeming transhistorical and transcultural character of sexual behavior, but also by apparent cross-species similarities (depending upon the flexibilities of the language, sometimes extending over the full range of living organisms the idea of sexual capacity more often conceived of as instinct or drive than as appetite, Beach, 1956) is taken for granted, leaving individual theories to compete merely in accounting for the organization of its expression and assessing its importance or power. The most influential recent thought about human sexuality falls very much within this tradition: the biogenetic model of Freud, the comparative zoological approach of Kinsey, and the medical model of Masters (Masters & Johnson, 1966).

One major consequence of this intellectual tradition has been a marked tendency to see the sexual as a subject matter in its own right, requiring approaches to motivation all its own. Even more common has been the tendency to submerge a concern for motivation within a developmental perspective; accounting for the appearance of some form of sexual behavior seemingly obviates the need for accounting for the meaning and uses of that behavior for the individual. This has been particularly true in our handling of sexual deviance, where etiological concerns dominate the literature (or have until very recently), and attention to conventional sexual development is limited to blandly generalized statements (Simon & Gagnon, 1967). Once again, the assumption that the sexual is something akin to a primary act allows us to assume a meaning, feeling, or experience without having to acknowledge the profound variability that characterizes the meanings, feelings, and experiences of sexual actors, in categories of both the conventional and the deviant. (The problem of the relationship between sexual development and sexual behavior is critical, being the point where we might distinguish between developmental and motivational perspectives; we will return to it shortly.)

The emphasis upon cross-species or phylogenetic continuity with reference to the sexual, among other effects, has most generally colored our thinking about the sexual in two somewhat contradictory respects. On one hand, we have seen the reproductive aspect of sexual behavior as something of an organizing principle, almost as if a powerful and direct commitment to species responsibility were programmed as an attribute of all individual actors, except perhaps the maldeveloped (Tiger, 1969). On the other hand, it is seen in terms of a primitive and powerful force that is presocial; it is viewed as hostile to the rational and, when unchecked by social regulation, dangerously antisocial in its expression (Davis, 1971).

This "naturalistic" view of the sexual, with an almost inevitable stress upon its passionate and primitive character, is further reinforced by our very sense of the conventional heterosexual coital act, particularly as seen (more typically imagined) through that rather rich and vivid language used to describe it in lay, literary, or scientific terminology. We tend to view it as a universally understood drama ("the primal scene") that contains its own definition and generates its own recognition, if only on preconscious levels. Yet it is precisely at this point, where behavior appears in its most powerful garb, that the extreme behaviorist position provides the least insight. Imagine, if you will, a panel of matched penises entering an equal number of matched or randomized vaginas: the penises all thrust the identical number of thrusts, all simultaneously achieve orgasms of equal magnitude, and all withdraw at the same time, leaving all vaginas in an equal state of indifference. What can we possibly know about the character of any of these acts? Or any of the involved actors? Let me suggest, if I may, some reasonable candidates for this panel: (a) a lower-class male, having a mild sensual experience, though glowing with the anticipation of the homosocial acknowledgment he will receive as long as the vagina did not belong to his wife; (b) an upper-middle-class male crushed by his inability to bring his partner to orgasm; (c) a male achieving unusual orgasmic heights because his partner is a prostitute or someone else of equally degraded erotic status; (d) a stereotyped Victorian couple "doing their thing" —or is it "his thing"?—or possibly, natives of contemporary rural Ireland; (e) a husband fulfilling his marital obligations while dreaming dreams of muscular young truck drivers; (f) a couple performing an act of sexual initiation in the back seat of a VW; and (g) a Belgian nun being raped by a Hun.

Similarly, we may well ask whether or to what degree a pair of homosexual lovers in the Athens of Socrates bears any resemblance to a pair of homosexual lovers in midtown Manhattan, or whether either of these resembles a pair of homosexual lovers here in Lincoln, Nebraska? It is possible that, aside from the not inconsiderable issue of gender preference, differences between all pairs may exceed similarities.

Further, were we able to characterize accurately an entire community's population with regard to general aspects of the sexual, it is likely that all categories of sexual preference (except for the dramatically deviant, at best an extremely small proportion) would be represented, though in differing proportions. Were we, for example, to identify all of those for whom the sexual was currently very salient, those who were actually going to engage in some form of sexual activity (whether or not it is salient), or those for whom a sexual experience would be productive of demoralization and self-alienation—or, if you prefer, productive of ecstasy, recreation, and self-actualization—such categories (i.e., the salient, the active, the negative, and the positive) would contain homosexuals and heterosexuals, as well as other types of sexual preferences.

It is, in many ways, a mark of the intellectual backwardness of the field that our nearly exclusive concern, on theoretically responsive levels, has been with the being of sexuality rather than the doing of sex, and in ways that do not appear to be leading toward any approach to the doing of sex. Alternately, the recent growth of attention to the doing of sex that has followed upon the landmark work of Masters and Johnson (1966), has for the most part occurred in an intellectual or theoretical vacuum. To link these two dimensions—the being and the doing—would require that the sexual be denied its currently isolating, privileged status, a status that has been nurtured by our continuing and questionable assumptions about the universal and "natural" nature of the sexual. It would also require that we expect the developmentalist to abandon a view of the sexual as something with an implicit agenda all its own, to be used as a marker for other aspects of development, and view it as a problematic outcome that requires explanation.[2] Moreover, it would also require that our concern for sexual behavior be seen in the broad context of individual lives, individual decision making, and the social context within which the actors function, and seen in conceptual language appropriate to the fullness of these. This, however, is obviously more easily said than done, given both the unevenness of the data we have accumulated and the probably societal intolerance for the kinds of inquiries that would have to be undertaken, as such inquiries would necessarily threaten the preciously guarded capacity of the sexual to feed our anxieties and our fantasies.

The sex act is, if nothing else, an extremely complicated act, one that—as we have attempted to argue—explains little by itself and, more often than not, requires both a complex explanation and an equally complex description (Gagnon & Simon, 1973). We might begin by considering three conceptually distinct, though highly interactive and interdependent, dimensions, all three contributing to the motivation to be sexual—whatever form that might take—and, at the same time, almost incapable of independent effect. These are the *sensual* (bodily responses and the meanings we attribute to them), the *erotic* (the changing images and icons of our personal, but rarely unique, sexual cultures), and the *social* (a somewhat residual category representing the nonsexual motivational inputs for sexually relevant decisions—residual not for its lack of importance, but rather for the heterogeneous quality that makes simple definition virtually impossible).

Of the three, it would appear that the first, the sensual, would be the one that, given the perspective that has marked most considerations of the sexual, should bear the major weight of the explanatory. And while it represents in most instances a minimal condition

2. For example, how "ready" for coital behavior is the upper-status female at age 14? What if we were to compare a 14-year-old of the era that first saw Shakespeare's Juliet with a comparable 14-year-old of the end of the nineteenth century, and then with a contemporary teenager?

(arousal and orgasm having immediate and important bodily dimensions), it is the sensual that may be the most *dependent* of the three components. It becomes particularly important, since an *attitude* toward the sensual is almost definitionally required in establishing one's sexual posture (ranging from high levels of sexual activity to extremely low levels), but in no way that I can see does this reflect a direct or compelling message from the organism as such. The major near exceptions may be found in such phenomena as extremes of hormonal production and physical impairment or maldevelopment as such. However, on this level, the evidence points far more consistently in the direction of negative consequences than positive ones and explains the absence of sexual activity or its decline more often than activity itself.

The conception of the body as a source of compelling messages persists, even within the scientific community, on a level not too far removed from the adolescent male's common fantasy concerning some obscure part of the female anatomy which, once it has been "touched," magically transforms the most repressed of females into eager, if not lustful, partners. Much of the material on foreplay that appears in both the research and applied literatures suggests something akin to this; the process, as they describe it, resembles nothing so much as a car owner's manual explaining how to get a car started on a cold morning.

This is not to say that the body is purely passive, nor to imply that the sexual response is an invention of the mind. Rather, the suggestion, again, is merely to urge a reevaluation of the role traditionally assigned to the instinctive life of the human organism in shaping the expression of sexual behavior. The best evidence for the need for reevaluation is to be found in the manifest discrepancy between physiological capacities for sexual activity that describe in general the two genders and the reported differences in rates of sexual activity observed in most cultures (Masters & Johnson, 1966; Ford & Beach, 1951; Kinsey, et al., 1948, 1953). More specifically, one might point to the relative ineffectiveness of orgasm as a reinforcer for subsequent sexual activity for females. I have in mind here not only the relative ease with which most females in contemporary American society manage relative sexual inactivity during adolescence (Douvan & Adelson, 1966), and the characteristic for limited orgasmic experience for adolescent females to be not associated with continued or increased sexual activity (masturbatory or sociosexual) (Simon, Gagnon, & Berger, 1972), but also the relative ease with which females in a postmarital status report the managing of sexual "deprivation" (Kinsey, et al., 1953). Still stronger evidence can be found in the work of Money and Green demonstrating the primacy of social and psychological conditioning in the determination of "core gender identity" over biological determinants (Green & Money, 1969; Money & Ehrhardt, 1972).

In sum, then, against the prevailing notions of significant biological determination of sexual behavior—a model suggestive of the notion of an internal battery that may vary among subjects in both power and the way with which it is integrated with the larger structure of personality, but that links in a fixed and direct way with man's phylogenetic heritage—I would argue the need for developing a model focusing upon the learning or invention of sexual commitments or identities, based at best upon a limited biological capacity or, in Beach's term, appetite (Beach, 1956).

It is worth recalling, at this point, an observation made by Beach at an earlier meeting of this symposium: of the several biologically rooted forms of human behavior, it is almost uniquely an aspect of the sexual that inactivity (or the more loaded term, deprivation) is not necessarily followed by some negative consequence. Individuals have lived lives of total celibacy or have been celibate for long periods of time without manifesting impairment or deterioration that could be directly linked to their abstention. Moreover, others, predominantly females, have engaged in sexual behavior with little or no conscious sensual response. (A mark of the record of sexism that covers much of the human record—a history that colors much of our thinking about the sexual in subtle and almost preconscious ways—is the fact that women have rarely been selected for a role in sexual activity on the basis of their own erotic commitments or capacities.) Victorian woman may well have been more fact than myth; it was, as I recall, George Eliot who described her husband as a "perfect gentleman" because, among other things, he "used her but once or twice a month."

The other two dimensions of sexuality belong to the world of socialization, social learning, and symbol systems. And while there are substantial differences between what I have called the erotic and the social, they are similar in that they are prepossessingly assimilated, organized, and expressed in terms of that uniquely human capacity (or perhaps, uniquely human necessity) to have virtually all experience, including the experiencing of self, mediated by symbols and symbolic meanings (Schachtel, 1959). The content of symbols and symbol systems is obviously learned and, in that sense, may be conceived for some purposes as a kind of "dependent variable." However, at the same time, insofar as they also organize experience, they may also be conceived as "independent variables." This quality of "independence" partly derives from the fact that they are not totally dependent upon external influence or experience for subsequent modification, either in content or function. Somewhat autonomously, there is an important and frequently neglected potential for the merger of meanings, the establishment of linkages between otherwise unrelated and even disparate orders of experience, and a corresponding reordering of meanings that derives from the peculiarly plastic and abstract character of symbolic processes.

Both the language and perspective being invoked at this point obviously belong to Kenneth Burke, whose insistence that we learn to treat symbolic materials—both collective and personal—in terms of their intrinsic resources and capacities, as against the standard, more behavioristic approaches of the behavioral sciences that tend to view them as being little more than passive instruments or reflections of the ongoing social process, has rarely been given the kind of consideration it deserves (Burke, 1935).

It is this capacity for interchanges of meaning (and, implicitly, of the complexity and power of particular symbols or aspects of symbolic universes) that generates the complexity that potentially characterizes the sexual and, moreover, that creates the *scripted character* of sexual behavior, or, for that matter, the scripted character of much of human behavior per se. This migratory or changeful potential was clearly recognized by the psychoanalytic tradition in the concept of sublimation, where behavior serves as a "container" for the expression of many needs, interests, or emotions, which are related to one another primarily through the invisible (at least on the level of mere observation or even of superficial analysis) structure of meaning or a personal version of a symbolic universe. Implicit in the psychoanalytic concept of sublimation, however, was the notion of an underlying motive, meaning, or reality and a superficial meaning or—in a limited sense—pseudoreality. While we are able, from this view, to play games with libido, or turn it to uses alien to its basic nature, it remains at its root and source "faithful" to its original and continuing nature. Libido may be rechanneled or disguised in its expression, but only at cost to the actor, and moreover, while it will alter the character of behavior to which it has been harnessed, its character cannot be said to change.

The perspective I am proposing would postulate a continuing potential for reordering of meanings (and, implicitly, of motives as well) of a fundamental character, a reordering that has permanent consequences in the sense that later changes are at the very least as significant in informing current behavior as were the original or earlier meanings and, in many instances, more significant. For example, as Burke observed over thirty years ago, the linking of sexual and political metaphors (or motives), which can occur as an almost totally "internal" operation, creates effects that operate on both levels, affecting the sexual and the political. As the political (to follow classical psychoanalytic or libido theory) becomes a vessel for the expression of latent or disguised sexual motives (Freud, 1966), so, too, can the sexual become a vessel for the expression of latent or disguised political motives (Simon & Simon, 1962). Norman Mailer remains something of the apotheosis of this particular union, as not merely one whose political and sexual styles cannot be understood without reference to the other, but whose development on either side cannot be understood without reference to the other (Mailer, 1971).

The term *script* or *scripted behavior* immediately suggests the dramatic, which is appropriate; but it also suggests the conventional dramatic narrative form, which, more often than not, is inappropriate. The latter tendency is reinforced by our most general notion of the sex act itself, which is seen as a dramatic event with continuous cumulative action. This is suggested, for example, by the language of Masters and Johnson (1966)—arousal, plateau, climax, and resolution—a conception resembling somewhat an Aristotelian notion of the dramatic or the design for a nineteenth-century symphony. However, the sources of arousal, passion, or excitement (the recognition of a sexual possibility), as well as the way the event is experienced (if, indeed, an event follows), derive from a complicated set of layered symbolic meanings that not only are difficult to comprehend from the observed behavior, but also may not be shared by the participants. Even where there is a minimal sharing of elements of a script by persons acting toward each other (which, while not necessary, clearly facilitates execution of the acts with mutual satisfaction), they may be organized in different ways and invoked at different times (see Gagnon article, pp. 27–60).

Again, the same overt gesture may have a different meaning and play a different role in organizing the sexual "performance." It is not unlikely that the identical gesture undertaken during sexual activity may be read by one participant with a content that might resemble that of De Sade or Sacher-Masoch, while the other derives from *Love Story.*

As we will see in a moment, elements entering into the performance may be both relatively remote to the erotic (or what is conventionally defined as remote to the erotic) as well as immediately and intrinsically erotic. Moreover, the logic of organization may more closely follow the nonnarrative qualities of modern poetry, the surrealistic tradition, or the theater of the absurd than conventional narrative modes. The sexual, with more commonality with other, nonsexual forms of behavior, provides us with a situation where the mere invocation of some powerfully organizing metaphor links behavior to whole universes of meaning, a situation where the power of a metaphorically enriched gesture, act, characteristic, object, or posture cannot be determined by the relative frequency with which it occurs. Such organizing metaphors need only be suggested for their effects to be realized.

An example of this may be seen in Kosinski's novel *Steps* (1968), where the nameless hero finds himself looking down upon a fellow office worker (female) whom he has long desired sexually and who is at the moment in a posture of unrestrained sexual accessibility. Though it is a moment he has long desired, he finds himself unable to become aroused. He then recalls the occasion of his initial sexual interest, a moment in which, while watching her in the act of filing papers with uplifted arms, he caught a fleeting glimpse of her bra. This trivial image, originally arousing, remains arousing, and the hero goes on to complete the act. It is that image (and what it links to) that both names her as an erotic object in terms of his sense of the erotic and also names what he is about to do to her. Though the image need only be briefly suggested (both in its origins and subsequent utilization) and remains unknown to the behaviorist observer, it becomes critical to the performance. Its meanings could be several. It could mean, for example, that the sexual becomes erotically enriched when it is hidden, latent, or denied, or when it is essentially violative (deriving from unintended exposure). It also legitimates the appropriate name for the behavior. Consider the possible "labels" our hero could have invoked that could have been applied to the behavior, each with its own powerful and powerfully distinct associations: making love, making out, fucking, screwing, humping, doing, raping.

Recall, if you will, two of the penises from our hypothetical panel of penises: the male who is achieving a powerful orgasm (or feels that it was an unusually powerful orgasm) because his partner is a prostitute or one of comparably degraded status and the male who was bothered by his inability to bring his partner to orgasm. Both of these can be not only the same individual at different stages of development or the same individual in different social locations during the same stage of development, but can also be experiencing both as he reacts to the same, single experience—one individual reacting complexly to the same coital act, with the same partner, at the one moment. In this illustration it could be a wife or girl friend who provides, either unknowingly or complicitly, the imagery of the prostitute. Once again, literature provides us with an excellent example of just the process in O'Hara's early novel, *Appointment in Samara* (1934), where the hero expresses his very inability to manage a world of mounting social strains through aggressive sexual performances which his wife facilitates by wearing, at those moments, a black negligee which both refer to as her "whoring gown." Now this might appropriately be taken as being symptomatic of a complex, if not ambivalent, attitude toward sex, but it may equally be approached as a manifestation of a complex and/or ambivalent attitude toward dominance and submission—power, if you will—that may derive from experiences initially remote to the sexual.

Something similar to this can be found in the observation that homosexual content is sometimes present in the dreams or fantasies of minimally heterosexual men who are experiencing occupational stresses, particularly where the problems of managing authority relationships are involved (Ovesey, 1950).

The erotic component, we can assume, is minimally necessary if sexual activity is to occur; that is, it gives the activity its very importance. (A dramatic exception, of course, includes many women whose participation in sexual activity has often—historically, possibly more often than not—had little to do with their own sense of the erotic.) On the other hand, a preoccupation with the erotic may reach obsessive proportions without overt sexual behavior necessarily following. Thus, like the sensual component, it can be described as simultaneously being of critical importance and also insufficient by itself to be either fully descriptive or predictive of actual sexual careers.

While the importance of the erotic can be asserted, it may be the most difficult to elaborate, as a concern for the erotic—the acquisition of sexual culture—is possibly the least well understood or attended aspect of sexual behavior. We know very little about how it is acquired or, for that matter, the ways in which it influences both our sexual and nonsexual lives. Persistence of concepts like libido or the sex drive obviate need for this knowledge. For those who hold these or comparable positions, the body is frequently seen as being both wise and articulate, recognizing and speaking a compelling language. Still others have assumed, in too unexamined a way, a direct link between collective sexual cultures and private sexual cultures, despite the fact that, for many, what is collectively defined as erotic may not be associated with sexual response or that much that the collectivity defines as non- or even antierotic may become part of the private sexual culture of a given individual (e.g., various kinds of full and partial fetishisms). As a result, much of the research on responses to erotic materials often begins with the dubious assumption that experimental stimuli are recognizable in terms of a conventional social definition.

It is clear that, for contemporary society, erotic imagery or metaphors are, for the most part, discontinuously or only latently a part of the images or metaphors of nonsexual identity or social life. (The exceptions are those social roles that are specifically assumed to have a "known" erotic aspect, such as the prostitute, the homosexual, the stewardess, and the divorcee, all of whom we tend to see as either fully erotic or unusually erotic to the point where we have difficulty seeing them in anything but erotic terms.) Thus, for conventional actors in relatively conventional settings, the invocation of the erotic, necessary for sexual arousal, frequently requires a series of rituals of transformation before either of the partners or the setting license, as it were, the sexual moment. For example, much of precoital petting or foreplay may serve less as facilitators of a physiological process than as elements in a ritual drama, allowing one or both actors to rename themselves, their partners, as well as various parts of the body in terms of this "special" purpose. The intrusion of nonerotic, manifest meanings to images (i.e., parts of the body or nonsexual role commitments of one or another of the actors) is experienced as disruptive of sexual interest and/or capacity, if only because such commitments are rarely predictive of sexual role needs. For most, as a consequence, the sexual flourishes best in a sheltered and, in some sense, isolated universe, a landscape denuded of all but the most relevant aspects of identity.

At the same time, the larger part of identity and the sense of the rest of social life frequently intrudes in an indirect way. The elaboration of the erotic or its direct expression is often constrained by an anticipation of the return to that larger social role, that more continuous sense of self. For some, this may involve merely the insulation of silence. For others, there may be symbolic reinterpretation and condensation: for example, an intensity of pressure that allows the actor to represent by that gesture passion (or convey the message that uncharacteristic behavior is explained); love or affection (meaning that the actor is the same as he or she is in a more conventional mode of relating); and sadistic aggression (illuminating a complicated fantasy rehearsed and experienced sufficiently that the gesture successfully evokes most of the emotional density generated by a long and frequently complicated scenario).

Beyond the very general level, little can be said. Important questions dealing not only with origins but careers have yet to be examined even provisionally. Where do such images come from? In terms of what sexual and nonsexual experiences do their meanings change? Is there need for elaboration? These, and many more, are the questions that we may have to examine before sexual activity, which all too often can be described as a dumb show for its participants, becomes something other than that for behavioral science.

Unfortunately, there is little likelihood that research on the development, content, and uses of erotic capacities will be undertaken in the near future. The very conditions that are presently necessary for sex research often actually serve to preclude a concern for the erotic component. The de-eroticization of the sexual appears necessary to allay the anxieties of the research subjects and the funding sources, as well as the researcher himself or herself. As it has in the past, the erotic will most likely remain a neglected frontier of sex research or, worse, remain in the hands of those whose interests are "overdetermined" and whose research skills and sense of professional responsibility will remain "underdeveloped."

The erotic obviously provides in a very direct way the basis for much of *sociosexual behavior*, which, in turn, might be defined as the organization of social activity and social space in order to facilitate sexual behavior. Of equal, if not greater, importance is what might be termed *sexiosocial behavior*, that is, the organization of the sexual in order to facilitate essentially nonsexual social and personal goals. To lapse into Freudian imagery, while *ego* must regulate libidinous impulses associated with *id*, seeking to confine or channel their expression into socially acceptable outlets, the relationship is not exclusively unidirectional. Ego has sexual interests of its own, independent of id—indeed, involving interests that generate a commitment to the sexual without necessarily being a reaction to the pressures of id. In many instances, for example, we might easily conceive of strong motivation to engage in sexual behavior that derives from a utilization of the sexual to realize the confirmation of ego's idealized sense of self. *In some instances, the pressures to perform sexiosocial activity deriving from ego's needs may exceed those deriving from any id-like or immediately sexual needs.* The clearest example of this may be the pressures upon young males to engage in coital behavior as part of a continuing need for masculinity confirmation (Gagnon & Simon, 1973). Further, many of the intraphysic conflicts that contemporary actors experience with the sexual may involve precisely this kind of problem. To anticipate some of our subsequent discussion, this may be seen in a conflict between pleasure (i.e., a concern for one's own orgasm) and competence (i.e., a concern for one's partner's orgasm).

The most obvious, and possibly most influential, of the social determinants of sexual scripting is the quality of nonsexual, gender role learning or gender identification. Moreover, given the general weight of evidence that points to rather early development of gender identity (Stollar, 1968; Green & Money, 1969), it is possible that the critical link between the very earliest experiences ("infantile sexuality") and subsequent adolescent and adult sexual patterns may not be direct, but indirect, as such early experience more importantly shapes gender identity, which in turn influences later sexual adaptations (Kagan & Moss, 1962).

Such concepts as "penis envy" and "castration fear," then, may affect later sexual development primarily through the elaboration and assimilation of gender role ideals. For females, this is more dramatically manifested in the differences with males in terms of masturbation. Not only do significantly fewer females masturbate than do males, but frequencies are strikingly lower. About half of those females who do masturbate do so only after having had the experience of orgasm in some kind of sociosexual context (as against males, for whom masturbation is nearly the universal introduction to orgasm); moreover, the frequencies for females during adolescence suggest the failure for orgasm to provide substantial conditioning impact (Kinsey, et al., 1948; Kinsey, et al., 1953). For most females, the very sense of the sexual and of their own bodies that merges with female gender training almost precludes a substantial masturbatory capacity, since it points to the need for realizing self sexually only through an attachment to a male actor. From this perspective, the great emphasis upon masturbation that has been associated with "the women's movement," and for which it has received much criticism, is not totally misplaced.

Similarly, even homosexual adaptations tend to be strongly influenced by gender training. This makes sense in that we learn to be men or women before we learn to be sexual in any explicit sense. Thus, the lesbian's chronological ordering of psychosexual development, including the actual entry into sociosexual activity, the patterns of masturbation, the conditions associated with sexual arousal, and even the number of partners, tends to approximate closely that of heterosexual women. Similarly, patterns of male homosexual behavior, while often differing significantly from heterosexual male patterns, still is best explained within the context of male socialization—but male socialization "uncorrupted" by the retraining (if not the resocialization) imposed by greater commitments to both heterosexuality and heterosociality (Gagnon & Simon, 1973).

While gender identity and training provide the most general framework within which sexual scripts are elaborated, they point to specific sexual adaptation only in highly probabilistic ways. Among other contributing factors is one of major significance: commitment to the religious-moral system of a social order. In western societies, to learn about sex is almost simultaneously to learn about sin and guilt, making the sexual both more powerful as well as more problematic. Much as the early protestant looked to economic success as signifying his moral status (Weber, 1930), the sexual is taken in contemporary society as an indicator of moral status. Possibly, as the scope of the society enlarges, the sexual becomes one of the few areas of social life where "significant" moral behavior becomes possible (Simon, 1973). As a mark of this, in the research of Kinsey (1948; 1953) and virtually all the research that has followed (Reiss, 1967; Simon, et al., 1972; Miller, et al., 1973), religious participation was among the most predictive variables. Ritual elaboration of devices to provide for the management and focusing of guilt and anxiety surely must become a major part of the sexual scripts of most individuals. The erotic, I suspect, depends critically on a tenuous balance between guilt and anxiety as amplifiers of the experience (making it more powerful and passionate), not as inhibitors of the experience.

One consequence of the intellectual isolation within which most of our current knowledge about human sexuality has been developed is that we tend to view sexual gratification without reference to the social context. In no way that I can see is there a way of establishing the meaning of sexual pleasure, particularly with reference to the meaning and valuation of other sources of pleasure. Once again, most of our assumptions about the compelling attractiveness and intensity of sexual gratification are derived from the commonly held

assumptions about the sexual as an expression of an equally compelling instinctive drive. However, once this position is abandoned,
we must begin to confront the sexual as merely one of a number of
component elements that are an individual's *repertoire of gratifications*.
The balance of such components and their relative importance and
value shift over time, both in a historical sense and in the sense of
movement through the life cycle.

With historical change, we can expect changes in the economic
value and accessibility of given gratifications. The meaning and
power of the sexual should differ radically between those subject to
the "anomie of deprivation" and those subject to the "anomie of
affluence" (Simon & Gagnon, 1972). In situations of extreme deprivation we might expect the sexual to have only limited value, as
other gratifications more closely tied to immediate survival take
precedence. It is in situations of moderate or relative deprivation
that the sexual should take on maximum value, given the relatively
greater resources potentially allocable to sexual pursuits and the
relatively greater costs (or risks) associated with other modes of
gratification. The latter suggests that the sexual in some situations
becomes a vehicle for focusing a number of unrealized aspirations,
beyond those involving the sexual itself. Lastly, situations of
affluence might well produce a complex response; for some, particularly those for whom affluence was an unexpected outcome, sexual
experience might achieve greater significance, as other goals that
once focused aspirations are realized and found existentially wanting.
For still others, essentially those for whom affluence is the assumed
condition of life, the sexual may take on less significance as it cannot
as easily substitute for other, less available, gratifications and when,
generally, repertoires of gratification are more likely to be fashioned
in terms of great existential realism.

Similarly, we might consider the differential role of the sexual
and the motivation to be sexual as individuals move through the life
cycle. The larger part of societal attention to the sexual in recent
years has been focused upon the young and near young. This is not
unexpected, as it is just during such periods that the sexual looms
the largest, both because it is commonly experienced as more problematic (in a multiple sense), and because the sexual is most significant
then in determining public status. Extramarital sex has received

increasing attention. However, marital sex, where most adults in our society spend most of their years, remains largely unattended. Sex among the aged has only recently been raised as a legitimate concern—for the aged or for social scientists.

The predominant imagery in our society depicting "active" sexuality is currently limited to the several years of later adolescence and young adulthood (with a satiric gesture to the "dirty old man"), the main point, again, in life when one's sexuality has quasi-public status. The assumption is frequently made that most of what follows can be ascribed to biological decline. Not only does this position do manifest injustice to patterns of female sexuality, it does an injustice to sexuality per se. What does change, with possibly greater significance—for some, with gentle continuity, for others, strident disjuncture—are the repertoires of gratification, within which changing sexual potentials must find their place.

A final aspect of social determination: I am reminded of White's paper given at these meetings a number of years ago (White, 1960). In that paper, White argues for the affirmation or experience of competence as a mode of gratification that competes rather effectively with the pleasures of the immediately sensual. This, I feel, makes a great deal of sense, explaining more of sexual behavior as a social and psychological event than most interpretations. Here we might recall the example from our panel of penises of the penis owner who is extremely nervous about his ability to bring his partner to orgasm and whose sense of that experience is heavily shaped by that nervousness. The current, almost obsessive, concern with technique might also be taken as something of a triumph of competence over the erotic.

Some research indicates that orgasm reached through masturbation may quite often be a more powerful event in terms of gross physiological effects than that reached through forms of sociosexual activity. This makes some sense in that during masturbation one need only attend to one's own needs, without having to cope with the uncertainties of a body controlled predominantly by someone else—a problem Gagnon has described for us at these meetings. At the same time, however, such orgasms are generally reported to be less powerful. Perhaps what subjects are saying is that it was less gratifying. And this, I think, may be read, in turn, as: masturbation is less gratifying, not because it fails to fill erotic needs, but rather because it leaves the actor feeling incompetent—socially first, and then sexually. (Gratification is probably also lessened by guilt for making demands upon one's partner that are virtually never made outside of fantasy.)

A final observation, linked more directly to concepts of competence than to the erotic, is that purely status considerations often produce powerful sexual interests: making it with the prom queen or the star quarterback, any one of the Beautiful People, or the Playmate of the Month. Important to Mailer's version of the American dream is to make it big with some black stud's woman, then beat him up, and then get him to like you—the simultaneous triumph of the sexual, the physical, and the liberal mind (Mailer, 1964). This is preeminently the world of the sexiosocial. The impact of status needs, as contrasted with the power of the sexual, may be seen in the following: Suppose one had the opportunity to choose between spending the night with some near-mythic sexual celebrity without anyone knowing about it, or having the entire world believe it had happened, when in fact it had not. Which of us would not prefer the reputation to the actual experience?

What I have attempted to provide is a view of the sexual experience as complex rather than simple; unnatural rather than an expression of our phylogenetic inheritance; variable rather than constant in its most fundamental aspects, not only across generations, but also within a single life's experience; and, ultimately, a part of the human experience that requires explanation more often than it provides explanation. In sum: sexual behavior is scripted behavior in the sense that its very sources and meaning (except for that part of it which becomes habit and ritual, which may actually be a great deal of it) derive from structures of meaning and possible motivation that cannot be understood or inferred from the observed behavior. Two largely unmet challenges in sex research are the understanding of the elements that enter these structures and the ways in which they are organized—a strategy of strategies, in the language of Kenneth Burke. Until we respond to these challenges, sex research will resemble nothing so much as a science of icebergs that is based exclusively upon above-surface observations.

REFERENCES

Beach, F. Characteristics of masculine "sex drive." In M. R. Jones (Ed.), *Nebraska Symposium on Motivation, 1956*. Lincoln: University of Nebraska Press, 1956. Pp. 1–32.

Berkowitz, L. Social Motivation. In G. Lindzey and E. Aronson (Eds.), *The Handbook of social psychology*. (2d ed.) Vol. 3. Reading, Mass.: Addison Wesley, 1969. Pp. 52–135.

Burke, K. *Permanence and change*. New York: New Republic, 1935.

Davis, K. Sexual behavior. In R. K. Merton and R. Nisbet (Eds.), *Contemporary social problems*. (3rd ed.) New York: Harcourt Brace Jovanovich, 1971. Pp. 313–405.

Douvan, E., & Adelson, J. B. *Adolescent experience*. New York: John Wiley & Sons, 1966.

Fischer, D. H. *Historical fallacies*. New York: Harper Torchbooks, 1970.

Ford, C. F., & Beach, F. A. *Patterns of social behavior*. New York: Harper, 1951.

Freud, S. Three Essays on Sexuality. In *Complete psychological works*. (Std. ed.) Vol. 7. London: Hogarth, 1953. Pp. 135–245.

Freud, S. *The complete introductory lectures on psychoanalysis*. Trans. and ed. by James Strachey. New York: W. W. Norton, 1966.

Gagnon, J., & Simon, W. *Social sources of human sexuality*. Chicago: Aldine, 1973.

Green, R., & Money. J. (Eds.). *Transsexualism and sex reassignment*. Baltimore: Johns Hopkins University Press, 1969.

Kagan, J., & Moss, H. A. *From birth to maturity*. New York: John Wiley & Sons, 1962.

Kinsey, A. C., et al. *Sexual behavior in the human male*. Philadelphia: Saunders, 1948.

Kinsey, A. C., et al. *Sexual behavior in the human female*. Philadelphia: Saunders, 1953.

Kosinski, J. N. *Steps*. New York: Random House, 1968.

Mailer, N. *American dream*. New York: Dial Press, 1964.

Mailer, N. *Prisoner of sex*. Boston: Little, Brown & Co., 1971.

Marcus, S. *The other victorians*. New York: Basic Books, 1966.

Masters, W. H., & Johnson, V. E. *Human sexual response*. Boston: Little, Brown & Co., 1966.

Miller, P. Y.; Simon, W.; & Cottrell, C. B. Some social and psychological correlates of adolescent sexuality. Paper presented at the annual meeting of the Pacific Sociological Association at Scottsdale, Arizona, May, 1973.

Money, J., & Ehrhardt, A. A. *Man and woman, boy and girl: Differentiation and dimorphism of gender identity from conception to maturity*. Springfield, Ill.: Charles C. Thomas, 1972.

O'Hara, J. *Appointment in samara*. New York: Random House, 1934.

Ovesey, L. Homosexual conflict: An adaptational analysis. *Psychiatry*, 1950, **17**, 243–250.

Reiss, I. L. *Social context of premarital sexual permissiveness*. New York: Holt, Rinehart & Winston, 1967.

Schachtel, E. G. *Metamorphosis*. New York: Basic Books, 1959.

Simon, W. Management and men. In E. C. Bursk (Ed.), *Challenge to leadership: Management in a changing world*. New York: Free Press, 1973. Pp. 275–297.

Simon, W., & Gagnon, J. Homosexuality: The formulation of a sociological perspective. *Journal of Health and Social Behavior*, 1967, **8**, 177–185.

Simon, W., & Gagnon, J. Anomie of affluence: A post-Mertonian conception. Mimeographed, 1972.

Simon, W.; Gagnon, J.; & Berger, A. Beyond fantasy and anxiety: The coital experience of college youth. *Journal of Youth and Adolescence*, 1972, **1** (3), 203–221.

Simon, W., & Simon, M. Past the visceral sleuth: Reflections on the symbolic representation of deviance. *Studies in Public Communication*, 1962, **4**, 71–84.

Stoller, R. *Sex and gender: On the development of masculinity and femininity*. New York: Science House, 1968.

Tiger, L. *Men in groups*. New York: Random House, 1969.

Weber, M. *Protestant ethic and the rise of capitalism*. New York: Charles Scribner's Sons, 1930.

White, R. Competence and the psychosexual stages of development. In M. R. Jones (Ed.), *Nebraska Symposium on Motivation, 1960*. Lincoln: University of Nebraska Press, 1960. Pp. 97–141.

Paternal and Sex-Role Factors in Cognitive and Academic Functioning

HENRY B. BILLER

University of Rhode Island

This paper is a beginning step in analyzing the multifaceted interaction of the father-child relationship and sex-role development in the young child's cognitive and academic functioning. Until quite recently, relatively little attention was paid to the father's role in child and personality development. Parental influence was considered to be primarily maternal influence. The father was seen as important only insofar as he was usually the breadwinner and the primary determiner of the family's socioeconomic status. He was not seen as a major factor in the socialization of the child. However, considerable research, especially during the past decade, has modified more traditional views, and now the impact of paternal influence and father absence is being increasingly recognized (Biller, 1971a).

A major purpose of this paper is to examine the relationships between variations in paternal behavior, both qualitative and quantitative, and the child's cognitive functioning and his classroom adjustment. This is an extremely complex area, and in the current discussion there is an attempt to delineate deficiencies in previous studies and to suggest new avenues of research. Serious methodological criticisms can be directed at much of the research that has been conducted concerning father-child relationships. For example, investigators have often ignored variations among father-absent families and have also implicitly made the tenuous assumption that father presence ensures an active father-child relationship. Furthermore, the potential interactions of paternal influence with factors such as variations in mothering, sociocultural variables, and constitutional-genetic variables have generally not been taken into account.

The child's sex-role development has been frequently considered a mediating link between paternal influence and cognitive functioning. For instance, sex-role inadequacies are often associated with both paternal deprivation and academic underachievement. Unfortunately, researchers have generally not attended to the complexity and multidimensionality of the sex-role development process and have usually worked with very limited measures of sex role. In this paper, some consideration is given to findings concerning fathering and sex-role development and to findings concerning sex-role development and cognitive functioning. However, such topics are covered only to the extent that they are relevant to the relationships among paternal influence, academic performance, and cognitive functioning. A more detailed discussion of fathering and sex role and the many antecedents and correlates of sex-role development can be found elsewhere (e.g., Biller, 1971a; Biller, 1973).

FATHERING AND COGNITIVE FUNCTIONING

The first section of this paper includes a description of research efforts which in some way have explored the relationship between fathering and cognitive functioning. Results from several investigations have suggested that boys who have inadequate relationships with their fathers are more likely to be academic underachievers.

Kimball (1952) studied highly intelligent boys enrolled in a residential preparatory school. She compared twenty boys who were failing in school with a group of boys who were randomly selected from the total school population. Interview and psychological test material consistently revealed that the underachieving boys had very inadequate relationships with their fathers. Many of the fathers were reported to work long hours and to be home infrequently, or to attempt to dominate and control their sons by means of excessive discipline. Using a specifically designed sentence completion technique, Kimball found further evidence that significantly more of the boys in the underachieving group had poor relationships with their fathers. Responses suggesting feelings of paternal rejection and paternal hostility were considerably more frequent among the underachieving boys. Projective test data also suggested that the boys had much hostility toward their fathers because they perceived that their fathers had rejected them.

Through the use of extensive clinical interviews, Grunebaum et al. (1962) examined the family life of elementary school boys who had at least average intelligence, but were 1 to 2 years below expectation in their academic achievement (Metropolitan Achievement Test). These boys seemed to have very poor relationships with their fathers. Their fathers were reported to feel generally inadequate and thwarted in their own ambitions, and to view themselves as failures. The fathers appeared to be particularly insecure about their masculinity and did not seem to offer their sons adequate models of male competence. Most of the fathers viewed their wives as being far superior to them, and their wives generally shared this perception. Most of the mothers perceived both their husbands and sons as inadequate and incompetent, and seemed to be involved in undermining their confidence. This study was of an exploratory clinical nature, but it did suggest some of the ways in which the dynamics of the husband-wife relationship can affect the child's academic functioning. It is also interesting to note that boys with inadequate sex-role development are often found in families in which the mother dominates the father and undermines his attempts to be decisive and competent (Biller, 1969a; Hetherington, 1965).

Shaw and White (1965) conducted an investigation of the familial correlates of high and low academic achievement among high school students with above-average intelligence. Adjective checklist rating scales were administered to the students and their parents, who were instructed to describe themselves and other members of their family. High-achieving boys (B average or better) perceived themselves as more similar to their fathers than did low-achieving boys (below a B average). The high-achieving boys also perceived themselves as more similiar to their fathers than their mothers, but low-achieving boys did not. Among the high-achieving group, but not among the low-achieving group, father and son self-ratings were correlated. Such results suggest that father-son closeness and identification are related to academic achievement.

I worked with a group of high school boys who were involved in a project designed to motivate them to utilize their academic potential (Biller, 1966b). In general, these boys had superior intelligence, but their academic functioning was below grade level. Most of the boys were alienated from their fathers. Many of their fathers were quite successful, but according to their son's reports, they were much more devoted to their work than to their families.

Mutimer, Loughlin, and Powell (1966) compared children who were relatively retarded in their reading ability with children who were reading above grade level. Children in both groups were generally well above average in intelligence. On a task involving various choice situations, boys who were high achievers in reading more often indicated that they would prefer to be with their fathers than did boys who were poor readers. Although not statistically significant, similar differences were noted among the girls.

Both Katz (1967) and Solomon (1969) described a strong positive association between paternal interest and encouragement and academic achievement among lower-class black elementary school boys. Katz's findings were based on the boys' perceptions of their parents, whereas Solomon had ratings of parent-child interactions while the boys were performing a series of intellectual tasks. Interestingly, in both studies the father's behavior appeared to be a much more important factor than the mother's behavior.

The studies so far discussed have dealt with paternal factors and their association with academic achievement. In addition, there is evidence that the quality of fathering is related to the child's performance on intelligence and aptitude tests.

Radin (1972) found both the quality and quantity of father-son interactions strongly associated with 4-year-old boys' intellectual functioning. Father-son interactions during an interview with the father were recorded and later coded for frequency of paternal nurturance and restrictiveness. The overall number of father-son interactions was positively correlated to both Stanford-Binet and Peabody Picture Vocabulary Test Intelligence Test scores. However, the strongest relationship observed was between paternal nurturance (seeking out the child in a positive manner, asking information of the child, meeting the child's needs, etc.) and the intelligence test measures. On the other hand, paternal restrictiveness (demands for obedience, etc.) was negatively correlated with level of intellectual functioning. The quality of the father's behavior, particularly paternal nurturance, appeared to be more important than the total number of father-son interactions.

In a subsequent study, Radin (1973) reported evidence indicating that the amount of paternal nurturance at the time of the initial study was still positively related to the boys' intellectual functioning 1 year later. In addition, a questionnaire measure of paternal involvement in direct teaching activities (e.g., teaching the child to count, read, etc.) at the time of the initial study was positively associated with the boys' intellectual functioning both at that time and 1 year later.

Radin (1972, 1973) also found some interesting social-class differences. For the middle-class subsample, the relationship between paternal nurturance and intellectual functioning was much more clear-cut. Middle-class fathers were found to interact more with their children and to be more nurturant than lower-class fathers. These findings are consistent with those of Davis and Havighurst (1946), who reported that middle-class fathers spent more time with their children in activities such as taking walks, as well as in educational functions, than did those from the lower class. Boys with nurturant fathers seem to become motivated to imitate their fathers' instrumental behaviors, cognitive skills, and problem-solving abilities.

Individual Differences

Correlational data do not prove that a positive father-son relationship directly facilitates the boys' intellectual functioning. For example, a father may be much more available, accepting, and nurturant to a son who is bright and performs well in school. On the other hand, disappointment with the son's abilities may lead the father to reject him, and/or the son's performance may further weaken an already flimsy father-son relationship. Individual differences in the child's constitutional predispositions and behavior can have much influence on the quality of interactions between father and child (Biller, 1971a).

Fathers are reported to be much less tolerant of severely intellectually handicapped children than are mothers (Farber, 1962). They seem to develop particularly negative attitudes toward retarded sons (Farber, 1962; Tallman, 1965). The father who highly values intellectual endeavors is especially likely to reject a retarded child (Downey, 1963). Paternal deprivation lessens the probability that the retarded child will maximize his intellectual potential or have adequate sex-role development (Biller, 1971a; Biller & Borstelmann, 1965).

In addition to being the antecedents of some forms of mental retardation, constitutional predispositions and genetic factors may be related to other types of influences affecting the father-child relationship. Father and son can manifest cognitive abilities in the same area primarily as a function of a similar genetic inheritance. Poffenberger and Norton (1959) found that attitudes of fathers and their college freshman sons toward mathematics were similar, yet were not related to closeness of father-son relationship. These investigators speculated that genetic factors are involved in the degree of success in mathematics and can predispose similar father-son attitudes toward mathematics. However, Hill's (1967) findings suggest that more than genetic factors are involved in the child's attitude toward mathematics. In studying the relationship between paternal expectations and upper-middle-class seventh grade boys' attitudes toward mathematics, Hill found that positive attitudes toward mathematics were more common among boys whose fathers viewed mathematics as a masculine endeavor and expected their sons to behave in a masculine manner.

Father Availability

Much of the evidence concerning the father's importance in cognitive development has come indirectly from studies in which father-absent and father-present children have been compared. The first investigator to present data suggesting an intellectual disadvantage among father-absent children was Sutherland (1930). In a rather ambitious study involving Scottish children, he discovered that those who were father-absent scored significantly lower than did those who were father-present. Unfortunately, specific analyses concerning such variables as length of father's absence, sex of child, and socioeconomic status are not included in his report. A number of more recent and better controlled studies are also generally consistent with the supposition that father-absent children, at least those from lower-class backgrounds, are less likely to function well on intelligence and aptitude tests than are father-present children (e.g., Blanchard & Biller, 1971; Deutsch & Brown, 1964; Lessing, Zagorin, & Nelson, 1970; Santrock, 1972).

Maxwell (1961) reported some evidence indicating that father absence after the age of 5 negatively influences children's functioning on certain cognitive tasks. He analyzed the Wechsler Intelligence Test scores of a large group of 8-to-13-year-old children who had been referred to a British psychiatric clinic. He found that children whose fathers had been absent since the children were 5 performed below the norms for their age on a number of subtests. Children who had become father-absent after the age of 5 had lower scores on tasks tapping social knowledge, perception of details, and verbal skills. Father absence since the age of 5 was the only family background variable which was consistently related to subtest scores; it seems surprising that there were no findings related to father absence before the age of 5.

Sutton-Smith, Rosenberg, and Landy (1968) explored the relationship between father absence and college sophomores' aptitude test scores (American College Entrance Examination). These investigators defined father absence as an absence of the father from the home for at least 2 consecutive years. Compared to father-present students, those who were father-absent performed at a lower level in terms of verbal, language, and total aptitude test scores. Although father absence appeared to affect both males and females, it seemed to have more influence on males. Some interesting variations in the effects of father absence as a function of sex of subject and sex of sibling were also reported; for example, in 2-child father-absent families, boys with brothers appeared to be less deficient in academic aptitude than boys with sisters. On the other hand, the father-present girl who was an only child seemed to be at a particular advantage in terms of her aptitude test scores.

In a related investigation, Landy, Rosenberg, and Sutton-Smith (1969) found that father absence had a particularly disruptive effect on the quantitative aptitudes of college females. Total father absence before the age of ten was highly associated with a deficit in quantitative aptitude. Their findings also suggested that father absence during the age period of 3 to 7 may have an especially negative effect on quantitative aptitude.

Lessing, Zagorin, and Nelson (1970) conducted one of the most extensive investigations concerning father absence and cognitive functioning. They studied a group of nearly 500 children (ages 9 to 15) who had been seen at a child guidance clinic and explored the relationship between father absence and functioning on the Wechsler Intelligence Test for Children. They defined father absence as separation from the father for 2 or more years, not necessarily for a consecutive period of time. Father absence, for both boys and girls, was associated with relatively low ability in perceptual-motor and manipulative-spatial tasks (e.g., Block Design and Object Assembly). Father-absent boys also scored lower than father-present boys on the arithmetic subtest. In terms of our society's standards, such tasks are often considered to require typically male aptitudes.

The results of this study suggest some rather complex interactions between father absence and social class. Among working-class children, those who were father-absent performed at a generally lower level than did those who were father-present. They were less able in their verbal functioning as well as in perceptual-motor and manipulative-spatial tasks. In comparison, middle-class children did not appear to be as handicapped by father absence. They earned lower performance scores (particularly in Block Design and Object Assembly), but they actually scored higher in verbal intelligence than did father-present children.

Lessing, Zagorin, and Nelson also found that previously father-absent children who had a father surrogate in their home (e.g., a stepfather) did not have intelligence test scores that were significantly different from those of father-present children. (In general, children with no father figure in the home accounted for most of the differences between father-absent and father-present children.) These findings can be interpreted in terms of a stepfather presenting a masculine model and/or increasing stability in the home. There is other evidence indicating that father surrogates and male siblings and peers can facilitate the child's sex-role and personality development if they are competent and effective models (Biller, 1971a).

The Lessing, Zagorin, and Nelson study is interesting and impressive. In many ways it is a vast improvement over earlier research in which there was an attempt to link father absence and intellectual deficits. For example, there is more detail in the analysis of sex differences, social class, and specific areas of intellectual functioning. In general, the investigators show awareness of potential variables that may interact with father absence. Nevertheless, a number of serious questions can be raised in regard to the methodology of the research. The investigation can be criticized because it is based solely on findings from a clinic population. Of even more direct relevance, the study has the weakness, similar to almost all of its predecessors, in that the variables of father absence and father presence are not clearly enough defined. Two years of not necessarily consecutive separation from the father was used as the criterion for father absence. An obvious question is whether age at onset of father absence is related to intellectual functioning. There is also no consideration as to the amount of availability of father-present fathers or the quality of father-child interactions within the intact home. Similar inadequacies may account for the lack of clear-cut findings concerning father absence and academic functioning in some studies (e.g., Coleman, et al., 1966; Engemoen, 1966; Herzog & Sudia, 1970).

Early Paternal Deprivation

Blanchard and I attempted to specify different levels of father availability and to ascertain their relationship to the academic functioning of third-grade boys (Blanchard & Biller, 1971). We examined both the timing of father absence and the degree of father-son interaction in the father-present home. The boys were of average intelligence and were from working-class and lower-middle-class backgrounds. Four groups of boys were studied; early father-absent (beginning before age 3), late father-absent (beginning after age 5), low father-present (less than 6 hours per week), and high father-present (more than 2 hours per day). In order to control for variables (other than father availability) which might affect academic performance, there was individual subject matching in terms of the characteristics of the early father-absent group. The subjects were matched so that each boy from the early father-absent group was essentially identical with a boy from each of the other three groups in terms of age, IQ, socioeconomic status, and presence or absence of male siblings.

Academic performance was assessed by means of Stanford Achievement Test Scores and classroom grades. (The teachers did not have the children's achievement test scores available to them until after final classroom grades had been assigned.) The high father-present group was very superior to the other three groups. With respect to both grades and achievement test scores, the early father-absent boys were generally underachievers, the late father-absent boys and low father-present boys usually functioned somewhat below grade level, and the high father-present group performed above grade level.

The early father-absent boys were generally handicapped in their academic performance. They scored significantly lower on every achievement test index as well as in their grades. The early father-absent group functioned below grade level in both language and mathematical skills. When compared to the high father-present group, the early father-absent group appeared to be quite inferior in skills relating to reading comprehension. Citing previous research relating to sex-role and cognitive development, Winebrenner (1971) has speculated that father absence often interferes with the male child's attempts to develop reading competency.

Santrock (1972) reported additional evidence which indicated that early father absence can have a very significant debilitating effect on cognitive functioning. He studied lower-class junior high and high school children and generally found that those who became father-absent before the age of 5, particularly before the age of 2, had scored significantly lower on measures of IQ (Otis Quick Test) and achievement (Stanford Achievement Test) that had been administered when they were in the third and sixth grades. The most detrimental effects occurred when the father's absence was due to divorce, desertion, or separation, rather than death. This study also revealed some support for the positive remedial effects of a stepfather for boys, especially when the stepfather joined the family before the child was 5 years of age.

At this point, it is relevant to note that there is other evidence indicating that early father absence can have a profound effect on the boy's personality development, especially with respect to masculinity of his self-concept (Biller, 1968a, b; Biller & Bahm, 1971; Burton, 1972; Hetherington, 1966). Among lower-class boys, father absence before the age of 2 has been reported to be associated with feelings of inferiority and a low level of trust and perseverance (Santrock, 1970). The early father-absent boy, especially if he is from a lower-class background, often enters school with much uncertainty about himself and his ability to succeed.

In contrast, boys who have consistently experienced high paternal availability and involvement are much more likely to actualize their intellectual potential. Highly available fathers seem to afford their sons models of perseverance and achievement motivation. The father can provide his son a model of a male functioning successfully outside of the home atmosphere. Frequent opportunity to observe and imitate his father may facilitate the development of the boy's overall instrumental competence and problem-solving skill. But a highly competent father would not facilitate his son's cognitive development if he were not consistently accessible or if the father-son relationship were negative in quality (e.g., the father generally critical and frustrating in his relationship with his son).

When the father has intellectual interests, a positive father-child relationship can greatly stimulate the child's academic achievement. If the father's activity involves reading, writing, or mathematics, it is likely that the boy will develop skills in these areas. Frequent observation of a father who enjoys intellectual activities does much to further a child's cognitive development. However, if the father does not enjoy such activities, the child is less likely to excel in school.

Cognitive Styles

There is a wealth of evidence documenting sex differences in intellectual functioning (Garai & Scheinfeld, 1968; Maccoby, 1966). Analytical, mathematical, spatial, and mechanical skills are generally more developed in males, whereas females usually perform at a higher level on most types of tasks requiring verbal fluency, language usage, and perception of details, including reading. The father may greatly influence the acquisition of certain sex-typed intellectual skills in his children (Biller, 1971a).

Carlsmith (1964) made an interesting discovery concerning the relationship between father absence and differential intellectual abilities. She examined the College Board Aptitude Test scores of middle-class and upper-middle-class high school males who had experienced early father absence because of their fathers' military service during World War II. Boys who were father-absent in early childhood were more likely to have a feminine patterning of aptitude test scores. Compared to the typical male pattern of math score higher than verbal score, males who had experienced early separation from their fathers more frequently had a higher verbal score than math score. She found that the earlier the onset of father absence and the longer the father absence, the more likely was the male to have a higher verbal than math score. The effect was strongest for students whose fathers were absent at birth and/or were away for over 30 months. Higher verbal than math functioning is the usual pattern among females, and Carlsmith speculated that it reflects a feminine-global style. Results from other studies have also indicated a relationship between father absence and a feminine patterning of aptitude test scores among males (e.g. Altus, 1958; Maccoby & Rau, 1962; Nelsen & Maccoby, 1966).

A study with adolescent boys by Barclay and Cusumano (1967) supports the supposition that difficulties in analytical functioning are often related to father absence. Using Witkin's rod-and-frame procedure, Barclay and Cusumano found that father-absent males were more field-dependent than those who were father-present. Field-dependent individuals have difficulties in ignoring irrelevant environmental cues in the analysis of certain types of problems (Witkin et al., 1962).

On the other hand, there is evidence suggesting that a close father-son relationship is conducive to the development of analytical thinking and field independence. Bieri (1960) found that boys who perceived themselves as more similar to their fathers and as having a close relationship with their fathers did better on an embedded-figures test, an indication of their field independence, than did boys who were not close to their fathers.

Dyk and Witkin (1965) reported that field-independent boys were more likely to perceive warm father-son relationships in a projective story task (TAT) than were field-dependent boys. Dyk and Witkin also described the results of a study by Judith Seder

(1957). Fathers of field-independent boys participated more actively with their sons than did fathers of field-dependent boys. Father-son participation in sports, outings, and trips was more frequent among the field-independent boys. In contrast, fathers of field-dependent boys spent relatively little time with their sons. Boys who have neglecting or passive fathers appear to be more likely to adopt a global rather than an analytical conceptual style (Witkin, 1960).

Lynn (1969) hypothesized that there is a curvilinear relationship between paternal closeness and field independence. Low paternal availability, Lynn assumed, makes the boy very dependent on his mother. He speculated that moderate father availability is most conducive for the development of field independence. According to Lynn, when the father is moderately available, the boy has an outline of the masculine role but has to interact actively with his environment to develop his masculinity. However, if the father is highly available to his son, Lynn argued, then the task of becoming masculine will be very easy for the boy and he will not develop an analytical, independent stance in interacting with his environment.

Lynn reasoned that research with Eskimo children supports his contention that high father availability actually leads to field dependence among boys. Eskimo boys spend a great deal of time with their fathers, and they seem from an early age to engage in much imitation of the father. Nevertheless, among Eskimo children, boys are not more field-independent than girls (Berry, 1966; MacArthur, 1967). Lynn also cited a study by Sherman and Smith (1967) in which orphans who received full-time care from male counselors were less field-independent than males from normal families.

Availability of a father or father surrogate per se is not sufficient to promote independent and analytical behavior. There are some data which indicate that many fathers who are constantly at home play rather unassertive roles in their families (Biller, 1968a). Lynn noted that the male caretakers of the orphan boys in the Sherman and Smith (1967) study performed some typically mothering functions. Unless the father's or the father surrogate's behavior has a clear analytical-independent component, it will not directly facilitate the boy's problem-solving ability. Lynn's analysis is interesting, but available data suggest that there is a generally positive relationship between the adequacy of the boy's analytical ability and the amount of interaction he has with a salient, competent father.

Behavior Problems

In addition to certain intellectual skills, other abilities which are important in academic success also appear to be hampered by paternal deprivation. There is evidence that paternally deprived children have difficulty in controlling their impulses and accepting authority. Such difficulties seem to be particularly frequent among children whose fathers are continually absent. Aggressive outbursts and delinquent behavior are reported to be more common among father-absent children, especially those from lower-class backgrounds, than among father-present children. Academic success requires the capacity to concentrate, delay gratification, and plan ahead. These abilities are less likely to be well developed among paternally deprived children than among well-fathered children (e.g., Biller, 1971a; Biller & Davids, 1973; Hoffman, 1971; Mischel, 1961).

Paternally deprived boys frequently lack a secure masculine self-concept and have difficulties in peer relationships. Such boys are usually much more interested in getting the attention of their peers than in concentrating on schoolwork. Anxiety also seems to be more intense among paternally deprived children than among well-fathered children. Lower-class boys who are paternally deprived and insecure in their underlying sex-role orientations, even though they may be quite masculine in other facets of their behavior, are often very anxious and defensive about their intellectual abilities (Biller, 1971a).

The quality and quantity of the father-child interactions can influence the child's overall adjustment, responsibility, and motivation for success. Bronfenbrenner (1961) found a positive association between the amount of time fathers spent with their adolescent sons and the degree of leadership and responsibility the boys displayed in school. Results from a study by Reuter and me indicate that both the quality and quantity of father-son relationships must be taken into account (Reuter & Biller, 1973). For example, we found that college males who perceived their fathers as both nurturant and available had very adequate scores on personality adjustment measures, whereas those who perceived their fathers as highly available but low in nurturance, or as high in nurturance and low in availability, had very inadequate scores on personality adjustment measures.

Mussen et al. (1963) reported that instrumental achievement striving was more frequent among adolescent males who had warm relationships with their fathers than among those who had poor relationships with their fathers. Cervantes's (1965) results revealed an association between inadequacy of the father and the child's not completing high school. Results from other studies have suggested that males who have been father-absent during childhood have both lower achievement motivation and less career success than do those who have been father-present (McClelland, 1961; Terman & Oden, 1947; Veroff et al., 1960).

Independence, competence, and achievement motivation can be much stimulated by an involved father. Rosen and D'Andrade (1959) found a high level of paternal encouragement among adolescent boys with strong achievement strivings. The father can facilitate his child's independence and achievement by giving him a model of effective behavior and allowing him to make his own decisions. The quality of the father-mother relationship is also very important. A man who is consistently dominated by his wife is not an effective model for his child. Several research projects have suggested that boys from maternally dominated families are overly dependent and unsuccessful in their academic performance (e.g., Devereux, Bronfenbrenner, & Suci, 1962; Elder, 1962; Smelser, 1963).

The father who is involved in his family and is viewed as a salient family decision maker can do much to facilitate his child's personality development and cognitive functioning. The father's self-confidence, encouragement, and involvement can be significant factors in the development of the child's academic and problem-solving skills. However, in addition to being a competent model, the father must allow his child to function in an independent and assertive manner. Paternal interference and pressure can hamper the child's ability to think flexibly and independently (Busse, 1969; Rosen & D'Andrade, 1959). Paternal as well as maternal domination can undermine the child's competency by not allowing him sufficient opportunity to solve his own problems. Some research has indicated that rigid paternal subordination of the mother and child by the father stifles the boy's achievement strivings (Strodtbeck, 1958).

Many other studies have revealed that father-absent children have a high rate of behavior problems relating to school adjustment, both academic and interpersonal (e.g., Crescimbeni, 1964; Hardy, 1937; Holman, 1953; Kelly, North, & Zingle, 1965; Risen, 1939; Rouman, 1956; Rowntree, 1955; Russell, 1957). Unfortunately, methodological limitations make for difficulties in interpreting the findings of most studies linking father absence with maladjustment in school. For example, such studies have usually lacked analyses relating to the potential effects of such variables as age at onset and length of father absence, socioeconomic background, and sex of child (Biller, 1971a).

Sex Differences

Most of the research concerning paternal influence and the child's personality development and cognitive functioning has focused on the father-son relationship. However, the quantity and quality of fathering can affect girls as well as boys, as is evident from data reviewed here and elsewhere (Biller, 1971a, b; Biller & Weiss, 1970; Fish & Biller, 1973; Hetherington, 1972; Johnson, 1963). Although boys and girls are both influenced, current evidence suggests that paternal deprivation has a somewhat more negative effect on the cognitive abilities of boys (e.g., Landy, Rosenberg, & Sutton-Smith, 1969; Lessing, Zagorin, & Nelson, 1970; Santrock, 1972).

Nevertheless, there is increasing evidence that the behavior of fathers can do much to stimulate their daughters' cognitive functioning and intellectual attainment. Data from a number of studies, when taken together, indicate that high paternal expectations in the context of a warm father-daughter relationship are conducive to the development of autonomy, independence, achievement, and creativity among girls (Crandall et al., 1964; Helson, 1967; Honzik, 1967; Nakamura & Rogers, 1969). The type of model that the father represents to the girl can be very important, as is suggested by Bing's (1963) findings of a positive association between the amount of reading fathers do at home and their daughters' verbal ability. On the other hand, paternal rejection seems related to deficits in females' functioning in certain types of cognitive tasks (Heilbrun et al., 1967).

The degree and direction of sex differences vary with respect to which components of cognitive functioning are considered. As with other issues relating to paternal influence, there is a need for much more research. But we do know that a warm relationship with a competent father is a very significant factor in the personality development of both boys and girls. Children who have positively involved fathers develop more adequate self-concepts and are more effective in their interpersonal and cognitive functioning than are children who have been paternally deprived or inadequately fathered (Biller, 1971a).

Sociocultural Variables

Paternal deprivation is often a contributing variable in the complex and debilitating process leading to cultural disadvantage (Bronfenbrenner, 1967). Father absence appears to particularly hamper lower-class black children. Some investigators have reported that among lower-class black children, those who are father-absent score considerably lower on intelligence and achievement tests than do those who are father-present (e.g., Deutsch, 1960; Deutsch & Brown, 1964; Mackie et al., 1967).

With respect to such findings, Kohlberg (1966) has suggested that the relatively immature cognitive development of the lower-class father-absent child is the key factor associated with differences in the sex-role development of father-absent and father-present boys. Kohlberg proposed that sex-role development is a dimension of the general process of cognitive development. He reasoned that if father-absent and father-present boys were matched in intelligence, differences in sex-role development would not be found or would be very small. He cited the data of one of his students (C. Smith) which suggest that differences in sex-role preference are considerably lessened when father-absent and father-present boys are matched in terms of intellectual level. Other research has indicated that there is a generally positive correlation between intelligence and sex-typed preferences among young children (Biller & Borstelmann, 1965, 1967; Kohlberg & Zigler, 1967).

However, there is no clear-cut linear relationship between intelligence and sex-role preference among older children. Some data suggest that intelligence, at least as measured by the usual verbal-oriented tests, may be negatively correlated with masculinity of sex-role preference among lower-class boys (Radin, 1972). Also, as individuals gain wider experiences and education, there is usually a broadening of interests, so that their preferences often become less sex-typed (Biller & Borstelmann, 1967). To further complicate the situation, all aspects of sex role are not equally affected by rate of cognitive development (Biller, 1968a; Biller & Borstelmann, 1967).

General knowledge about social norms does seem to be related to age and experience. Father-absent children, at least after they reach elementary school, are not usually deficient with respect to their awareness of cultural values concerning sex typing (e.g., Biller, 1968b; Thomes, 1968). Nevertheless, such awareness is not sufficient to promote a positive and secure sex-role development (Biller, 1968b, 1971a). For example, even when matched in terms of intelligence and social class, father-absent boys have been found to have less secure masculine sex-role orientations (Biller, 1969b; Biller & Bahm, 1971). The sex-role development process involves much more than the acquisition of social norms.

Socioeconomic and sociocultural variables have to be considered more carefully if there is to be a greater understanding of the effects of paternal deprivation on cognitive development. A problem in some research is that there are not specific enough comparisons among individuals from different social backgrounds. In particular, culturally disadvantaged groups and members of stable blue-collar occupations (e.g., teamsters, skilled factory workers) are often both placed under the rubric of lower class. Such generalized groupings seem to obscure possible relationships (Biller, 1971a). For example, the incidence of continual father absence is much higher among culturally disadvantaged families than among working-class families. The classifications become very difficult to untangle because a family that has been considered working-class may be redefined as disadvantaged or lower-class if it becomes father-absent (Miller, 1958). In a cogent analysis, Herzog and Sudia (1970) pointed out that there have been inadequate controls for income level in research with disadvantaged children. They emphasized that differences in income level between father-absent and father-present families may be more closely related to intellectual disadvantage than is father absence per se. They cited some studies which suggest that when family income is taken into account, there is little or no difference between father-absent and father-present children on measures of cognitive functioning.

In any case, paternal deprivation seems to be associated with much more serious consequences among lower-class children than among middle-class children (Biller, 1970, 1971a). Some research already discussed in this paper has suggested that among father-absent children, those who are from working-class backgrounds are more consistently handicapped in their cognitive functioning than are those from middle-class backgrounds (Lessing, Zagorin, & Nelson, 1970). A general depression in academic achievement associated with father absence has usually been found with working-class or lower-class children (Blanchard & Biller, 1971; Santrock, 1972). Middle-class, father-absent children often do well in situations requiring verbal skills. Carlsmith's (1964) middle- and upper-middle-class father-absent group apparently were equal or superior to her father-present group in verbal aptitude, although inferior in mathematical aptitude. Lessing, Zagorin, and Nelson (1970) found that middle-class father-absent children had higher verbal scores, although lower performance (e.g., perceptual-manipulative) scores, than did father-present children. Because academic achievement, particularly in elementary school, is so heavily dependent on verbal and reading ability, father-absent middle-class children do not seem to be very handicapped.

Maternal Influence

The middle-class mother seems to influence strongly her father-absent son's intellectual development. In an interview study in a university town, Hilgard, Neuman, and Fisk (1960) found that men who lost their fathers during childhood tended to be highly successful in their academic pursuits despite, or maybe because of, a conspicuous overdependence on their mothers. Clinical findings presented by Gregory (1965) also suggest that many upper-middle-class students who have been father-absent do well in college. Evidence reviewed by Nelsen and Maccoby (1966) reveals that high verbal ability in boys is often associated with a close and restrictive mother-son relationship. Levy (1943) reported that middle-class maternally overprotected boys did superior work in school, particularly in subjects requiring verbal facility. However, their performance in mathematics was not at such a high level, which seems consistent with Carlsmith's (1964) results.

Middle-class mothers are much more likely to place strong emphasis on academic success than are lower-class mothers (Kohn, 1959). Among lower-class mothers, those without husbands appear more preoccupied with day-to-day activities and less frequently think of future goals for themselves or for their children (Heckscher, 1967; Parker & Kleiner, 1966). Compared to the middle-class mother, the lower-class mother usually puts much less emphasis on long-term academic goals and is also generally a much less adequate model for coping with the demands of the middle-class school.

In homes in which the father is absent or relatively unavailable, the mother assumes a more primary role in terms of dispensing reinforcements and emphasizing certain values. A father-absent boy who is strongly identified with an intellectually oriented mother may be at an advantage in many facets of school adjustment. He may find the transition from home to the typically feminine-oriented classroom quite comfortable. Such father-absent boys might be expected to do particularly well in tasks where verbal skills and conformity are rewarded.

Although they may stimulate the paternally deprived child's acquisition of verbal skills and his adaptation to the typical school environment, middle-class overprotecting mothers often inhibit the development of an active problem-solving attitude concerning the environment. A mother who is excessively overprotecting and dominating is likely to interfere with the development of the child's assertiveness and independence (e.g., Biller, 1969; Biller & Bahm, 1971). The psychological adjustment of the mother is a crucial factor; a mother who is emotionally disturbed and/or interpersonally handicapped can have a very negative effect on the father-absent child's self-concept and ability to relate to others (e.g., Pedersen, 1966; McCord, McCord, & Thurber, 1962). On the other hand, mothers who are self-accepting, have high ego strength, and are interpersonally mature can do much to facilitate positive personality development among their paternally deprived children (Biller, 1971a, c).

Variations in fathering can influence the child's cognitive development, but it must be emphasized that fathering is only one of many factors which have an impact on the child's intellectual functioning. Sociocultural, maternal, and peer-group values are especially important. For example, among children in the lower class, paternal deprivation usually intensifies lack of exposure to experiences linking intellectual activities with masculine interests. Many boys, in their desperate attempts to view themselves as totally masculine, become excessively dependent on their peer group and perceive intellectual tasks as "feminine." The school setting which presents women as authority figures and makes strong demands for obedience and conformity is particularly antithetical to such boys' fervent desires to feel masculine.

THE FEMINIZED CLASSROOM

In this section, the emphasis is on the academic and interpersonal difficulties encountered by boys in elementary school, especially in the acquisition of reading skills, which is often a focal point of conflict. Evidence relating to the feminine atmosphere of the classroom and the potential effects of male teachers are also discussed.

Much of the difficulty that many boys encounter in adjusting to the school atmosphere is related to the interaction of inadequate fathering and the feminized classroom. Many boys enter school with intense motivation to behave in a masculine manner. However, as a result of paternal deprivation, they are very insecure in their basic sex-role orientations. Their insecurity is exacerbated because of the omnipresence of female authority figures and a general atmosphere which reinforces behavior antithetical to their expectations of the masculine role. The emphasis is on conformity, neatness, and passivity. In addition, on a maturational level, the boys are often at a disadvantage in relation to girls, and this adds to their feelings of insecurity.

Reading Skills

The superiority of girls as compared to boys in terms of language development is well documented (e.g., Garai & Scheinfeld, 1968; Maccoby, 1966). Both earlier maturation and more social reinforcement from the mother (at least in our society) seem to be involved. It is not surprising, given the positive relationship between reading and verbal development, that girls generally do better in reading than do boys.

Much concern has been focused on the fact that boys are much more likely to have reading disabilities than are girls. Compared to girls, about four times as many boys are referred to reading clinics (Bentzen, 1963; Kopel and Geerded, 1933; Marzurkrewicz, 1960).

Part of the sex difference in reading ability may be due to less visual maturity among boys (Anderson, Hughes, & Dixon, 1962) as well as the general verbal maturity of girls (Garai & Scheinfeld, 1968). Constitutionally related sex differences stemming from genetic and prenatal factors may, to some extent, account for boys' more frequent problems in impulse control and related academic problems. The situation is very complicated, in that males may be more vulnerable to disadvantaged environments than are females. For example, there is some evidence that more males than females are neurologically handicapped because of poor nutrition and/or lack of adequate medical assistance during the prenatal period (e.g., Bronfenbrenner, 1967).

In terms of many reading criteria relating to motivation as well as ability, girls seem to far exceed boys. Girls are more interested in reading at all ages and read more than boys (Anderson, Hughes, & Dixon, 1962). Among elementary school children, girls attach more social prestige to reading and are more highly motivated to read well in class (Strang, 1968). Girls begin to read earlier than boys. By the age of 6, more than half of the girls are reading, compared to less than 40% of the boys (Baker, 1948). The sex differences observed in reading ability seem to be manifested throughout the elementary school years (Gates, 1961).

Sex differences in reading are reflected in interest areas as well as in amount of time spent reading. Masculine material relating to adventure, exploration, science, technical matters, and sports is preferred by boys, whereas girls are more likely to prefer books concerning family life and romance (Anastasi, 1958). A number of studies in the United States and Europe have indicated that with the exception of a strong interest in politics, boys have more circum-scribed reading interests than do girls. Usually (as with their general preferences), boys' reading interests tend to be more sex typed than do girls' (Garai & Scheinfeld, 1968).

It is interesting to note that boys in kindergarten seem to learn to read as well as do girls when programmed techniques are used (McNeil, 1964). Such techniques may be more consistent with masculine role demands for autonomy and independence. There is some evidence suggesting that boys who have clear-cut masculine sex-role preferences prior to first grade are more mature and develop better reading skills than boys who manifest an uncertainty about their sex-role preferences (Anastasiow, 1965). In any case, girls do better when taught by teachers in small reading groups, which may be a reflection of their sensitivity to adults, particularly females. It should also be noted that girls are usually much in the majority among "high" reading groups, and this, too, may work to discourage boys in developing their reading skills.

Teacher Bias

Both boys and girls report that female teachers react less favor-ably to boys during reading instruction (Davis & Slobodian, 1967; McNeil, 1964). However, research involving ratings of teacher behavior during reading instruction have not confirmed the suppo-sition that female teachers react in a more negative manner with boys than they do with girls (Brophy & Laosa, 1971; Davis & Slobodian, 1967).

Nevertheless, there is much evidence indicating that compared to girls, boys are at a general disadvantage in terms of the reactions of female teachers. Certainly if boys feel that female teachers have negative attitudes toward them, it is probably going to hamper their classroom performance. Moreover, some researchers have found that female teachers give girls better grades even when boys have objectively achieved a higher level of performance (Carter, 1952; Hanson, 1959). Boys receive more negative reactions and criticisms and less supportive feedback from their teachers than do girls (Davis & Slobodian, 1967; Meyer & Thompson, 1956; Lippitt & Gold, 1959).

Fagot and Patterson's (1969) data suggest that female teachers direct most of their disapproval toward assertive and aggressive behaviors and toward activities that are usually labelled masculine. In their study of the interactions between female teachers and nursery school children, they found that teachers reinforced boys about six times as often for "feminine" behaviors as they did for masculine behaviors. Boys as well as girls received more teacher reinforcement when they were engaged in quiet, sedentary-type activities and appeared to be generally ignored and/or criticized for relatively mechanical or rough-and-tumble activities. Although such teacher reaction per se did not seem to feminize the boys, the fact that teachers reacted in such a nonreinforcing manner toward masculine behavior probably led many boys to the conclusion that boyish behavior and success in school do not go together. A recent study with nursery school children suggested that female teachers initiate far fewer contacts with boys than with girls; they seem to make fewer requests for information and give less information to boys (Biber, Miller, & Dyer, 1972).

Many boys spend much of their time involved in physically demanding sports activities and acquire considerable knowledge in the process. However, female teachers seldom have much interest in such endeavors, and this widens the gulf between teachers and masculine boys. Sports can also be a constructive outlet for aggressive and competitive feelings which may otherwise come out in a disruptive manner in the classroom. There is little opportunity in most elementary schools for intense physical activity, except for an occasional recess period.

Female teachers often react negatively to assertive behavior in the classroom and seem to feel much more comfortable with girls, who are generally quieter, more obedient, and conforming. Boys perceive that teachers are much more positive in responding to girls and to "feminine" behavior than they are to boys and "masculine" behavior. Unfortunately, the type of "feminine" behavior reinforced in the classroom is frequently of a very negative quality if one is using self-actualization as a criterion. For example, timidity, passivity, dependency, obedience, and quietness are usually rewarded. The boy or girl who is independent, assertive, questioning, and challenging is typically at a great disadvantage. Even though girls generally seem to adapt more easily to the early school environment, such an atmosphere does not seem conducive to their optimal development. Girls need to learn how to be independent and assertive just as much as do boys. We need more stress on inquiry and mastery methods of learning.

Sexton's (1969) essential thesis is that our educational system exerts a feminizing influence on children and teachers. Sexton labels feminization as inducing passive, conforming, uncreative types of behavior. According to her, masculine males are turned off by their experiences in the classroom and reject academically related intellectual endeavors. She argues that much of the reason for our high number of male problem children, of both the inhibited and acting-out variety, is our school system. Women are given too large a role in our school system (and in child rearing) and too small a role in our other institutions. The growing tendency toward suburban living also seems to have increased the salience of a community of women and children with little exposure to competent male models.

Sexton presents extensive data which indicate that our traditional conceptions of masculinity are incompatible with success in school. Her findings suggest that the top scholars in school are all too often feminized boys. (Males who are conforming, polite, obedient, and neat are favored.) She believes that there is no basic incompatibility between a healthy masculinity and academic achievement but that our present educational system works against such development. She is not arguing for a rigid adherence to masculine standards but that males (and females) be liberated and be given more flexibility and freedom.

She found that boys with high masculine standards did much more poorly in school than did those with relatively feminine values. Similar to other investigators, she reported that girls generally achieved higher grades than did boys and that more boys were identified as severely emotionally disturbed (e.g., being sent to see a psychiatrist). In most specific categories of problem behavior, over 70% of the children were boys. Almost one out of four boys was either a total failure or doing barely passing work (a D or F student).

Sex Role and School Achievement

Many of Sexton's conclusions fit well with other data reported in this paper. However, a major criticism of her research is that she did not put enough emphasis on how socioeconomic and socio-cultural factors interact with sex-role development and the education-al process. For example, there is no control for socioeconomic status in her analysis of the relationship between sex-role behavior and school success. Much of the relationship she finds between femininity and academic achievement seems to be due to the difference in values between working-class and middle-class individuals. It may be that, to some extent, middle-class individuals are generally more feminized (partly as a function of being more "educated") and less concerned with sex-role distinctions than are working-class indi-viduals, but it is also true that there are social class differences in the definitions of what is appropriate sex-role behavior. For ex-ample, middle-class adults have been found to stress intellectual competence in their definition of masculine behavior, while working-class adults stress physical prowess (Biller, 1966a). Sexton's sex-role measures essentially assess degree of interest in sports, mechanical, and technical areas. What is needed is a definition of masculinity with no incompatibility among physical, mechanical, and intellectual abilities.

A related criticism of Sexton's and other researchers' work is that overgeneralizations about the relationship between masculinity and academic functioning are often made on the basis of very restricted measures of sex role. For example, many investigators have used measures of sex-role preference which force the subject to choose between either a traditionally masculine or a traditionally feminine activity (e.g., being a mechanic or a librarian). On such procedures an individual cannot score both highly masculine and highly feminine; masculinity and femininity are conceived as polar oppo-sites. There is ample evidence that, with increasing education, individuals become more and more interested in many cultural activities traditionally labeled as feminine (Biller & Borstelmann, 1967; Kohlberg, 1966). However, this does not mean that the highly educated male has to give up his masculine interests; a well-rounded person of either sex probably has both a number of masculine and feminine interests. For example, many creative and productive people have a basic sex-role security which helps them transcend rigid sex-role stereotypes (Biller, Singer, & Fullerton, 1969; Helson, 1967; Maslow, 1960).

There is also considerable evidence that sex-role preference is more subject to variation as a function of increasing experience than are either sex-role orientation (masculinity-femininity of self concept) or sex-role adoption (masculinity-femininity of the individual's social and environmental interactions). Sex-role preference measures seem more influenced by temporary life situation factors and may be less meaningful representations of an individual's sex-role functioning than orientation or adoption measures. In any case, research attempting to relate sex-role behavior to other facets of personality functioning should take into account different aspects and patterns of sex role (Biller, 1971a, 1972; Biller & Barry, 1971).

A further criticism of Sexton's research is that she does not deal with the issue of varying academic performance as a function of grade level. Boys who perform the best in sixth grade are not necessarily the ones who do best in high school or college. She seems to make the assumption of a consistent homogeneity in the sex-role relatedness of school atmosphere and curriculum across grade level. Such an assumption is open to question (Kagan, 1964). For example, many males do much better in high school and/or college than they do in the earlier grades. This may be because the curriculum becomes more "masculinized." For these same reasons, females often have a more difficult time in the later stages of their education, particularly in college and graduate school. It is again important to emphasize that females, as well as males, are restricted in their cognitive development because of the rigidities and sex-role stereotypes associated with our educational process.

Stein's findings serve as an excellent illustration of the way in which sex-typing can affect the child's motivation in relation to particular areas of school achievement (Stein, 1971; Stein, Pohly, & Muellar, 1969; Stein & Smithells, 1969). Stein and Smithells (1969) found that children in both elementary and high school perceived reading, artistic, and social skills as feminine, and mathematical, spatial, mechanical, and athletic skills as masculine. Such results are consistent with studies concerning sex differences in abilities (Garai & Scheinfeld, 1968).

In the Stein and Smithells (1969) study, there was evidence that sex-typing of academic activities was stronger among older children. Sixth graders expressed higher attainment values and expectancies on tasks that they perceived as sex-appropriate (Stein, Pohly, & Muellar, 1969). Furthermore, the boys' achievement was clearly related to their expectations. The degree to which boys perceive tasks as sex-appropriate influences the extent of their involvement and achievement. There is other evidence that suggests that intellectual performance is higher for children when assessment is made in terms of problems that can be considered sex-appropriate (e.g., Epstein & Liverant, 1963; Milton, 1957). However, sex-role preference measures have not been found to be consistently related to specific areas of cognitive functioning (e.g., Maccoby, 1966; Stein, 1971).

In a study with sixth- and ninth-grade children, Stein (1971) focused on attitudes and expectancies concerning mechanical, athletic, mathematical, reading, artistic, and social skills. Girls tended to rate all the areas as relatively more feminine than did the boys, particularly reading, artistic, and social skills. Both sexes gave athletic, mechanical, and mathematical skills predominantly masculine ratings, while they gave generally feminine ratings to reading, artistic, and social skills.

Stein's prediction that boys would value masculine areas as important and girls feminine areas was generally supported. The findings were most clear-cut with the ninth-grade children; math was the only area in which the results were not as predicted. It is interesting to note that lower-class children of both sexes perceived reading as less important and had less expectancy of success than did middle-class children. Lower-class boys seemed to have a particularly negative attitude toward reading. There was also evidence that the more boys tended to perceive reading as feminine, the less likely they were to be motivated to read well. Unfortunately, individual differences were not examined separately in terms of social class. One might expect a particularly strong negative correlation between a view of reading as feminine and a lack of motivation in reading among boys of lower-class background.

Male Teachers

There are some data which suggest that among elementary school teachers, men are more emotionally mature, flexible, and objective in the classroom than are women. Ryans (1960) reported more emotional stability, permissiveness, and child-centeredness among male teachers. Arnold's (1968) findings indicated that compared to female teachers, male teachers are more objective and unbiased in assigning grades to children of both sexes. Such data could be used to support the notion that male teachers may generally be better models for both boys and girls than are female teachers.

Other data suggest that boys do better in school when they have male teachers. In contrast to the sex differences reported in the United States, Preston (1962) found that among fourth and sixth graders, German boys had significantly better reading scores than German girls. In addition, severe reading retardation was significantly less common among German boys than among German girls. Even at the elementary school level, teachers in Germany are usually males. The high frequency of male teachers may be a factor in the seemingly better reading performance of German boys. It is also important to note that intellectual endeavors such as reading are labelled as masculine within the German culture (Anderson & Ritscher, 1969). Apparently, the German culture makes it exceedingly difficult for girls to optimize their intellectual skills.

The facilitating influence that male teachers may have on boys is also indicated by a study with Japanese children cited by Kagan (1969). In contrast to the high rates of reading difficulties reported for American boys, there was no differential sex ratio in reading difficulties found for children living in a community of Hokkaido, a Japanese island, where about 60% of the teachers in the first and second grades were males.

Cascario (1971) found a tendency for male-taught children to earn higher reading achievement scores than female-taught children. Interestingly, some of her data suggest that father-absent children score higher in reading achievement when taught by a teacher of the same sex. Father-absent boys may be particularly responsive to an adult male who fulfills some of their needs for a masculine model. It is also relevant to note that children taught by males perceived teachers as reacting more positively to boys than to girls. Such data are, of course, in direct contrast to findings among children taught by female teachers. Hopefully, we can work toward a situation where all children feel they are valued and accepted by teachers, regardless of their sex or the teacher's sex.

Brophy and Laosa (1971) compared the behavior of children in a kindergarten conducted by a woman with the behavior of children in a kindergarten conducted by a man and a woman (husband and wife). In general, few differences were observed. The investigators found no consistent relationships between measures of the children's sex-typing as a function of whether or not they were taught by the male teacher. However, children of both sexes who were in the kindergarten with the male teacher performed better on tasks relating to spatial skills, and boys in this kindergarten seemed to enjoy a relatively higher peer status.

The care with which Brophy and Laosa developed and selected measures of sex-typing, the amount of data they collected, and the depths to which they analyzed their results are impressive. Nevertheless, the fact that their investigation was limited to two comparison groups seems to greatly restrict the generality of their findings. The question must also be asked whether one can deduce the potential effects of a male teacher when the male teacher is paired with a female teacher; at least, one must develop a research design to assess such factors. Perhaps more important, we do not know in any systematic way how adequate these teachers were in terms of their own sex-role behavior and what types of personality characteristics they possessed. This study would have been much improved if several different schools could have been compared, some having a male teacher, some having a female teacher, and some having both a male and a female teacher. (Obviously, such criticisms and limitations apply to other studies relating to the effects of male teachers.) In addition, careful personality assessment of the teachers might reveal important interactions among sex of teacher, personality of teacher, sex of child, and personality of child. For example, assertive male teachers may have the greatest effect on paternally deprived boys with aggressive characteristics but have little effect on well-fathered, moderately aggressive girls.

The Brophy and Laosa study is also limited in that the children studied are from primarily middle- and upper-middle-class backgrounds. The situation gets even more complicated when we consider the importance of sociocultural variables. For example, as emphasized earlier in this paper, among boys who are father-absent, those who come from lower-class backgrounds are particularly likely to perform inadequately on academic tasks. A male teacher, other things being equal, may have a greater effect on lower-class children than on middle-class children. These are obviously simplified examples, but they again point out the need for more research. The systematic evaluation of the effects of sex of teacher on social adjustment, cognitive functioning, and reading performance of children is a little-explored but provocative and promising area of research.

In a number of different educational and treatment contexts, I have observed some rather dramatic effects of paternally deprived children responding to the attention of an interested male adult. In practicing and supervising psychotherapy with young boys, I have often found an improvement in school work associated with explicit reinforcement from adult males. Some particularly interesting results were achieved by having books about sports and sports heroes available during therapy. In these cases, reading and talking about sports became a major focus of therapy. These boys needed to become aware that there was no incompatibility between intellectual endeavors such as reading and their conception of masculine behavior. It seemed particularly helpful to the boys that the therapist clearly exhibited athletic as well as reading skills and that, equally as important, he obviously enjoyed both reading and athletics. In therapy the emphasis was on modeling and joint participation in concretely reinforcing activities. Similarly, through the process of family therapy, positive involvement of the father (or father surrogate) has often been associated with a marked improvement in the child's academic functioning. However, clinical experiences are no substitute for systematic research.

Concluding Remarks

Our educational system could do much to mitigate the effects of paternal deprivation if more male teachers were available,

particularly in nursery school, kindergarten, and the early elementary school grades. Competent and interpersonally able male
teachers could facilitate the cognitive development of many children
as well as contribute to their general social functioning.

There is much need for greater incentives to attract more males
to become teachers of young children. There have to be more freedom and autonomy to innovate, as well as greater financial rewards.
We must make both men and women aware of the impact that males
can have in child development and also the importance of male
influence in the early years of the child's development. Just having
more male teachers is not going to be sufficient. The feminized
school atmosphere must become more humanized, and teachers
must be selected on the basis of interpersonal ability and overall
competency. If a man is basically feminized or allows himself to be
dominated by a restrictive atmosphere, he may be a particularly
poor model for children.

The remedy for the feminized classroom is not just having more
male teachers per se, but giving men and women a more equal
distribution of the responsibilities and decisions related to education.
As Sexton (1969) suggests, both boys and girls might be better off
if there were more women in top administrative positions as well
as more men in the classroom. As in the family situation, children
can profit much from opportunities of seeing males and females
interact in a cooperative, creative manner. Men and women in the
classroom could help each other better understand the different
socialization experiences of males and females.

Even if significantly more male teachers are not immediately
available, our school systems could better utilize existing personnel.
Many of the males who teach in the upper elementary school grades,
junior high, and high school could also be very effective with younger
children. Again, we need to put emphasis on the importance of males
interacting with young children (as well as with older children).
Programs could also be planned so that male teachers could spend
some of their time with a wider range of children, particularly in
tasks where they had much skill and enthusiasm. Perhaps their
responsibilities could be concentrated on father-deprived children.
In addition, other males, such as older students or retired men, may

be encouraged to participate in the educational process of young children.

There is a general need to make our schools more a part of the community and to invite greater participation, especially from fathers. Men in the community could be invited to talk about and demonstrate their work. Participants could include members of various professions, skilled craftsmen and technicians, politicians, and athletes.

Sexton (1969) suggests that we have more flexibility in educational job classifications. She advocates school job classifications such as resource person, group leader, and technical specialist. Such positions could be filled by individuals with skills or knowledge that would have more relevance to children. Individuals with various physical or interpersonal skills could be recruited. In addition, more paraprofessional teacher aides from the community could be hired. (Such jobs might do much to lower our unemployment rates.) Paraprofessionals could assist in specific school subjects and also instruct both teachers and children in certain areas.

An atmosphere in which older children help younger children or children help less able peers of their own age could go a long way toward encouraging males to gain the skills and experiences that are important in being competent fathers. Men from the community could come in during lunch breaks and eat with the children. They could also interact with children on the playground and ride with them on school buses. Hopefully, businesses and industries could regularly cooperate in giving men the opportunities and incentives to make such contributions. Another function that could be performed by business and industry would be to set up regular visits for children to various settings in their community. Such visits can be very educational and also can provide children with more experiences in interacting with competent adults of both sexes. Some of these, and other suggestions, have also been made by a number of observers who have criticized the lack of male influence in our educational system (e.g., Biller, 1971a; Garai & Scheinfeld, 1968; Grambs & Waetjen, 1966; Ostrovsky, 1959; Sexton, 1969).

It should be emphasized that there are many practical implications which transcend our school system. We generally need greater participation of men in child rearing and in various situations relating to adult-child interaction. Practical implications relating to family life, therapy, and other phases of community interaction are outlined elsewhere (Biller, 1971a).

REFERENCES

Altus, W. D. The broken home and factors of adjustment. *Psychological Reports,* 1958, **4**, 477.

Anastasi, A. *Differential psychology: Individual and group differences in behavior.* New York: Macmillan, 1958.

Anastasiow, N. S. Success in school and boys' sex-role patterns. *Child Development,* 1965, **36**, 1,053–1,066.

Anderson, I. H.; Hughes, B. O.; & Dixon, W. R. The rate of reading development and its relation to age of learning to read, sex, and intelligence. *Journal of Educational Research,* 1962, **65**, 132–135.

Anderson, R., & Ritscher, C. Pupil progress. In R. Ebel (Ed.), *Encyclopedia of educational research.* London: Macmillan, 1969.

Arnold, R. D. The achievement of boys and girls taught by men and women teachers. *Elementary School Journal,* 1968, **68**, 367–372.

Baker, E. Reading problems are caused. *Elementary English,* 1948, **25**, 360.

Barclay, A. G., & Cusumano, D. Father-absence, cross-sex identity, and field-dependent behavior in male adolescents. *Child Development,* 1967, **38**, 243–250.

Bentzen, F. Sex ratios in learning and behavior disorders. *American Journal of Orthopsychiatry,* 1963, **33**, 92–98.

Berry, J. W. Temne and Eskimo perceptual skills. *International Journal of Psychology* 1966, **1**, 207–229.

Biber, H.; Miller, L. B.; & Dyer, J. L. Feminization in preschool. *Developmental Psychology,* 1972, **7**, 86.

Bieri, J. Parental identification, acceptability, and authority, and within-sex differences in cognitive behavior. *Journal of Abnormal and Social Psychology,* 1960, **60**, 76–79.

Biller, H. B. Adults' conceptions of masculinity and femininity in children. Unpublished study, Emma Pendleton Bradley Hospital, Riverside, R.I., 1966. (a)

Biller, H. B. Experiences with underachieving adolescents enrolled in an academic potential project. Unpublished manuscript, Emma Pendleton Bradley Hospital, Riverside, R.I., 1966. (b)

Biller, H. B. A multiaspect investigation of masculine development in kindergarten age boys. *Genetic Psychology Monographs,* 1968, **76**, 89–139. (a)

Biller, H. B. A note on father-absence and masculine development in young lower-class Negro and white boys. *Child Development,* 1968, **39**, 1,003–1,006. (b)

Biller, H. B. Father dominance and sex-role development in kindergarten age boys. *Developmental Psychology,* 1969, **1**, 87–94. (a)

Biller, H. B. Father-absence, maternal encouragement, and sex-role development in kindergarten age boys. *Child Development,* 1969, **40**, 539–546. (b)

Biller, H. B. Father-absence and the personality development of the male child. *Developmental Psychology*, 1970, **2**, 181–201.

Biller, H. B. *Father, child, and sex role.* Lexington, Mass.: D.C. Heath, Heath Lexington Books, 1971. (a)

Biller, H. B. Fathering and female sexual development. *Medical Aspects of Human Sexuality*, 1971, 5, 116–138. (b)

Biller, H. B. The mother-child relationship and the father-absent boy's personality development. *Merrill-Palmer Quarterly*, 1971, **17**, 227–241. (c)

Biller, H. B. Sex role learning: Some comments and complexities from a multi-dimensional perspective. Paper presented at the annual meeting of the American Association for the Advancement of Science, Sec. 1, Symposium on Sex Role Learning in Childhood and Adolescence, Washington, D.C., December 1972.

Biller, H. B. *Sex role development.* Monterey, Calif.: Brooks/Cole, 1973, in preparation.

Biller, H. B., & Bahm, R. M. Father-absence, perceived maternal behavior, and masculinity of self-concept among junior high school boys. *Developmental Psychology*, 1971, **4**, 178–181.

Biller, H. B., & Barry, W. Sex role patterns, paternal similarity, and personality adjustment among college males. *Developmental Psychology*, 1971, **4**, 107.

Biller, H. B., & Borstelmann, L. J. Intellectual level and sex-role development in mentally retarded children. *American Journal of Mental Deficiency*, 1965, **70**, 443–447.

Biller, H. B., & Borstelmann, L. J. Masculine development: An integrative review. *Merrill-Palmer Quarterly*, 1967, **13**, 253–294.

Biller, H. B., & Davids, A. Parent-child relations, personality development, and psychopathology. In A. Davids (Ed.), *Issues in abnormal child psychology.* Monterey, Calif.: Brooks/Cole, 1973, in press.

Biller, H. B.; Singer, D. L.; & Fullerton, M. Sex role development and creative potential in kindergarten age boys. *Developmental Psychology*, 1969, **1**, 291–296.

Biller, H. B., & Weiss, S. The father-daughter relationship and the personality development of the female. *Journal of Genetic Psychology*, 1970, **114**, 79–93.

Bing, E. Effect of child-rearing practices on development of differential cognitive abilities. *Child Development*, 1963, **34**, 631–648.

Blanchard, R. W., & Biller, H. B. Father-availability and academic performance among third grade boys. *Developmental Psychology*, 1971, **4**, 301–305.

Bronfenbrenner, U. Some familial antecedents of responsibility and leadership in adolescents. In L. Petrullo and B. M. Bass (Eds.), *Leadership and interpersonal behavior.* New York: Holt, Rinehart and Winston, 1961. Pp. 239–272.

Bronfenbrenner, U. The psychological costs of quality and equality in education. *Child Development*, 1967, **38**, 909–925.

Brophy, J. E., & Laosa, L. M. The effect of a male teacher on the sex-typing of kindergarten children. *Proceedings of the 79th Annual Meeting of the American Psychological Association*, 1971, **6**, 169–170.

Burton, R. V. Cross-sex identity in Barbados. *Developmental Psychology*, 1972, **6**, 365–374.

Busse, T. W. Child-rearing antecedents of flexible thinking. *Developmental Psychology*, 1969, **1**, 585–591.

Carlsmith, L. Effect of early father-absence on scholastic aptitude. *Harvard Educational Review*, 1964, **34**, 3–21.

Carter, E. S. How invalid are marks assigned by teachers? *Journal of Educational Psychology*, 1952, **43**, 218–228.

Cascario, E. F. The male teacher and reading achievement of first-grade boys and girls. Unpublished doctoral dissertation, Lehigh University, 1971.

Cervantes, L. F. Family background, primary relationships, and the high school dropout. *Journal of Marriage and the Family*, 1965, **27**, 218–223.

Coleman, J. S.; Campbell, E. Q.; McPartland, J.; Mood, A. M.; Weinfeld, F. D.; & York, R. L. *Equality of educational opportunity*. Washington, D.C.: Office of Education, 1966.

Crandall, V.; Dewey, R.; Katkovsky, W.; & Preston, A. Parents' attitudes and behaviors and grade-school children's academic achievements. *Journal of Genetic Psychology*, 1964, **104**, 53–56.

Crescimbeni, J. Broken homes affect academic achievement. *Education*, 1964, **84**, 440–441.

Davis, A., & Havighurst, R. J. Social class and color differences in child rearing. *American Sociological Review*, 1946, **11**, 698–710.

Davis, O., & Slobodian, J. Teacher behavior toward boys and girls in first grade reading instruction. *American Educational Research Journal*, 1967, **4**, 261–269.

Deutsch, M. Minority group and class status as related to social and personality factors in scholastic achievement. *Monograph of the Society for Applied Anthropology*, 1960, **2**, 1–32.

Deutsch, M., & Brown, B. Social influences in Negro-white intelligence differences. *Journal of Social Issues*, 1964, **20**, 24–35.

Devereaux, E. C., Jr.; Bronfenbrenner, U.; & Suci, G. J. Patterns of parent behavior in the United States and the Federal Republic of Germany: A cross-national comparison. *International Social Science Journal*, 1962, **14**, 488–506.

Downey, K. J. Parental interest in the institutionalized severely mentally retarded child. *Social Problems*, 1963, **11**, 186–193.

Dyk, R. B., & Witkin, H. A. Family experiences related to the development of differentiation in children. *Child Development*, 1965, **36**, 21–55.

Elder, G. H., Jr. *Adolescent achievement and mobility aspirations*. Chapel Hill, N.C.: Institute for Research in Social Science, 1962.

Engemoen, B. L. The influence of membership in a broken home on test performance of first grade children. Unpublished doctoral dissertation, North Texas University, 1966.

Epstein, R., & Liverant, S. Verbal conditioning and sex role identification in children. *Child Development*, 1963, **34**, 99–106.

Fagot, B. I., & Patterson, G. An in vivo analysis of reinforcing contingencies for sex-role behaviors in the pre-school child. *Developmental Psychology*, 1969, **1**, 563–568.

Farber, B. Effects of a severely mentally retarded child in the family. In E. P.

Trapp and P. Himelstein (Eds.), *Readings on the exceptional child.* New York: Appleton-Century-Crofts, 1962. Pp. 227–246.

Fish, K. D., & Biller, H. B. Perceived childhood paternal relationships and college females' personal adjustment. *Adolescence*, 1973, **8**, 415–420.

Garai, J. E., & Scheinfeld, A. Sex differences in mental and behavioral traits. *Genetic Psychology Monographs*, 1968, **77**, 169–299.

Gates, A. Sex differences in reading ability. *Elementary School Journal*, 1961, **61**, 431–434.

Grambs, J. D., & Waetjen, W. B. Being equally different: A new right for boys and girls. *National Elementary School Principal*, 1966, **46**, 59–67.

Gregory, I. Anterospective data following childhood loss of a parent: II. Pathology, performance, and potential among college students. *Archives of General Psychiatry*, 1965, **13**, 110–120.

Grunebaum, M. G.; Hurwitz, I.; Prentice, N. M.; & Sperry, B. M. Fathers of sons with primary neurotic learning inhibition. *American Journal of Orthopsychiatry*, 1962, **32**, 462–473.

Hanson, E. H. Do boys get a square deal in school? *Education*, 1959, **79**, 597–598.

Hardy, M. C. Aspects of home environment in relation to behavior at the elementary school age. *Journal of Juvenile Research*, 1937, **21**, 206–225.

Heckscher, B. T. Household structure and achievement orientation in lower-class Barbadian families. *Journal of Marriage and the Family*, 1967, **29**, 521–526.

Heilbrun, A. B.; Harrell, S. N.; & Gillard, B. J. Perceived child-rearing attitudes of fathers and cognitive control in daughters. *Journal of Genetic Psychology*, 1967, **111**, 29–40.

Helson, R. Personality characteristics and developmental history of creative college women. *Genetic Psychology Monographs*, 1967, **76**, 205–256.

Herzog, E., & Sudia, C. E. *Boys in fatherless families.* Washington, D.C.: Office of Child Development, 1970.

Hetherington, E. M. A developmental study of the effects of sex of the dominant parent on sex-role preference, identification, and imitation in children. *Journal of Personality and Social Psychology*, 1965, **2**, 188–194.

Hetherington, E. M. Effects of paternal absence on sex-typed behaviors in Negro and white pre-adolescent males. *Journal of Personality and Social Psychology*, 1966, **4**, 87–91.

Hetherington, E. M. Effects of father absence on personality development in adolescent daughters. *Developmental Psychology*, 1972, **7**, 313–326.

Hilgard, J. R.; Neuman, M. F.; & Fisk, F. Strength of adult ego following bereavement. *American Journal of Orthopsychiatry*, 1960, **30**, 788–798.

Hill, J. P. Similarity and accordance between parents and sons in attitudes towards mathematics. *Child Development*, 1967, **38**, 777–791.

Hoffman, M. L. Father absence and conscience development. *Developmental Psychology*, 1971, **4**, 400–406.

Holman, P. Some factors in the etiology of maladjustment in children. *Journal of Mental Science*, 1953, **99**, 654–688.

Honzik, M. P. Environmental correlates of mental growth: Prediction from the family setting at 21 months. *Child Development*, 1967, **38**, 338–364.

Johnson, M. M. Sex-role learning in the nuclear family. *Child Development*, 1963, **34**, 319–333.

Kagan, J. Acquisition and significance of sex-typing and sex-role identity. In M. L. Hoffman and L. W. Hoffman (Eds.), *Review of child development research*. Vol. 1. New York: Russell Sage, 1964. Pp. 137–167.

Kagan, J. Sex typing during the preschool and early school years. In I. Janis; G. Mahl; J. Kagan; & R. Holt (Eds.), *Personality: Dynamics, development, and assessment*. New York: Harcourt, Brace and World, 1969.

Katz, I. Socialization of academic motivation in minority group children. In D. Levine (Ed.), *Nebraska Symposium on Motivation*, Lincoln: University of Nebraska Press, 1967. Pp. 133–191.

Kelly, F. J.; North, J.; & Zingle, H. The relation of the broken home to subsequent school behaviors. *Alberta Journal of Educational Research*, 1965, **11**, 215–219.

Kimball, B. The sentence completion technique in a study of scholastic underachievement. *Journal of Consulting Psychology*, 1952, **16**, 353–358.

Kohlberg, L. A cognitive-developmental analysis of children's sex-role concepts and attitudes. In E. E. Maccoby (Ed.), *The development of sex differences*. Stanford: Stanford University Press, 1966. Pp. 82–173.

Kohlberg, L., & Zigler, E. The impact of cognitive maturity on the development of sex-role attitudes in the years 4–8. *Genetic Psychology Monographs*, 1967, **75**, 89–165.

Kohn, M. L. Social class and parental values. *American Journal of Sociology*, 1959, **64**, 337–351.

Kopel, D., & Geerded, H. A survey of clinical services for poor readers. *Journal of Educational Psychology Monograph*, 1933, **13**, 209–224.

Landy, F.; Rosenberg, B. G.; & Sutton-Smith, B. The effect of limited father-absence on cognitive development. *Child Development*, 1969, **40**, 941–944.

Lessing, E. E.; Zagorin, S. W.; & Nelson, D. WISC subtest and IQ score correlates of father absence. *Journal of Genetic Psychology*, 1970, **67**, 181–195.

Levy, D. M. *Maternal overprotection*. New York: Columbia University Press, 1943.

Lippitt, R., & Gold, M. Classroom social structure as a mental health problem. *Journal of Social Issues*, 1959, **15**, 40–58.

Lynn, D. B. *Parental and sex role identification*. Berkeley: McCutchan, 1969.

MacArthur, R. Sex differences in field dependence for the Eskimo: Replication of Berry's findings. *International Journal of Psychology*, 1967, **2**, 139–140.

Maccoby, E. E. Sex differences in intellectual functioning. In E. E. Maccoby (Ed.), *The development of sex differences*. Stanford: Stanford University Press, 1966. Pp. 25–55.

Maccoby, E. E., & Rau, L. Differential cognitive abilities. Final report, U.S. Office of Education, Cooperative Research Project No. 1040, 1962.

Mackie, J. B.; Maxwell, A. D.; & Rafferty, F. T. Psychological development of culturally disadvantaged Negro kindergarten children: A study of the selective influence of family and school variables. Paper presented at the meeting of the American Orthopsychiatric Association, Washington, D.C., March, 1967.

Marzurkrewicz, A. J. Social-cultural influences and reading. *Journal of Developmental Reading*, 1960, **3**, 254–263.

Maslow, A. H. Creativity in self-actualizing people. In H. H. Anderson (Ed.), *Creativity and its cultivation*. New York: Harper, 1960. Pp. 83–95.

Maxwell, A. E. Discrepancies between the pattern of abilities for normal and neurotic children. *Journal of Mental Science*, 1961, **107**, 300–307.

McClelland, D. C. *The achieving society*. Princeton, N.J.: Van Nostrand, 1961.

McCord, J.; McCord, W.; & Thurber, E. Some effects of paternal absence on male children. *Journal of Abnormal and Social Psychology*, 1962, **64**, 361–369.

McNeil, J. D. Programmed instruction versus usual classroom procedures in teaching boys to read. *American Education Research Journal*, 1964, **1**, 113–119.

Meyer, W., & Thompson, G. Sex differences in the distribution of teacher approval and disapproval among sixth grade children. *Journal of Educational Psychology*, 1956, **47**, 385–396.

Miller, W. B. Lower-class culture as a generating milieu of gang delinquency. *Journal of Social Issues*, 1958, **14**, 5–19.

Milton, G. A. The effects of sex-role identification upon problem solving skill. *Journal of Abnormal and Social Psychology*, 1957, **55**, 208–212.

Mischel, W. Father-absence and delay of gratification. *Journal of Abnormal and Social Psychology*, 1961, **62**, 116–124.

Mussen, P. H.; Young, H. B.; Godding, R.; & Morante, L. The influence of father-son relationships on adolescent personality and attitudes. *Journal of Child Psychology and Psychiatry*, 1963, **4**, 3–16.

Mutimer, D.; Loughlin, L.; & Powell, M. Some differences in the family relationships of achieving and underachieving readers. *Journal of Genetic Psychology*, 1966, **109**, 67–74.

Nakamura, C. V., & Rogers, M. M. Parents' expectations of autonomous behavior and children's autonomy. *Developmental Psychology*, 1969, **1**, 613–617.

Nelsen, E. A., & Maccoby, E. E. The relationship between social development and differential abilities on the scholastic aptitude test. *Merrill-Palmer Quarterly*, 1966, **12**, 269–289.

Ostrovsky, E. S. *Father to the child: Case studies of the experiences of a male teacher*. New York: Putnam, 1959.

Parker, S., & Kleiner, R. J. Characteristics of Negro mothers in single-headed households. *Journal of Marriage and the Family*, 1966, **28**, 507–513.

Pedersen, F. A. Relationships between father-absence and emotional disturbance in male military dependents. *Merrill-Palmer Quarterly*, 1966, **12**, 321–331.

Poffenberger, T. A., & Norton, D. Factors in the formation of attitudes toward mathematics. *Journal of Educational Research*, 1959, **52**, 171–176.

Preston, R. Reading achievement of German and American children. *School and Society*, 1962, **90**, 350–354.

Radin, N. Father-child interaction and the intellectual functioning of four-year-old boys. *Developmental Psychology*, 1972, **6**, 353–361.

Radin, N. Observed paternal behaviors as antecedents of intellectual functioning in young boys. *Developmental psychology*, 1973, **8**, 369–376.

Reuter, M. W., & Biller, H. B. Perceived paternal nurturance-availability and personality adjustment among college males. *Journal of Consulting and Clinical Psychology*, 1973, **40**, 339.

Risen, M. L. Relation of lack of one or both parents to school progress. *Elementary School Journal*, 1939, **39**, 528–531.

Rosen, B. C., & D'Andrade, R. The psychosocial origins of achievement motivation. *Sociometry*, 1959, **22**, 185–218.

Rouman, J. School children's problems as related to parental factors. *Journal of Educational Research*, 1956, **50**, 105–112.

Rowntree, G. Early childhood in broken families. *Population Studies*, 1955, **8**, 247–253.

Russell, I. L. Behavior problems of children from broken and intact homes. *Journal of Educational Sociology*, 1957, **31**, 125–129.

Ryans, D. B. *Characteristics of teachers*. Washington, D.C.: American Council on Education, 1960.

Santrock, J. W. Influence of onset and type of paternal absence on the first four Eriksonian developmental crises. *Developmental Psychology*, 1970, **3**, 273–274.

Santrock, J. W. Relation of type and onset of father-absence to cognitive development. *Child Development*, 1972, **43**, 455–469.

Seder, J. A. The origin of differences in extent of independence in children: Developmental factors in perceptual field dependence. Unpublished doctoral dissertation, Radcliffe College, 1957.

Sexton, P. C. *The feminized male: Classrooms, white collars, and the decline of manliness*. New York: Random House, 1969.

Shaw, M. C., & White, O. L. The relationship between child-parent identification and academic underachievement. *Journal of Clinical Psychology*, 1965, **21**, 10–13.

Sherman, R. C., & Smith, F. Sex differences in cue-dependency as a function of socialization environment. *Perceptual and Motor Skills*, 1967, **24**, 599–602.

Smelser, W. T. Adolescent and adult occupational choice as a function of family socioeconomic history. *Sociometry*, 1963, **4**, 393–409.

Solomon, D. The generality of children's achievement-related behavior. *Journal of Genetic Psychology*, 1969, **114**, 109–125.

Stein, A. H. The effects of sex-role standards for achievement and sex-role preference on three determinants of achievement motivation. *Developmental Psychology*, 1971, **4**, 219–231.

Stein, A. H.; Pohly, S. R.; & Muellar, E. Sex-typing of achievement areas as a determinant of children's motivation and effort. Paper presented at the meeting of the Society for Research in Child Development, Santa Monica, California, March, 1969.

Stein, A. H., & Smithells, J. Age and sex differences in children's sex role standards about achievement. *Developmental Psychology*, 1969, **1**, 252–259.

Strang, J. B. Students' reasons for becoming better readers. *Education*, 1968, **89**, 127–131.

Strodtbeck, F. L. Family interaction, values, and achievement. In D. C. McClelland, et al. (Eds.), *Talent and society*. New York: Van Nostrand, 1958. Pp. 135–194.

Sutherland, H. E. G. The relationship between I.Q. and size of family in the case of fatherless children. *Journal of Genetic Psychology*, 1930, **38**, 161–170.

Sutton-Smith, B.; Rosenberg, B. G.; & Landy, F. Father-absence effects in families of different sibling compositions. *Child Development*, 1968, **38**, 1,213–1,221.

Tallman, I. Spousal role differentiation and the socialization of severely retarded children. *Journal of Marriage and the Family*, 1965, **27**, 38–42.

Terman, L. M., & Oden, M. H. *The gifted child grows up*. Stanford: Stanford University Press, 1947.

Thomes, M. M. Children with absent fathers. *Journal of Marriage and the Family*, 1968, **30**, 89–96.

Veroff, J.; Atkinson, J.; Feld, S.; & Gurin, G. The use of thematic apperception to assess motivation in a nationwide interview study. *Psychological Monographs*, 1960, **74** (Whole No. 499).

Winebrenner, R. Father absence effects and sons' abilities; A review of the literature and its relationship to reading. Unpublished master's thesis, Indiana University, 1971.

Witkin, H. A. The problem of individuality in development. In B. Kaplan & S. Wapner (Eds.), *Perspectives in psychological theory*. New York: International Universities Press, 1960. Pp. 335–361.

Witkin, H. A.; Dyk, R. B.; Faterson, H.; Goodenough, D. R.; & Karp, S. A. *Psychological differentiation: Studies of development*. New York: Wiley, 1962.

Parent Identification and Filial Sex-Role Behavior: The Importance of Biological Context

ALFRED B. HEILBRUN, JR.

Emory University

It has been commonly observed that human social responses are of such complexity as to deny us clear understanding of their antecedents. It is my belief that our behavior as social scientists has been profoundly influenced by this realization so that we have held on to simplifying theories and outrageously simplistic research tools long after they have served whatever heuristic value they have for our scientific enterprise. Since I can see nothing being gained by delaying the inevitable scientific confrontation with complexity, I would like to devote this paper to that end, using human sex-role behavior as the focus of discussion.

We will proceed by first identifying the simplifying theories which hinder our progress toward understanding human sex-role behavior and to argue for their relinquishment. We will then consider the importance of a relatively unexplored variable in explaining the ontogeny and character of sex-role behavior in the child. Sex-role behavior of a parent model or of the modeling child occurs in the context of an established biological sex-gender role. Psychological masculinity can be observed, for example, in either a biological male or female. We will use the term *congruity* to describe the fit between psychological masculinity and biological maleness and between psychological femininity and biological femaleness, with *incongruity* applied to femininity in the male and masculinity in the female. It will be our contention that the development and character of the child's sex-role behavior can be better understood if we consider the congruity factor in parent models as this may interact with the sex of the child. Masculinity or femininity in males is different from masculinity or femininity in females, whether we are looking at parents or at their children.

PROBLEMS OF DEFINITION AND CONCEPTUALIZATION

It is necessary to consider several of the issues surrounding the key concept of parent identification and that of sex-role behavior in order to lay the groundwork for our biological context proposals. These issues will range from the most basic concerns about how we should define our subject matter to more abstract considerations regarding the explanation of behavioral outcome. It should become clear to you in the development of this section that my resolution to these issues is only one of innumerable ways that the social scientist could order his thinking about identification and sex-role behavior. I am convinced, however, that what I shall propose has promising heuristic value and can open the way to an acceleration of scientific progress.

Problems in Defining Parent Identification

Identification as process or outcome? Among the problems inherent in defining parent identification discussed at length by Urie Bronfenbrenner (1958), the most compelling problem of definition to me was that of distinguishing process from outcome in identification research. While it is generally agreed that identification of a child with his parent should result in some degree of learned similarity between the two, there is no reason to believe that identification is the only basis for similarity. Parent-child similarity could be the result of genetic endowment, parental reinforcement of their own behavioral styles, or the response of both parent and child to the same cultural influence (including common pressures to conform or not conform to prescribed sex roles).

Since our research measures of parent-child similarity fail to distinguish between sources, Bronfenbrenner points out that we measure multiply determined outcome and not the identification process as a singular source of parent-child similarity. Even granting the aptness of this observation, it is worth pointing out that a danger exists in confounding our current methodological limitations with the definition of our subject matter. If we admit that we cannot distinguish between sources of the parent-child similarity which our measures reflect, this does not preclude our defining parent identification as a process. It does mean that we must acknowledge the imperfect nature of our measure with the genetic, reinforcement, and common influence factors introducing an unknown amount of error variance.

In a way, the measurement problem is similar to that facing those investigating any facet of learning. A distinction must be maintained between performance (what we measure) and learning (one source of performance variance). Learning theorists, at least those in the Hull-Spence tradition, identified several other sources of performance variance besides learning, including both drive and inhibition variables. Given that identification of a child with the parent is a learning process, the social scientist must contend with the fact of life that his measure of similarity reflects performance, only part of which can be justifiably attributed to identification learning. This problem has not stopped other learning research; why should it stop ours? I also reassure myself with the solid hunch that behavioral similarity between parent and child, if properly measured, is related in a far more important way to identification than to other sources of variance.

What type of learning is involved in the identification process? It has been specified that parent identification, the process by which a child comes to increase the similarity between his covert and overt behaviors and those characterizing one or both parents, is accomplished by some form of learning. There probably would be very little argument regarding this assumption among social scientists, or with the more specific contention that modeling or imitative learning assumes major importance in understanding the manner in which identification occurs. However, I undoubtedly join somewhat more select company in my assumption that imitative learning represents the only form of learning which is systematically involved in parent identification.

A brief working definition of parent identification for purposes of this paper would be as follows: *Parent identification is a process of imitative learning which occurs over an extended period of time and results in behavioral similarities between the child and one or both parents.* This source of learned behavior must be distinguished from learning occurring within the family context which involves direct tuition of the child by a parent or learning resulting from schedules of reinforcement, whether intentionally devised by the parent or not. Clear separation of behaviors learned in any of these three ways is exceedingly difficult, if not impossible, since a given behavior may be facilitated in the child by more than one of these learning conditions. For example, a boy may be exposed to an aggressive father as a model, a father who continually lectures his son on the virtue of "standing up for your rights" or "going after what you want" and who rewards his son for aggressive action and punishes him for passivity. Now if the boy turns out to be aggressive, should we attribute this behavior outcome to modeling, tuition, or the schedule of reinforcement?

While I cannot offer any panacea for the identification researcher who must contend with this possible confounding between learning sources, I would warn against one tempting avenue of escape. Many would include within their definition of identification the stipulation that the process is an unconscious one; somehow the imitative learning occurs beyond the awareness of the child. If this were so, we could use level of awareness as a rough criterion of learning source, for, after all, the child should certainly be aware of what his parents have told him (direct tuition) and the behaviors which have been systematically reinforced. Be this as it may, I intuitively reject the assumption that imitation of a parent (or others, for that matter) occurs beyond the awareness of the child. I submit that both intrinsic and extrinsic rehearsal of behavior observed in a model may occur within the full awareness of the child, and furthermore, he is likely to be aware of his own motivation to be like the other person. While imitation without awareness may occur, it is misleading, in my opinion, to offer it as a precondition for identification.

What reinforcement is involved in the identification process? There is no particular interest at this point in raising the thorny issue of whether reinforcement is necessary for learning to occur. There is a vested interest, however, in distinguishing between types of reinforcement, as far as their contribution to modeling is concerned, since I hope to make use of such a distinction later in this paper. It seems to me that what little evidence exists fails to indicate the importance of secondary (learned) reinforcement as instrumental to imitative learning. A secondary-reinforcement hypothesis would contend that the continued association between a potential parent model and primary reinforcement (e.g., feeding) results in the establishment of a secondary drive for the presence of the physical properties or the behaviors of that model, which have assumed secondary reinforcing value. To behave like the model should, in theory, allow the child to secondarily reinforce himself, thereby stamping in these behaviors through reinforced rehearsal.

Bandura presented evidence in an earlier Nebraska Symposium (1962) which not only failed to support the importance of secondary reinforcement for imitation of a model (Bandura, Ross, & Ross, 1963a) but which clearly suggested the importance of vicarious reinforcement in mediating this effect in nursery-age children (Bandura, Ross, & Ross, 1963a; 1963b). Children tend to imitate models whom they observe to be successful in attaining their goals or see in a position of power to control a variety of resources which the child desires. People love winners and children are no exception, and we are left to assume that behaving like a winner is vicariously rewarding.

I propose that vicarious reinforcement is the primary type of reward involved in parent identification, with no assumption that all such modeling is reinforced. Other types of reinforcement may be more important to strengthening a response after the behavior has been incorporated into the child's repertoire through imitation.

Problems in Conceptualizing Parent Identification

The psychoanalytic legacy. The impact of Freud's thinking upon developmental theory and research is undeniable, not to mention its effect upon popular "psychologizing" at the cocktail-party level.

An entire symposium could be dedicated to weighing the evidence as it might or might not support psychoanalytic developmental theory, and I shall not be so presumptuous as to try to digest this evidence in a brief review. However, I would presume to identify a few ways in which psychoanalytic theory has deterred our progress in understanding parent identification. Parenthetically, it is to be understood that these comments are generated from the perspective of a modeling theorist.

The first problem which the psychoanalytic legacy has created for us is the emphasis laid upon behavior dynamics which have nothing to do with why people learn in a social context. Freud's postulation of a conflictual crisis faced by the child in his or her competition with the same-sex parent for the sexual-affectional favor of the opposite-sex parent is probably as well known as any attempt to explain human behavior. Our concern over the years with whether the Oedipus or Electra complex is really a universal, whether the young child is really capable of adult sexuality, or whether boys really notice the absence of the phallus in the female, has been, in my opinion, a gigantic "red herring." We have allowed ourselves to be distracted by a theory of identification which is not only oversimplistic but whose terms are irrelevant to an explanation of how a child learns to be like a parent.

Our efforts should have been and should be now directed toward identifying those factors which relate to imitative learning as it occurs in the social context of the family. The present paper will be an effort in that direction in that we have chosen one of the more obvious variable conditions under which modeling must occur and have pursued the implications of this variable for identification outcome. It seems obvious that, given modeling behavior on the part of the child, his sex-role outcome must be influenced to some extent by the sex role of the model. Our question will be whether this sex-role influence is moderated by the biological context of the presenting model or the identifying child.

A second conceptual pitfall bequeathed to us by psychoanalytic theory is the stipulation that parent identification occurs within a circumscribed period around the middle of the first decade of life. The "incorporation" of the parent, Freud's identification, must await the child's diminished ardor for toilet behavior and his discovery of the pleasures of the phallic area. Yet the chronological facts of identification from a modeling point of view would hardly be expected to correspond to these parameters. I suggest that modeling theory would more likely consider identification as a continuous process, at least through the period from birth to 18 years within which the child maintains exposure to the parent models. Furthermore, serious adherence to a learning theory would require us to fix the age at which parent imitation might begin by determining those physical and psychological markers in development which must be present before the child is capable of true imitative behavior. We also would attend carefully to the developmental point at which behavior, identification-mediated or not, becomes so fixed in the youngster that parent modeling no longer serves as a major influence in shaping behavior.

I do not pretend to know precisely where these two chronological markers should be placed, although I certainly would not look for the beginnings of effective modeling behavior until the second or third year of life and would expect the effectiveness of modeling to dwindle some time before the child typically leaves the family home. To return to my original point, rather than restrict our attention to some more or less discrete happening which will occur at about 5 to 6 years of age, we should extend our range of interest to a continuous process occurring over a much broader developmental period.

The increased complexity of conceptualizing parent identification as a long-term continuous learning process stands in stark contrast to the vast oversimplification of psychoanalytic theory. Not only must we contend with the likelihood that model behaviors may have differential imitative pull at different chronological periods for the child, but the further likelihood that parents may change as models over time adds to our conceptual burden. If taking into account the child's changing priorities for imitation and the parents' shifting behaviors as models appears to create a conceptual hardship, we should not fail to mention the fact that the final registration of imitative behavior depends upon the behaviors already present in the child's repertoire. Two children may model after the same behavior in a parent with somewhat different outcomes if the blend with existing behavior differs. For example, I would expect the behavior of Child X to differ from that of Child Y, given that each modeled after an assertive father, if the former child had modeled after his mother's passivity previously and the latter child had not.

The successive-identification problem. It has been commonly proposed that identification with parents is a two-step procedure. As the proposal goes, children of both sexes make an initial identification with the mother, following which boys change their identificatory model to the father and girls maintain the mother as their primary model. While this contention has been attributed to Freud, I have been unsuccessful in finding its original source. However, successive identification has been given credence by both psychologists (Lynn, 1969; Sears, 1957) and sociologists (Parsons, 1958; Parsons & Bales, 1955) alike. Where such writers have been explicit, the initial identification of both sexes with the mother as a model occurs within the first year or so of life and follows from her singular importance as a caretaker during this period. Here, again, I would submit that we have been led down a conceptual path to an assumption which is at best unnecessary and at worst misleading.

I have already offered my opinion that modeling behavior requires a level of psychomotor development not found in the infant. Implicit or explicit rehearsal of behavior patterns observed in a parent model and the contingent vicarious reinforcement is simply not within the range of capacities of the child within the first year and would be expected to unfold gradually as a capacity following that.

The importance of the successive-identification assumption to sex-role development is to account for the presence of feminine qualities in a male when they are observed and for the absence of masculine qualities in females, who are presumably incapable of such behavior. After all, the father (masculine) identification of the boy is simply an overlay of the earlier mother (feminine) identification; scratch the tough surface of his personality and you will find the soft qualities endowed by his mother. Girls, who have looked only to the mother as a model, have had no opportunity to take on the qualities of masculinity.

I would point out that these phenomena, for which the notion of successive identification has been held to account, are themselves of dubious credibility. The expected femininity in men far too often is difficult to observe, just as the presence of masculine behaviors in women is difficult to miss. Perhaps one can sum up the successive-identification hypothesis most succinctly by noting that it is completely unnecessary, given the task of accounting for mixed or articulated sex-role behavior. The nuclear family provides the child two parents, either of whom can incorporate his or her own admixture of masculine and feminine behaviors as a model. Any sex-role outcome, usual or unusual, could be expected, depending upon the host of factors which influence modeling behavior.

What appears to have happened is that theorists have confused parental identification with another behavioral phenomenon of the first year, the formation of a social attachment to the primary caretaker. The initial social attachment of the infant, almost always to the mother, has been documented empirically by Schaffer and Emerson (1964) and Ainsworth (1967). Their findings suggest the presence of a social-responsivity factor in the infant, partially determined by the amount of nurturant care offered by the maternal caretaker and partially determined by something perhaps constitutional, which the infant brings to the mother-child interaction. If it could be demonstrated that these individual differences in social responsivity make some lasting contribution to the personality of the child, we would have a sex-role behavior influenced by the child's relationship with the mother during his first year without invoking the identification process at all. Girls *and* boys who emerge from their initial social attachments as more socially responsive individuals would be pointed toward a more feminine identity.

Differentiating attachment formation in the first year and identification which follows further psychological and physical maturation of the child also helps, in my way of thinking, to align the contribution of reinforcement to learning. We have surmised previously that secondary reinforcement is of negligible significance to later identification learning. However, the conditions of intense caretaking offered by the mother during the first year open the way to a close association between her stimulus properties and primary drive reduction. This would lead us to expect secondary reinforcement to contribute to attachment development. As the child develops the capacity for vicarious experience and the intimate relationship with the mother dissipates, vicarious reinforcement would become the important contributor to identification learning and secondary reinforcement would lose its importance.

Problems in Defining Human Sex Roles

The nature and development of human sex roles, at least from a social-learning perspective, are aptly summarized by Professors Rosenberg and Sutton-Smith in a recent publication (1972) when they state:

> Masculinity and femininity are not simply the result of birth as a boy or a girl. The gender role is assigned to the child at this time based on his biological sex, and he is subsequently treated as a member of that sex. In accord with cultural prescription regarding the manner in which boys and girls are viewed, different attitudes are evidenced toward children of different sexes, and different behaviors of these children are reinforced. A set of rules is established for the child which is based on his sex (his sex role), and the aim of the parent is to provide those reinforcements which conduce to the adoption and assimilation of that role. [P. 52–53]

As their book further illustrates, the contribution of learning to the adoption of sex roles increases as we consider species higher in the phylogenetic scale. Whereas constitutional factors (genetic endowment, physiological variables, physical differences) may play a singularly influential role in lower species, masculinity or femininity in the human is most reasonably considered the product of the child's experience with other human beings.

Since sex roles are culturally transmitted in humans, we are left with intriguing questions relating to how the cultural expectations were generated in the first place. Perhaps answers to such questions are best left to cultural anthropologists or sociologists, but we should recognize that the man-made character of sex-role expectations does contribute its own brand of difficulty to the social scientist's attempt to investigate the phenomenon. We are exposed to the continuous danger of definitional slippage as previous role assignments erode and what was at one time a clear behavioral differentiation between the biological sexes assumes a blurred character. While attitudes of "make love, not war" among our youthful males and the outspoken rejection of traditional marital or maternal goals by their female peers may have some merit, the consequent blurring of sex-role distinctions offers no advantage to our already imprecise research methodologies.

A WORKING METHODOLOGY FOR INVESTIGATING PARENT IDENTIFICATION AND SEX-ROLE BEHAVIOR

Before directing our attention to the central topic of concern, the moderating influences of biological context upon sex-role behavior, it is important to understand the procedures by which we have generated our data. This is true if for no other reason than the fact that the investigation of parent identification and sex-role identity has often proceeded with woefully inadequate methodologies. It follows that inquiry into method is essential within this realm of research. While our procedures, by which I mean our measurement approaches, are hardly above criticism, I have long maintained the conviction that they are as good as any and better than most.

Measurement of Parent Identification

Conceptualizing parent identification in almost any terms, but most certainly in modeling terms, requires some procedure for measuring the degree of behavioral similarity between the child and his parents. The various approaches to this type of measurement, usually psychometric, have fallen into three categories—perceived similarity, real similarity, or ideal similarity. Differences between these categories are basically instrumental in character. Perceived similarity is inferred from the child's description of parental behavior and his own behavior; real similarity is based upon independent descriptions of behavior obtained from the parents and the child or from an outside observer; ideal similarity would be based upon the expressed ideal behaviors of parents and child.

Preferences among these categories of measures should depend on the scientific payoff of each approach, but I suspect that subtle conceptual biases are more often paramount. My own biases are clear. Ideal similarity is of little value unless the investigator is influenced by psychoanalytic theory. Real similarity is a misleading bit of nomenclature. As standardly applied it represents the degree of correspondence in the adult's perception of his own behavior and the child's perception of his own behavior. While the term *real* may evoke surplus meanings relating to scientific credibility, we should not lose sight of the fact that this procedure does nothing more than relate one person's perceptions to those of another. Perhaps the somewhat noxious term *real* may be more reasonably applied to a methodology within which an independent observer discerns the behavior of both the parent and child, but the dependence upon fallible human perception must still be acknowledged.

My preferred approach has been to establish the degree of perceived child-parent similarity, using the child as the source of information. The simple reason for this preference is that modeling behavior represents the child's attempts to reproduce the responses of another person *as the child perceives these responses*. Given this assumption, it follows that gauging the extent to which modeling has occurred is most reasonably effected by establishing the child's perceived model against which one compares the child's own behavior. Whether the child's behavior is measured through self-assessment or by some other route depends upon a variety of considerations, including age of the child and expected subject motivation.

Depending on what you are after, any of these three categories of measures might be preferred. If interest is focused upon conscience development, similarity in idealized behaviors could be of interest. If interest is directed toward our closest approximation to the actual similarity between a parent and a child, use of an outside observer would be recommended. Such a real-similarity measure could generate only a by-product index of parent identification. Identification conceptualized as a process occurring totally within the child gains the potential for direct measurement only from a methodology which involves the child's perceptual system and his conception of the model he has held up for emulation, the perceived-similarity approach.

Our psychometric procedure for establishing the degree and type of parent identification for the child was described orginally several years ago, along with a series of studies relevant to its construct validity (Heilbrun, 1965a). The technique involves two sets of ratings which are obtained from our late-adolescent subject with no instructional liaison between them. Our impression has been that subjects are usually unaware of the object of our measurement, although this has not been systematically tested.

The first ratings obtained from the subject are self-assessments on the Adjective Check List (ACL) (Gough & Heilbrun, 1965), a compendium of 300 commonly used behavioral adjectives. Among the personality scales which can be scored from the ACL are 15 which measure variables originally catalogued by Murray (1938) as normal manifest need dispositions and subsequently adopted by Edwards for his Personal Preference Schedule (1957). These 15 personality variables and their brief definitions, taken from the ACL Manual, are as follows:

1. Achievement: To strive to be outstanding in pursuits of socially recognized significance.

2. Dominance: To seek and sustain leadership roles in groups or to be influential and controlling in individual relationships.

3. Endurance: To persist in any task undertaken.

4. Order: To place special emphasis on neatness, organization, and planning one's activities.

5. Intraception: To engage in attempts to understand one's own behavior or the behavior of others.

6. Nurturance: To engage in behaviors which extend material or emotional benefits to others.

7. Affiliation: To seek and sustain numerous personal friendships.

8. Heterosexuality: To seek the company of and derive emotional satisfactions from interactions with opposite-sex peers.

9. Exhibition: To behave in such a way as to elicit the immediate attention of others.

10. Autonomy: To act independently of others or of social values and expectations.

11. Aggression: To engage in behaviors which attack or hurt others.

12. Change: To seek novelty of experience and avoid routine.

13. Succorance: To solicit sympathy, affection, or emotional support from others.

14. Abasement: To express feelings of inferiority through self-criticism, guilt, or social impotence.

15. Deference: To seek and sustain subordinate roles in relationships with others.

Raw scores on each of these scales have been normed with *T*-score averages set at 50 and standard deviations at 10.

The second set of ratings provided by the subject involves assessment of his parents' behavior. He is given descriptions of behaviors associated with each of the 15 personality variables scaled on the ACL, and for each set of behaviors he is asked to identify the parent for whom the behaviors are more characteristic. The score depicting the relative similarity of the offspring to the father or the mother is generated by summing the algebraic deviations of the subject's personality scores from the norm of 50, using the rated behavior of the same-sex parent as the guide for assignment of positive or negative sign.

A set of examples might be useful. Consider only one of the 15 personality variables, let us say, the achievement variable. If the subject is male, there are four possible ways in which his achievement score could be related to the achievement rating for his parents: (a) If the son is a high achiever (e.g., has a score of 60 on the ACL) and his father is selected as the more likely achiever model of the two parents, a *plus* is assigned to the 10-point deviation from 50. (b) If the son is a high achiever (e.g., has a score of 60 on the ACL) and his mother is selected as the more likely achiever model of the two parents, a *minus* is assigned to the 10-point deviation from 50. (c) If the son is a low achiever (e.g., has a score of 40 on the ACL) and his father is selected as the more likely achiever model of the two parents, a *minus* is assigned to the 10-point deviation from 50. (d) If the son is a low achiever (e.g., has a score of 40 on the ACL) and his mother is selected as the more likely achiever model of the two parents, a *plus* is assigned to the 10-point deviation from 50. Plus scores, then, are achieved by the son's similarity to the father or dissimilarity to the mother; minus scores are assigned given the son's dissimilarity to the father or similarity to the mother.

The same principles of scoring are applied to female subjects, with the assignment of plus values readjusted to mean greater similarity to the mother or dissimilarity to the father and minus signs signifying dissimilarity to the to the mother or similarity to the father. The deviation raw scores have been normed for late adolescents so that a T score of 50 (standard deviation of 10) for males represents the average similarity to the father and a score of 50 for females indicates their average similarity to their mothers. As we have standardly used this pyschometric technique, a score above 50 is interpreted as primary identification with the same-sex parent model and a score of 50 or below as primary identification with the cross-sex parent.

The third operation involved in the identification measurement procedure is a parent sex-role model scoring procedure. Nine of the 15 personality variables for which parent behavior ratings are made by the subject within the perceived-similarity procedure qualified as sex-typed by a criterion imposed in earlier research (Heilbrun, 1964). Behaviors qualifying as masculine included achievement, dominance, endurance, and autonomy, and those qualifying as feminine were the personological variables of nurturance, affiliation, succorance, abasement, and deference. The sex-role model score is derived by a count of the number of parent ratings out of these nine which identified the appropriate parent, biologically speaking, as better characterized by the sex-typed behavior in question. This added dimension allows the researcher to discern not only the degree of relative similarity to one parent or the other but also the sex-role appropriateness or inappropriateness of the parent models.

Measurement of Masculinity-Femininity of the Child

While there were several published psychological tests of sex-role identity available in the 1960's (e.g., Brown, 1957; DeLucia, 1963; Gough, 1957; Hathaway & McKinley, 1951; Terman & Miles, 1936), the courage of our conviction that parent model sex-role identity was a critical addition to identification measurement led us to reorder our thinking about the measurement of masculinity and femininity in the child. The issue was a simple one. If the sex-role learning of the child is influenced in an important way by the sex-role behaviors of the parent model selected for primary identification, then this fact should be represented somehow in our procedures for measuring masculinity and femininity. The decision was to empirically derive a bipolar scale, using the ACL as our basic instrument, by contrasting the behaviors of psychologically and biologically extreme criterion groups—adolescent males identified with masculine fathers versus adolescent females identified with feminine mothers (Cosentino & Heilbrun, 1964).

The expectation that this extreme group comparison would give us an unadulterated measure of masculinity at one end and femininity at the other attains face validity simply by inspecting the behavioral adjectives which were empirically identified (Table 1). If you will indulge my own subjective clustering of these attributes, it strikes me that almost all of them can be considered as correlates of one of seven dimensions. These would include three bipolar dimensions (a to c) and four unipolar dimensions (d to g): (a) masculine aggressiveness versus feminine nurturance, (b) masculine dominance versus feminine submission, (c) masculine emotional unresponsiveness versus feminine emotional responsiveness, (d) masculine egocentrism, (e) masculine ingenuity, (f) feminine socialization, and (g) feminine immaturity. I have been struck with the correspondence between these dimensions of sex role which surfaced from our empirical search and Parsons's (1958; Parsons and Bales, 1955) proposed differences between the sex roles. He proposes that the essence of masculinity resides in the instrumental character of the person. This is defined by his ability to maintain a behavioral orientation which transcends the immediate interpersonal situation, his use of the interaction as a means to an end, and his insensitivity to the emotional responses engendered in others by his behavior. The essence of femininity is an expressive orientation which directs the person's concern to the immediate interpersonal situation and to how others are reacting to her and to one another. Instrumental goal-seeking of the masculine person is readily translated into the aggressiveness, dominance, emotional unresponsiveness, egocentrism, and ingenuity that we have identified. Similarly, the expressive-relationship orientation would most certainly be mediated by the nurturant, submissive, emotionally responsive, and socialized but immature (childlike) behavior of the feminine person identified on our empirically derived scale.

The final version of the Masculinity-Femininity (MF) Scale

TABLE 1

BEHAVIORAL ADJECTIVES DISTINGUISHING
MALE ADOLESCENTS IDENTIFIED WITH
MASCULINE FATHERS FROM FEMALE
ADOLESCENTS IDENTIFIED WITH FEMININE
MOTHERS

Males more often:	Females more often:
aggressive	appreciative
arrogant	cheerful
assertive	civilized
autocratic	complaining
conceited	considerate
confident	contented
cool	cooperative
cruel	dependent
cynical	disorderly
deliberate	emotional
dominant	excitable
egotistical	fearful
enterprising	feminine
forceful	fickle
foresighted	forgiving
frank	friendly
handsome	frivolous
hard-headed	generous
individualistic	helpful
industrious	immature
ingenious	jolly
inventive	meek
masculine	modest
opportunistic	praising
outspoken	reliable
progressive	self-pitying
reckless	sensitive
self-confident	sentimental
sharp-witted	sincere
shrewd	submissive
stern	sympathetic
strong	talkative
tough	thoughtful
vindictive	timid
	trusting
	unaffected
	warm
	wholesome
	worrying

included 54 of the 73 adjectives listed in Table 1, those for which conventional statistical significance ($p < .05$) was achieved for the criterion-group difference. (Table 1 includes those which reached the 10% level of probability or less.) Scale scores are treated in the same fashion as other ACL scales, with the norm set at $T = 50$ and the standard deviation at 10; higher scores indicate masculinity and lower scores, femininity.

The nature of the MF Scale derivation requires that there will be a certain degree of mechanical dependency between Identification Scale scores and MF Scale scores; a person who is psychometrically portrayed as identifying with a masculine father usually will have a higher (masculine) score on the sex-role scale, and a feminine-mother identification will commonly be associated with a lower (feminine) score. Data taken from a previously published study (Heilbrun, 1969) illustrate this point. Compared with college norms of $T = 50$ on the MF Scale for males and females, mean MF scores for masculine-father identified (58.1) and feminine-mother identified (36.7) offspring fell at the extremes. The MF means for feminine-father identified (48.1) and masculine-mother identified (49.3) subjects were intermediate and indistinguishable from the general norm.

SEX ROLE OF THE PARENT-IDENTIFICATION MODEL AND ADJUSTMENT OF THE CHILD

The particular category of research which triggered my interest in the effects of congruity or incongruity between biological and psychological sex related primarily, though not exclusively, to the adjustment value of various identification patterns in late-adolescent college students. I shall make no pretense of representative coverage of the research literature in this area of investigation, since it is not central to this paper. Furthermore, I can illustrate the progress in method and inference which took place between 1962 and 1970 by parading my own mistakes without surveying what has been a uniquely undistinguished body of research.

Heilbrun (1962a) noted in the evidence of two other studies (Heilbrun, 1960; 1962b) a suggested relationship between parental identification and adjustment in college. The former investigation had found personality differences between maladjusted males from a counseling center and randomly selected controls indicating a feminine personality pattern to be associated with poorer adjustment.

A similar comparison for females failed to reveal any clear association between sex-role identity and behavioral effectiveness. The latter paper reported on the personality correlates of early dropout from college in girls, with the results showing the more feminine personality traits to be associated with the failure to make the adjustment to the college environment. These findings led to the prediction in the 1962a study that a father identification in male college students would be conducive to better adjustment, whereas a mother identification in the female would mediate the opposite effect.

The identification-adjustment relationship for the male late adolescents was reasonably clear; those who had personal problems (i.e., counseling center clients) received a lower score (45.5) on the Identification Scale (IS) than did their male controls (50.29). Maladjusted males were less identified with their fathers, a finding entirely consistent with what many others had reported for boys.

The relationship between identification and adjustment for females was also entirely consistent with the findings reported by other investigators; it was equivocal. Although the identification of college female clients hinted of stronger modeling after the mother (53.4) than was the case for their controls (51.3), statistical confirmation of a difference was not found. A second sample of females was drawn in an attempt to clarify the equivocal findings. While the identification score for the maladjusted girls was higher (51.7) than for the control subjects (46.1), again suggesting a mother identification to be nonadaptive, the difference did not achieve statistical significance.

It was sometime after this initial study of identification and adjustment that belated recognition occurred of the methodological flaw previously discussed. If one is to place importance upon the sex-role behaviors of adolescents in explaining differences in behavioral effectiveness (which I had), then it is necessary to introduce some measurement of mediated parent sex-role attributes into the identification index (which I had not).

The investigation (Heilbrun & Fromme, 1965) which succeeded our initial venture not only plugged the gap left by the absence of a model sex-role index but also increased the levels of adjustment studied from two to three. *Maladjusted,* as before, was defined as the presence of personally disruptive problems in a counseling center client, and *adjusted* essentially meant a randomly selected student from the subject pool. Intermediate to these levels we inserted those who utilized the counseling center for vocational or educational guidance. The stepwise progression in behavioral effectiveness of these three groups would not be difficult to document.

Table 2 includes the findings of the Heilbrun and Fromme study relevant to our current discussion. These data can be approached in either of two ways, depending upon whether one is a horizontal or a vertical scanner. Unfortunately, in 1965 I apparently was a horizontal scanner. In reading the data this way, I was led to one conclusion I am now convinced is incorrect and, in addition, managed to miss a major point.

TABLE 2

RELATIONSHIPS BETWEEN MASCULINITY-FEMININITY OF THE PARENT MODELS
AND IDENTIFICATION AT THREE LEVELS OF ADJUSTMENT

| | Identification Scores for Sons | | | | Identification Scores for Daughters | | | |
| | Given Masculine Father and Feminine Mother[a] | | Given Feminine Father and Masculine Mother[a] | | Given Masculine Father and Feminine Mother[a] | | Given Feminine Father and Masculine Mother[a] | |
Level of Adjustment	N	Mean	N	Mean	N	Mean	N	Mean
Adjusted	41	53.9	47	48.3	31	48.4	42	53.7
Intermediate	32	49.3	28	49.1	31	51.0	41	49.2
Maladjusted	21	46.5	17	50.1	16	60.2	32	51.0

[a] Masculinity of the father or femininity of the mother was defined by scores of 8–9 on the parent model ratings; femininity of the father or masculinity of the mother was defined by scores of 0–5.

If you examine the mean identification scores for the male late adolescents in Columns 1 and 2 of Table 2, you will note a systematic reversal of identification with the father as a function of his sex-role properties relative to the mother and the level of adjustment of the son. Specifically, adjusted males had identified with the father more (53.9) when he was masculine than when he was feminine (48.3); males intermediate in adjustment had not differentially identified with the masculine (49.3) and feminine (49.1) father; and males who were maladjusted had identified less with the masculine father (46.5) than with his more feminine counterpart (50.1). These results were totally in keeping with the accrued evidence on male sex-role adoption which had found masculine sex-role behavior to be reinforced in our culture.

A similar comparison of means in Columns 3 and 4 of Table 1 seems to offer the opposite conclusion for daughters from that derived for sons. Whereas identification for the males with the appropriate parent model in terms of conventional sex-gender and sex-role expectations had been associated with the most effective behavioral outcome, greater identification of the females with the masculine mother relative to the feminine mother could be noted as we considered increasing levels of behavioral effectiveness. Our conclusion was that a feminine-mother identification tended to mediate ineffective adjustment, whereas modeling after a masculine mother facilitated an effective adjustment. While this conclusion did correspond to the systematic reversal of mean differences which are clear enough in the female data, there remained a nagging concern over the differences in group size which can be noted on the table. If masculine-mother identification was such a positive influence and feminine-mother identification was such a negative influence on subsequent adjustment of college female adolescents, why was the incidence of families with feminine father-masculine mother models actually less (58%) in our adjusted sample than it was (67%) in our maladjusted sample? Furthermore, identification with the masculine mother of the adjusted group (53.7) did not differ in any important way from that of the maladjusted group (51.0). Additional evidence, which we shall review shortly, confirmed our reservations about the salutary effects of a primary masculine-mother identification in adolescent girls.

I have alluded before to a point which could have been inferred from the Table 2 data but was not, at least at the time it was published. If one attends only to the within-column effects, it is clear that the means are lawfully ordered only within Columns 1 and 3. Given parents who present sex-role-appropriate models, the son's choice of the masculine father rather than the feminine mother as his primary basis for identification is a positive linear function of adjustment outcome ($46.5 \rightarrow 49.3 \rightarrow 53.9$). Given sex-role-appropriate parent models, the daughter's choice of the masculine father rather than the feminine mother for primary identification is also a positive linear function of adjustment outcome ($60.2 \rightarrow 51.0 \rightarrow$

48.4). (The reader should recall that scores below 50 are interpreted as identification with the opposite-sex parent.) However, given a reversal in conventional sex roles between parent models (Columns 2 and 4), no lawful relationships existed between identification and adjustment for sons (50.1 → 49.1 → 48.3) or daughters (51.0 → 49.2 → 53.7). The developmental implications of identification when an incongruity exists between the sex gender and sex roles of the parent models remained to be answered.

The implications of the 1965 Heilbrun and Fromme paper, regarding the contribution of parent-model congruity to the mediated effects of identification, lay dormant for some 5 years until the appearance of two studies in 1969 and 1970. One of these studies (Heilbrun, 1969) was directed toward the relationships between parent identification and the development of career interests in college late adolescents. Our procedures led us to relate the identification patterns to the indices of occupational interest on the Strong Vocational Interest Blank (1959). The most edifying aspect of the results, the relationships between identification and positive occupational interest, is reported in Table 3. Male late adolescents demonstrated the same lawful ordering of career interest development by identification pattern as had been noted earlier when the grosser criterion of behavioral effectiveness had been membership or nonmembership in a client group. Sons identified with masculine-father models evidenced the most highly developed set of occupational

TABLE 3

MEAN POSITIVE OCCUPATIONAL INTEREST SCORES[a] FOR LATE ADOLESCENTS VARYING IN TYPE OF PARENT IDENTIFICATION

	Parent Identification Pattern							
Sex of Child	Identified with Masculine Father		Identified with Feminine Father		Identified with Masculine Mother		Identified with Feminine Mother	
	N	Mean	N	Mean	N	Mean	N	Mean
Male	13	12.9	8	11.4	15	10.5	11	7.3
Female	9	3.4	7	4.6	11	4.9	6	2.7

[a] Mean scores based upon the number of "A" and "B+" scores from a total possible number of 54 occupations on the male form of the Strong Vocational Interest Blank and from the 33 occupations on the female form.

interests (12.9), whereas a feminine-mother identification was associated with the greatest restriction in career interest development (7.3). In contrast to these differences which appeared when the son had sex-role-appropriate models available to him, sex-role reversal of the parent models resulted in no relationship between identification and the criterion of adjustment (11.4 versus 10.5). It is noteworthy that a replication of these findings for males also was reported, using the measure of masculinity-femininity from the ACL as the basis for dividing our college client subjects; masculine late adolescents had significantly more career interests (10.4) than did their feminine male counterparts (8.2). Keep in mind that this Masculinity-Femininity Scale was derived from the performances of criterion groups identified with sex-role-appropriate masculine fathers and feminine mothers, so that this does represent a partial replication of the Table 3 male findings.

Despite the apparent restricted range of mean differences among the occupational-interest scores for the female identification groups reported in Table 3, there was a significant interaction effect. Here, again, we were more confounded than edified by the female findings. Unlike male late adolescents, these girls did not present sensibly ordered data when the parents represented appropriate sex-role models (3.4 versus 2.7) or when they represented inappropriate sex-role models (4.6 versus 4.9). In fact, this time it was the presence of an incongruity between sex gender and sex role in the parent model chosen for identification which was associated with more occupational interests. At this point we had progressed with our female subjects (if you wish to call it progress) from identifying the equivocal nature of the parent identification-level of adjustment findings (Heilbrun, 1962), to identifying the paradoxical nature of identification and adjustment findings when parent models assume appropriate sex roles (Heilbrun & Fromme, 1965), to identifying the confusing nature of the identification-adjustment findings when occupational-interest development is considered (Heilbrun, 1969).

A subsequent review chapter (Heilbrun, 1970a) sought to move us closer to solving some of the more plaguing questions which had been raised by prior investigation of the relationships between parent sex role, identification, and level of adjustment of the child.

This time incidence data was collected from a very large sample of college late adolescents (some 600) from which could be generated reliable base-rate estimates of primary identification with specific model types within the adjustment levels defined as before (adjusted, intermediate adjustment, maladjusted). Table 4 includes these data reported in percentage figures and should be read as follows: the first figure in Row 1, 33%, means that 33% of the males in the adjusted group had identified with a masculine father using our standard measurement procedures. Each row, then, should sum to 100%.

TABLE 4

INCIDENCE OF PARENT IDENTIFICATION PATTERNS
FOR MALE AND FEMALE COLLEGE STUDENTS
VARYING IN LEVEL OF BEHAVIORAL EFFECTIVENESS

Sex and Level of Adjustment of Child	Parent Identification Pattern			
	Identified with Masculine Father	Identified with Feminine Father	Identified with Masculine Mother	Identified with Feminine Mother
Male				
Adjusted	33%	22%	20%	25%
Intermediate	23%	18%	31%	28%
Maladjusted	21%	18%	23%	38%
Female				
Adjusted	32%	21%	22%	25%
Intermediate	20%	22%	34%	24%
Maladjusted	20%	21%	36%	23%

We can note in these percentage figures for males some reasonable consistency with previous findings. When you examine late adolescents who are not experiencing any extraordinary problems in adjustment, you will find that more have identified with a masculine father (33%) than with any other model type. At the other extreme, males who are finding it most difficult to make an adjustment have a high representation of feminine-mother identification (38%).

The female results added yet another interpretive wrinkle. We are informed by the Table 4 incidence data that it is identification with a masculine parent model which can facilitate either extreme of adjustment. Identifying with a masculine *father* is the most frequent pattern (32%) among the adjusted girls, whereas identifying with a masculine *mother* maintains the highest incidence rate among the most seriously maladjusted girls (36%) and among the girls with less debilitating problems of an educational-vocational nature (34%). In fact, as we look back at the male data again, the relatively high incidence (31%) of masculine-mother identification in the intermediate adjustment group can be found there as well.

Perhaps we can best conclude our preliminary considerations by quoting from the summary statements generated by the 1970 base-rate study:

> Perhaps the most promising direction that future inquiry might take would have to do with the sex role reversal feature of this pattern. It is unlikely that a woman can present as adequate a masculine model as the biologically male father. It seems possible that masculinity in a woman is more blended with feminine qualities, whereas masculine men are likely to behave discretely in masculine or, under special conditions, in feminine ways. If so, the sex role reversed masculine mother will present a somewhat blurred model of masculine and feminine behaviors for either the son or the daughter to emulate.
>
> ... The relationship between the biological-psychological sex of the parent chosen as the primary model for identification and subsequent competence of the daughter is a strange one. A masculine-father identification qualifies as the most facilitative of effectiveness for the girl, whereas a masculine-mother identification is seen to be the most likely correlate of ineffectiveness. Thus, while it is true that the girl is given greater leeway in adopting cross-sex role behavior in our society than is accorded the boy, it appears to be equally true that the mother who has taken advantage of this permissiveness presents the poorest identification model for her daughter.
>
> Although other observations might be made from the graph data, perhaps enough has been said to stress the importance of the *pattern* of parental identification, meaning here the combination of both the biological and psychological sex of the identification model, for behavior development into the college years. [Pp. 77–78]

CONGRUITY OF BIOLOGICAL SEX GENDER AND PSYCHOLOGICAL SEX ROLE IN PARENT MODELS AND THEIR CHILDREN

Having now reached the point in this paper where the central problem is to be confronted, let me hasten to narrow the scope of our concern to bring it within reasonable limits. Of the myriad questions which could be raised regarding the covariation of sex gender and sex role, only two general questions will be considered. First, what are the differences in outcome to be expected from congruity or incongruity of sex gender and sex role of the parent model with whom primary identification occurs? In the context of considering this question, we shall be interested not only in whether congruous masculinity in the father and femininity in the mother represent different identification conditions from incongruous masculinity in the mother and femininity in the father, but also in whether any mediated outcome differences might be contingent upon the sex of the child. The second question to be considered will bear upon whether psychological masculinity and femininity hold the same behavioral properties for the male and female late adolescent. For example, when we speak of a feminine boy and a feminine girl, to what extent does this describe the same behavior and to what extent does the meaning of femininity depend upon biological context?

Personality Profiles Accompanying the Primary and Secondary Sex-Role Systems

If, for the moment, we accept the premise that the biological context of sex-role behavior influences the stimulus value of the parent identification model, it seems reasonable to conclude that differing sex-role outcomes would be expected in the identifying child, dependent upon the congruous-incongruous character of model gender and role. I would like to label, for the sake of convenience, these differing outcomes as the primary and secondary sex-role systems, with their hypothesized origins resting in the following parent-identification patterns: (a) The primary sex-role system includes all behaviors which are systematically mediated by modeling after masculine behaviors of the father or feminine behaviors of the mother—congruous linkages of model gender and role. (b) The secondary sex-role system includes all behaviors which are systematically mediated by modeling after feminine behaviors of the father or masculine behaviors of the mother—incongruous linkages of model gender and role.

It should be added, parenthetically, that the term *system* as employed here is not to be understood in the strict dictionary sense of "an assemblage of objects united by some form of regular interaction or interdependence," at least, not as yet. It is used only to designate a collection of behaviors thought to have their origins in the same antecedent event.

Primary and secondary sex-role systems, as they are envisaged, are not mutually exclusive behavioral dispositions, but each would be represented to a variable extent in everybody. This follows in part from the fact that parent models would not be expected to represent pure sex role types to their children. Unadulterated masculine behavior, unsoftened as it is directed toward the child, would offer little basis for assuming a responsive paternal role. Similarly, the expressive extremes of pure femininity would render the mother incompetent in meeting her responsibilities within the family context; the toughness and tenacity of the mother which go into effective family functioning are often overlooked. In short, in almost every case of an intact nuclear family, the father will demonstrate some degree of femininity and the mother some degree of masculinity, and the potential for the development of both primary and secondary sex-role systems in the child will exist, their component nature depending upon the identification pattern followed by the child.

Even if we keep our thinking simple regarding primary and secondary sex-role adoption, as we must to keep pace with the limitations of our research methodology, it is necessary to conceive of at least four sex-role typologies rather than the usual two. Adolescents, with whom we shall continue to concern ourselves, need be thought of as not just masculine or feminine but as primary masculine (father mediated)–secondary masculine (mother mediated); primary masculine (father mediated)–secondary feminine (father mediated); primary feminine (mother mediated)–secondary masculine (mother mediated); or primary feminine (mother mediated)–secondary feminine (father mediated). In principle, half of these sex-role patternings have their origins in behaviors assimilated from both parents through identification; for the other half, modeling after both the masculine and feminine behavior of a single parent would be expected.

The approach to investigating the usefulness of these theoretical proposals was first to establish the personality profiles associated with primary sex-role identity and then to discern whether additional information about secondary sex-role status resulted in any significant reordering of the personality correlates. For example, if we select a group of adolescent males because they are masculine in the usual sense of the term, can we make any useful personological distinctions among them by identifying their secondary sex roles? If we cannot, the primary and secondary sex-role systems would appear redundant and the latter would be of no heuristic value. If further assignment of these masculine males to the secondary sex-role subgroupings results in discrete and more homogeneous behavior patterns, the secondary sex-role variable *may* be assumed to hold some explanatory significance.

Heilbrun's (1972d) approach to investigating this problem required that he first establish a procedure for measuring secondary sex-role identity. To do so, an approach paralleling earlier work was used. The derivation of the Masculinity-Femininity Scale of the ACL involved the selection of items differentiating males identified with masculine fathers and females identified with feminine mothers. Accordingly, we had available a scale by which we could measure the primary sex-role system. Some unanalyzed data generated by an earlier study (Heilbrun, 1965b) were used to establish by parallel format which ACL items would distinguish between males identified with a masculine mother and females identified with a feminine father. Those behavioral adjectives for which differences were obtained at the 10% confidence level (using *chi*-square procedures with Yates's correction) are presented in Table 5. The 23 adjectives received the same scalar organization as had been used with the MF Scale: masculine items were scored plus, feminine items were scored minus, and the algebraic sum of endorsed items provided the raw score.

Inspection of the Table 5 items and those found in Table 1 indicates quite clearly that males identified with masculine mothers and females identified with feminine fathers do not present the extensive contrast in behavior found with the previously compared masculine-father-identified males and feminine-mother-identified females. Less than a third of the number of discriminating items

were found in the secondary sex-role analysis than had been generated by the primary sex-role analysis.

The psychometric properties of the secondary sex-role scale,
which, for the sake of brevity, we shall refer to as the MFI (Masculinity-Femininity, Incongruous) Scale, included a 48% item overlap with the 54 items of the MF Scale, more than we would have
liked. However, the correlations of MF and MFI for males ($N = 88$)

TABLE 5

BEHAVIORAL ADJECTIVES DISTINGUISHING
MALES IDENTIFIED WITH MASCULINE
MOTHERS AND FEMALES IDENTIFIED WITH
FEMININE FATHERS

Males more often:	Females more often:
aggressive	awkward
clever	dependent
courageous	excitable
discreet	feminine
fault-finding	generous
forceful	unassuming
foresighted	
handsome	
individualistic	
insightful	
masculine	
opinionated	
opportunistic	
original	
rational	
sharp-witted	
tough	

and females ($N = 149$) of .45 and .46, respectively, suggest a sur-
prisingly low common variance of only 21% between the scales,
leaving ample opportunity for the two scale scores to represent
independent behavior dispositions.

Given the availability of the MFI Scale, we assigned a primary
and secondary sex-role score to each of 88 college males and 149
college females who had been administered the ACL. MF scores
were used to separate all subjects into primary masculine (>50)
and feminine (<51) groupings based upon published college
norms, whereas sample means were employed to further classify
subgrouping into secondary masculine and feminine. These sample

cutting scores were 7 = masculine for males and 2 = masculine for females.

The next step in the analysis involved the determination of personality profiles for groups differing only in primary sex-role identity. Since it is not difficult to trace the interdependence of identification scores, MF scores, and personality profiles, all obtained from the ACL, there should be no major surprises when these primary sex-role groups are compared. The profiles, contained in Table 6, attest to this fact. Both sets of primary sex-role profiles,

TABLE 6

PERSONALITY PROFILES FOR LATE-ADOLESCENT MALES AND FEMALES
DIFFERING IN PRIMARY SEX-ROLE IDENTITY

| | Mean Scale Score | | | |
| | Males | | Females | |
Personality Variable	Masculine ($N = 39$)	Feminine ($N = 49$)	Masculine ($N = 79$)	Feminine ($N = 70$)
Achievement	55.41	49.78	49.87	43.13
Dominance	56.49	48.27	51.57	43.25
Endurance	53.59	50.39	48.42	45.77
Order	52.28	50.47	48.51	46.79
Intraception	48.33	54.67	46.84	51.04
Nurturance	43.31	55.41	41.76	53.03
Affiliation	45.31	51.94	42.51	48.91
Heterosexuality	48.56	54.26	46.67	52.44
Exhibition	56.61	48.47	52.37	48.30
Autonomy	59.82	45.82	57.46	47.50
Aggression	57.20	47.24	56.90	47.43
Change	48.54	49.37	50.87	50.31
Succorance	44.28	50.78	48.03	54.49
Abasement	41.31	52.53	45.62	54.66
Deference	39.13	53.78	43.63	53.03

the male and the female, demonstrate the expected wide variance of personality scores. To illustrate this, the mean absolute difference across the 15 scales between masculine and feminine males is 7.66 *T*-score points, while this mean difference between masculine and feminine females is 6.40 points. Considering that these scales were devised to have an expected standard deviation of 10 points, these average discrepancies qualify as substantial.

The critical analysis for our purpose came next. Would a further assignment of our subjects to secondary sex-role groups offer any clearer delineation of personality patterns than that already demonstrated by the use of the primary sex-role system? If not, secondary sex-role identity would appear to be either redundant in meaning or an entirely irrelevant concept as far as social behavior is concerned. In Table 7 we find personality profiles for the four more refined male subgroups—primary masculine–secondary masculine, primary

TABLE 7

PERSONALITY PROFILES FOR LATE-ADOLESCENT MALES
DIFFERING IN PRIMARY AND SECONDARY SEX-ROLE IDENTITY

Personality Variable	Mean Scale Score			
	Primary Masculine		Primary Feminine	
	Secondary Masculine (N = 25)	Secondary Feminine (N = 14)	Secondary Masculine (N = 18)	Secondary Feminine (N = 31)
Achievement	57.24	52.14	54.56	47.00
Dominance	59.12	51.79	53.06	45.48
Endurance	55.68	49.86	53.67	48.48
Order	54.00	49.21	53.28	48.84
Intraception	51.56	42.57	56.28	53.74
Nurturance	46.76	37.14	55.61	55.29
Affiliation	49.40	38.00	54.17	50.64
Heterosexuality	51.28	43.71	56.06	53.22
Exhibition	58.56	53.14	52.39	46.19
Autonomy	58.40	62.36	48.72	44.13
Aggression	55.08	61.00	48.33	46.61
Change	47.64	50.14	53.83	46.77
Succorance	42.00	48.36	49.11	51.74
Abasement	39.28	44.93	49.33	54.39
Deference	39.84	37.86	49.11	56.48

masculine–secondary feminine, primary feminine–secondary masculine, and primary feminine–secondary feminine. Comparison of the secondary masculine and secondary feminine personality profiles in Table 7 indicates to me that these secondary designations are contributing something to personality description for males above and beyond their primary sex-role designations. Again, by way of illustration of this point, despite the fact that all males in the first two columns were masculine, using the primary sex-role measure, splitting into secondary sex-role designations resulted in an average absolute deviation across the personality scales of 6.16 *T*-score points. Similarly, primary feminine males split by secondary identity (Columns 3 and 4) demonstrated a mean absolute deviation of 4.58 points.

When the parallel comparisons were conducted for the female adolescents, a most unexpected finding emerged. Whether we were considering masculine or feminine girls, secondary sex-role assignment contributed essentially nothing to differentiation based upon

TABLE 8

PERSONALITY PROFILES FOR LATE-ADOLESCENT FEMALES
DIFFERING IN PRIMARY AND SECONDARY SEX-ROLE IDENTITY

	Mean Scale Score			
	Primary Masculine		Primary Feminine	
Personality Variable	Secondary Masculine (*N* = 46)	Secondary Feminine (*N* = 33)	Secondary Masculine (*N* = 25)	Secondary Feminine (*N* = 45)
Achievement	51.67	47.36	45.24	41.96
Dominance	53.22	49.27	44.36	42.64
Endurance	48.70	48.03	46.04	45.62
Order	49.72	46.82	48.08	46.07
Intraception	46.09	47.88	52.84	50.04
Nurturance	39.85	44.42	51.72	53.76
Affiliation	42.54	42.45	50.00	48.31
Heterosexuality	47.00	46.21	52.40	52.47
Exhibition	54.85	48.97	49.28	47.76
Autonomy	59.63	54.42	48.52	46.93
Aggression	58.43	54.76	47.84	47.20
Change	52.02	49.27	50.64	50.13
Succorance	48.26	47.70	54.80	54.31
Abasement	45.50	45.79	54.04	55.00
Deference	41.78	46.21	52.20	53.49

personality scores (Table 8). Summarizing the differentiation of personality patterns by the average absolute deviation statistic, we find that the discrepancy between the secondary sex-role subgroups for the masculine girls was 2.79 points and for the feminine girls, 1.40 points.

The conclusion that secondary sex-role status served a more important moderating function for male adolescents than female adolescents as far as personality variables were concerned was not difficult to substantiate by statistical means. The mean absolute deviation of personality scores for the secondary sex-role sub-groupings of masculine males (6.16) was significantly higher than the same mean difference score presented by masculine females (2.79); the t value of 4.06 (28 df) is associated with a probability of less than one in a thousand. These profile discrepancy scores for feminine males (4.58) and females (1.40) also differed reliably ($t = 5.05$; $df = 28$; $p < .001$).

Primary and Secondary Sex-Role Identity and Level of Adjustment

The finding derived from the comparison of personality profiles, that the secondary sex-role system was an important moderator variable for male adolescents but not (or less so) for female adolescents, was unexpected. Accordingly, it seemed important to obtain some additional empirical support for this sex difference.

The personality scales from which the profiles of Tables 6–8 were derived represent different modes of social interplay, many of which contribute critically to the student's adaptation to the college environment. An early study (Heilbrun, 1960) reported differences between adjusted and maladjusted male students on 10 of these 15 variables and differences between their female counterparts on 7. If differences in secondary sex-role status influence personality functioning for males and not for females, it follows that the secondary sex-role identity of the male adolescent should contribute systematically to behavior effectiveness on campus, but this would not be the case for the female. To investigate this, a 3-year (1969–72) time sample of clients from the Emory University student counseling center was collected from the files, including every client who had completed the ACL as part of a standard intake battery during that period. Levels of adjustment were constituted by the same defining operations as we described earlier in this paper: maladjusted subjects are those requesting psychotherapy for personal problems, intermediate adjustment means that the clients requested vocational or educational guidance, and adjusted refers to what is essentially a random sample of college late adolescents.

Table 9, which contains the primary and secondary sex-role scores for the adjustment level groups, lends itself to the same conclusion as had been drawn earlier. The secondary sex-role scores

TABLE 9

Secondary and Primary Sex-Role Scores for Late Adolescents
Varying in Level of Adjustment

Level of Adjustment	Secondary Sex-Role Score				Primary Sex-Role Score			
	Males		Females		Males		Females	
	N	Mean	N	Mean	N	Mean	N	Mean
Adjusted[a]	88	6.38	149	1.52	88	49.15	149	51.43
Intermediate	62	4.98	51	2.22	62	44.85	51	53.49
Maladjusted	90	3.22	87	1.64	90	43.14	87	50.55

Males Secondary: 6.38 / 4.98 $p < .05$; 4.98 / 3.22 $p < .005$. Females Secondary: 1.52 / 2.22 NS; 2.22 / 1.64 NS.

a These subjects were those previously employed in the study comparing personality profiles of groups differing in primary and secondary sex-role identity (Heilbrun, 1972a).

for males vary systematically from one level to the next, whereas no hint of systematic variation can be noted in the female data. Primary sex-role mean scores also are included and offer two additional conclusions. Primary masculinity-femininity is related to adjustment for males, although the relationship is curvilinear, with greater femininity being associated with both degrees of maladjustment. However, primary sex-role identity in the female, like secondary

TABLE 10

Incidence of Primary-Secondary Sex-Role Patterns
in Late Adolescents Varying in Level of Adjustment

Level of Adjustment Group	Sex-Role Identity Pattern[a]			
	Primary Masculine– Secondary Masculine	Primary Masculine– Secondary Feminine	Primary Feminine– Secondary Masculine	Primary Feminine– Secondary Feminine
Males				
Adjusted	28%	16%	21%	35%
Intermediate	19%	5%	15%	61%
Maladjusted	8%	11%	8%	73%
Females				
Adjusted	31%	22%	17%	30%
Intermediate	35%	20%	16%	29%
Maladjusted	28%	20%	19%	33%

a Assignment to masculine or feminine classes based upon the same cutting scores used in Heilbrun's 1972a study.

sex-role identity, holds no lawful relation with behavior effectiveness.

A second way to portray the importance of the secondary sex-role system in mediating behavioral effectiveness for male adolescents and not for female adolescents is to consider the incidence rates of primary-secondary sex-role patterns as a function of adjustment level. Our findings to this point would lead us to expect distinct differences in the frequency of representation for these patterns in the case of males and the absence of such differences for females. Table 10 percentage figures verify these expectations.

Biological and Psychological Sex of the Parent Identification Model: Further Evidence Regarding the Functional Significance of Congruity for Sons and Insignificance for Daughters

We have considered two empirical probes which clearly suggest the importance of the secondary sex-role construct for males and its functional insignificance for females. Model incongruity makes a difference for males but not for females. These observations require even firmer empirical establishment before we engage the questions of why this should be so and what social implications ensue. The initial selection of studies is intended to emphasize the daughter's use of either parent as an identification model, with a perplexing ability to disengage from model sex-role properties in her own sex-role identity. This will be followed by considering the opposite case for the son—his extraordinary sensitivity to the congruity between sex gender and sex role.

The first study (Heilbrun, 1965c) was concerned with the frequent assertion that the daughter's identification with her mother is likely to be stronger than the son's identification with his father (Lynn, 1959; Rosenthal, 1962; Stoke, 1950). The reasoning which tends to be associated with this expectation is that the more ready availability of the mother as a model makes it more likely that the daughter will adopt her specific behavioral properties, whereas the father offers a poorer identification model because his limited accessibility makes it more difficult to emulate his behavior.

The identification-measurement technique which had been established for our own program of research offered a way of testing this assertion of differential strength of identification. It may be recalled that the measurement procedure involves a comparison between the personality attributes of the offspring and those of both parents as rated by the offspring. If the differential-strength-of-identification hypothesis were correct, we would expect to find that the raw scores of female adolescents would reflect a strong similarity to the mother relative to the father; however, the father's absence as a specific model for identification would lead us to expect the male to have a more equal representation in his own makeup of the behaviors attributed to the father and mother. In short, females should have higher plus scores and males should have scores approximating zero. Reference to Table 11 provides the average behavioral

TABLE 11

SIMILARITY TO MALE AND FEMALE PARENTS FOR LATE
ADOLESCENTS VARYING IN LEVEL OF ADJUSTMENT

	Sex of Offspring			
	Males		Females	
Level of Adjustment	N	Mean Similarity Score	N	Mean Similarity Score
Adjusted	139	16.21	141	−.90
Maladjusted	73	−9.15	74	3.27

similarity between sons and daughters and their parents for adjusted and maladjusted college undergraduates, using our usual definitions of these levels of adjustment. Examination of Row 1 of the table reveals that the difference in similarity scores for the adjusted groups (significant at $p < .05$) runs counter to the differential-identification hypothesis; males demonstrate a more selective similarity to the specific attributes of their fathers, and females as a group demonstrate an unselective similarity to both parents. Maladjusted males, in contrast to their adjusted counterparts, established themselves as more similar to their mothers. The shift for these male groups from greater father-similarity (16.21) to greater mother-similarity (−9.15) was highly significant ($p < .01$). Maladjusted females, however, presented a mean similarity score which continued to approximate zero, again indicating no greater overall assimilation of behaviors from either parent. These data suggest that females are not inclined to selectively adopt the behaviors of the same-sex parent, and this nonselectivity fails to relate to their subsequent behavioral effectiveness. The opposite is true for males; they selectively model after the father, and the failure to do so is associated with poor adjustment.

Another study published the same year (Heilbrun, 1965b) was concerned with the question of which sex-gender-sex-role combination in the parent model facilitated maximum primary sex-role differentiation of the identified offspring. Put more simply, given identification of males and females with the same model type, under which of the four model-type conditions would we find the most masculine sons and the most feminine daughters? While the origins of the question raised in 1965 bear little similarity to those which concern us now, the methodology used can easily be brought to bear upon the currently more relevant question of whether the "laws" of identification, as they involve the sex-gender-sex-role attributes of the parent model, are simply different for the male and female offspring.

Questionnaires necessary to our identification-measurement technique were administered to 279 college undergraduates, approximately half of whom were males and half, females. Having discerned to which of the four identification pattern groups each subject belonged (e.g., identification with a masculine father), within-group *chi*-square comparisons on each of the 300 ACL behavioral adjectives were made between males and females showing that pattern. All discriminating adjectives were then submitted to four psychologists, who were asked to judge the instrumental (masculine), expressive (feminine), or indeterminate nature of each. Reasonably strict criteria of interjudge agreement were imposed to define masculine and feminine behaviors. We could at this point, then, ascertain which of the four identification conditions mediated a masculine sex-role outcome in the son and a feminine sex-role outcome in the daughter. The one condition which fostered not only the largest number of discriminating behaviors (35) but also the highest saturation of appropriate masculine behaviors in the son and feminine behaviors in the daughter (83%) was identification

with the masculine father. These figures for the remaining conditions were; feminine-mother identification, 28 behaviors, with
a 54% saturation; masculine-mother identification, 17, with a
41% saturation; feminine-father identification, 16, with a 38%
saturation.

Subsequent analysis compared the masculine-father-identified
females with their extreme same-sex counterparts identified with
feminine mothers. This analysis was conducted to determine whether
the apparent femininity of the masculine-father-identified girl
might be an artifact created by the extreme masculinity of the boy
to whom she was compared. The comparison of masculine-father-
and-feminine-mother-identified girls indicated very few differences
between these extremes. In fact, the eight differences which emerged
defied chance expectancy of 15 (i.e., 300 comparisons with the alpha
level set at .05). Heilbrun was led to conclude that

> the distinct instrumental-expressive behavior differences found when
> instrumental-father identified males and females were compared can
> be attributed to the presence of both instrumental qualities in the sons
> and expressive (but not passive) qualities in the daughter. [P. 796]

It seems safe to say that the surprising feature of these results has
nothing to do with the findings for males. That optimal outcome for
masculine sex-role development in the son would be associated with
modeling after a masculine father is entirely consistent with logic
and prior evidence. That the daughter could demonstrate a femininity in her sex-role development contingent upon a masculine-
father identification, defined in modeling terms, is both illogical and
(at that time) without empirical reference. The results do serve to
underscore our present theme, however. Parent identification and
behavioral-outcome relationships for the male and female offspring
are at variance, particularly with respect to the role played by
biological context of the parent model's sex-role behavior. Of course,
with these particular results, the daughter's femininity apparently
came from primary identification with a parent who was not only
a biological male but one whose sex-role attributes were masculine.

There were several unreported analyses forthcoming from the
1965b Heilbrun investigation which assume some relevance to our
present discussion. By and large, Heilbrun had proceeded by

comparing males and females identified with the same parent-model type. We might now turn the question around. To what extent will we find differentiated behavior outcomes for daughters having a primary identification with the four parent-model types? For sons? Differentiation here refers to the number of behavioral adjectives which received differing frequencies of endorsement

TABLE 12

NUMBER OF DIFFERENTIATING ($p < .10$) ADJECTIVES FOR MALE OFFSPRING
IDENTIFIED WITH DIFFERENT PARENT-MODEL TYPES AND FEMALE OFFSPRING
IDENTIFIED WITH DIFFERENT PARENT-MODEL TYPES

Identification Patterns Being Compared	Sex of Offspring		*Chi* Square
	Males	Females	
Masculine-Father-Identified Versus Masculine-Mother-Identified	35	16	6.94*
Feminine-Father-Identified Versus Feminine-Mother-Identified	15	8	1.63
Masculine-Father-Identified Versus Feminine-Father-Identified	26	33	.93
Masculine-Mother-Identified Versus Feminine-Mother-Identified	34	13	9.23*
Masculine-Father-Identified Versus Feminine-Mother-Identified	53	18	18.47**

* $p < .01$
** $p < .001$

between identification-pattern groups. Table 12 offers us the number of differentiating behavioral adjectives for the within-sex comparisons of identified offspring. Generally speaking, these data suggest that the biological attributes and the sex-role attributes of the parent model mediate more distinct behavioral outcomes for the son than for the daughter. The three significant findings each portray the more limited behavioral differentiation in girls associated with the choice of parent models varying in biological sex, sex role, or both.

It would be surprising if the reader, having followed the paper to this point, would not have questioned whether our data and, thus, the drift of our reasoning, might be an artifact of our measurement procedures. I am not alluding here to the use of psychometrics per se, since this is neither unusual in sex-role research nor, in my opinion, does it require apology. Rather, the question should be directed to the collection of all our information by means of ratings obtained from the child, so that the sex difference in the significance of parent-model attributes could be a by-product of some test-taking difference between males and females. Fortunately for our purposes, the results of a recent investigation conducted in another laboratory and using a different methodology help to answer the question of whether our results can be replicated when the scope of investigation is extended beyond the identifying child.

A study conducted by Mary Ann Grieser (1972) at the University of Nebraska was addressed to the relationships among parental identification, sex-role development of the child, and personal adjustment for the late-adolescent female. Her sample consisted of 88 college freshmen and their parents. Each member of the triad completed an inventory of values, and score similarity between parent and daughter on the non-sex-typed value scales defined parental identification. The sex-role identity of each parent and of the daughter was determined by scores on the sex-typed value scales. Personal adjustment of the child was ascertained by means of the California Psychological Inventory (Gough, 1957).

The results of this investigation indicated that either identification with a masculine father or with a feminine mother facilitated a feminine sex-role identity for the adolescent female. However, if the girl identified with a feminine mother in the absence of masculinity in the father, a negative effect upon her femininity could be observed. In contrast, identification with a masculine father when the mother was not feminine favorably influenced the daughter's feminine sex-role development. Finally, it was observed that either a same-sex or cross-sex parent model may be the object of identification without detrimental effects upon the girl's personal adjustment, although identification with a masculine father facilitated adjustment more than identification with a feminine father. According to the investigator, many aspects of her findings pointed to the importance of masculinity in the adolescent college girl for maintaining an effective adjustment.

We have in the Grieser study a set of results which correspond closely to those we have generated in our laboratory, despite the differences in measurement procedure which she employed. The most important of these results found late-adolescent girls demonstrating a feminine sex-role identity whether they identified with a masculine male parent or a feminine female parent. In fact, given but one sex-typical parent, a masculine-father identification presented a more facilitative process for engendering femininity in the daughter than identification with a feminine mother.

Many might find it paradoxical that the daughter's identification with a masculine father would culminate in a feminine sex-role identity. In strict keeping with imitative learning expectations, this empirical finding actually represents a conflict in terms, a fact we hope to deal with in a subsequent section. However, some of the mystery inherent in this relationship has been removed by a study coming out of our laboratory (Heilbrun, 1968).

All students in an undergraduate class were assigned a diverting task which required that they join small discussion groups of about six members. Each group contained both males and females, split as evenly as possible. The assignment to the class was to meet in the discussion groups for at least three hours outside of class time for the purpose of considering and reaching group consensus on several broad questions related to the course. The students were aware that each group would be required to present its consensual opinions in front of the class. These procedures were intended to provide the subjects sufficient observation of one another's behavior in these goal-oriented groups to allow reliable behavioral observations at the end.

When the period had elapsed within which the discussion groups were to meet, each subject was asked to make two behavioral ratings of each person in the group other than himself. One of the 6-point rating scales was concerned with the degree of expressive behavior demonstrated by the other person in the group. Parsons's construct of expressiveness, which we previously endorsed as a

critical component of femininity, was defined for the subjects as
follows:

> Concern with the relationships among the members of the group, con-
> cern with their attitudes and feelings toward each other. Tendency to
> cautiously avoid unpleasantness in relationships and by being likeable
> and understanding to seek positive responses from others. [P. 132]

The second 6-point scale measured instrumental tendencies.
Instrumentalness, the essence of masculinity for Parsons (again with
which we concur), was defined in these terms for the subjects:

> More concern with achieving the goal of the group than with the quality
> of personal interaction with its members. Unattentive to the immediate
> emotional responses of others directed toward her. Able to tolerate
> hostility from others in group. [P. 132]

Only the 30 females in the class were the object of study in this
investigation. Each was assigned an expressive score and an instrumental score based upon the average ratings of the five or six other
peer members of her group. The subjects were also classed as masculine or feminine, using their scores on the MF Scale of the ACL
with the college norm (T = 50) as the dividing point. You may
recall that this method of assigning subjects by sex role also will tend
to group them by parent-identification pattern, since identification with a masculine father (by males) and identification with a
feminine mother (by females) were used as criterion group definitions for purposes of MF Scale item selection. A subsequent check
confirmed this expectation; 64% of the feminine girls were identified with feminine mothers, and 62% of the masculine girls had a
masculine-father identification. I point these contingencies out now
as a reminder that the instrumental-expressive ratings are not only
relatable to the girl's sex-role identity but also in some measure to
her parent-identification pattern.

The mean instrumental and expressive ratings for masculine and
feminine late-adolescent girls (Table 13) revealed two significant
characteristics. Girls were generally more expressive than instrumental in their group behavior, but this tendency interacted with
sex-role identity. The interaction effect is the important finding. It
tells us that there is a common core of expressiveness to both feminine and masculine girls as we have defined them; all girls tend to

TABLE 13

INSTRUMENTAL AND EXPRESSIVE BEHAVIOR IN LATE-
ADOLESCENT GIRLS AS A FUNCTION OF SEX-ROLE
IDENTITY

	Sex-Role Identity	
Type of Rating Score[a]	Masculine ($N = 16$)	Feminine ($N = 14$)
Mean Instrumentalness	4.35	3.65
Mean Expressiveness	4.46	4.67

[a] Based upon 6-point rating scales extending from very low (1) to very high (6).

be expressive. It is in the realm of instrumental behavior that masculinity and femininity take on more distinct properties; masculine girls are more instrumental than feminine girls.

These findings seem to offer some explanation for the mysterious contingency between the daughter's identification with the masculine father and her feminine development. She does incorporate some degree of the father's instrumental qualities, as modeling theory would lead us to expect, but does not relinquish her expressive femininity. This reassures our logical sensibilities regarding the presence of a masculine component in girls who have modeled primarily after a masculine father. It still leaves the puzzling relationship between masculine-father identification and the presence of feminine expressiveness in the daughter. Even this seeming paradox receives some clarification in light of findings reported as an explanatory addendum to an earlier investigation (Heilbrun, 1965b). Ratings of paternal nurturance *as directed toward them* obtained from male and female late adolescents on two campuses gave the results presented in Table 14. As can be seen, masculine fathers were rated as less nurturant by their sons relative to feminine fathers. As far as affectional behaviors are concerned, fathers behave in keeping with sex type in relating to their sons. However, females viewed their masculine fathers to be just as nurturant toward them as feminine fathers were toward their daughters. Fathers do not maintain their sex-role distinctions in relating affectionally to their daughters; further, fathers as a whole are more nurturant to their daughters than they are to their sons. Both factors would contribute

TABLE 14

RATED NURTURANCE OF MASCULINE AND
FEMININE FATHERS

	Masculine Fathers		Feminine Fathers	
Sex of Child	N	Mean Nurturance	N	Mean Nurturance
Male				
Iowa	38	25.2	18	28.4
California	46	25.1	18	28.4
Female				
Iowa	38	30.7	22	30.4

NOTE: Both mean differences for the male samples significant
at $p < .05$.

to the likelihood that expressive behaviors would be available in the
behavior repertory of the masculine father as he presents himself as
a model to his daughter (but not to his son).

To this point we have reviewed studies which have focused
mainly upon the late-adolescent female in our effort to bolster the
observation that the congruity between biological and psychological
sex of the parent identification model is functionally significant to
sex role and adjustment outcomes in the son and functionally in-
significant for the daughter. Further evidence regarding the importance for the son of biological context for sex-role behavior in the
model has not been totally lacking, but I have to confess that the one
investigation within our laboratories which can qualify as relevant
(Wismar, 1971) does so only in light of that rare wisdom bestowed
by hindsight.

Wismar's study had as its goal the specification of some of the
conditions which might contribute to the learning of cross-sex behavior in the preschool-age boy. Considering only the father-son
relationship, Wismar wished to determine whether feminine behavior could be induced more effectively by the father's direct
social reinforcement of such behavior in the son or by the father's
modeling cross-sex behavior for the son. The question arose because
of the emphasis placed upon both modeling and social reinforcement as necessary components of the identification process by major
socio-behavioristic theorists such as Bandura and McDonald
(1963), Sears (1957), Gewirtz and Stingle (1968), and Kagan

(1958), but the inability of any of these theorists to establish the weight which should be assigned to either component.

Wismar used toy play as his dependent variable and for his subject sample, white middle-class boys ranging from 3 to 6 years of age. A baseline free-play period lasting for 3 minutes was provided for each child in a room furnished with six toys previously rated at the extreme of masculinity (airplane, tool set, dump truck) and femininity (cleaning set, doll buggy, cosmetics). Contact time with each class of toy was recorded, and the boys were then assigned to one of three groups, each representing a different experimental condition. Care was taken to match the groups for initial masculine- and feminine-toy preferences as well as for scores on the It-Scale for Children, devised by Brown (1957) to measure a child's preference for the masculine or feminine role.

Toys used to establish baseline toy preference were then put away and one of three experimental conditions was imposed. The *modeling* condition involved the replacement of the baseline toys with three new toys also rated at the extreme of femininity (doll wardrobe, dish cabinet, doll-house furniture). The subject was then told by the experimenter (a male graduate student in his mid-twenties) that "last time *you* played with the toys. Now it is *my* turn." The experimenter then sat on the floor and, with what we can only hope was an acting performance, proceeded to joyfully spend 1 minute playing with each of the three toys in a set order. The *reinforcement* condition also involved the replacement of the six baseline toys with the three new feminine toys, but the boy in this group was told that these were additional toys with which he could play. Verbal reinforcers were administered by the male experimenter on a prearranged schedule. Initial approach to a toy elicited a positive reinforcement, as did each 20 seconds of consecutive contact with a toy. Four positive statements, such as "you're doing fine" or "that's very good," were administered in rotating order. Three minutes of play time were provided. Finally, the *control* subjects were read a 3-minute story by the experimenter.

The test of whether modeling or reinforcement would facilitate a greater change in feminine-toy play for boys came with a replication of the initial phase of the experiment. Each boy was given 3 minutes of play time with the original set of six toys and contact time again was recorded. As might be expected, the toy preferences in the baseline period were for the masculine toys. The three groups of boys spent an average percentage of time in contact with masculine toys ranging between 85% and 89%. Did modeling or reinforcing feminine-toy play by the adult male make any appreciable dent in this strong preference? When we compare the mean increase in feminine play, it would appear that modeling ($\bar{X} = 31.94$ seconds) might have drawn the boys into more cross-sex behavior than social reinforcement ($\bar{X} = 12.18$ seconds). However, the control group demonstrated the greatest increase in feminine play ($\bar{X} = 37.44$ seconds), so we are left to conclude that modeling and, particularly, reinforcement by the adult male not only failed to enchance cross-sex behavior but even may have had a suppressive influence. Let me quickly add that Wismar's results were statistically negative, so that we cannot safely conclude that suppression effects were present to account for these mean differences.

However, careful examination of the individual performances among the boys in Wismar's study revealed that several of the more chauvinistic among them refused to make any contact with feminine toys either during the baseline phase or the final testing phase. If these more reluctant children are not considered, Wismar's results would look like what we see in Table 15. The mean feminine-toy play times for the three groups during the baseline period did not differ significantly ($F = 1.31$; $df = 2, 35$; $p > .25$). Following the intervening conditions, the contact time with feminine toys did vary reliably ($F = 4.91$; $df = 2, 35$; $p < .025$). Again, control

TABLE 15

TIME SPENT IN FEMININE-TOY PLAY BEFORE AND AFTER
SOCIAL REINFORCEMENT OR MODELING OF CROSS-SEX BEHAVIOR
(OMITTING BOYS WITH ZERO CONTACT TIME)

	Experimental Condition					
	Reinforcement		Modeling		Control	
Phase	N	Mean	N	Mean	N	Mean
Baseline	14	19.36 sec.	13	18.77 sec.	11	38.00 sec.
Testing	14	33.29 sec.	13	58.08 sec.	11	92.45 sec.

subjects spent the most time playing with feminine toys (51%) during the testing period, the modeling group somewhat less time (32%), and those boys receiving social reinforcement for feminine-toy play spent the least time in this activity (18%).

Whether the statistical verdict of this post hoc analysis is accepted or not, I believe that it is difficult to ignore the absence of effects for modeling and reinforcement when it would be no problem to document the effectiveness of either in altering the behavior of middle-class preschool children. I think now that what Wismar's results demonstrate is the importance of biological context of sex-role behavior for the boy. The incongruity of an adult male playing with feminine toys or reinforcing play with feminine toys vitiated his attractiveness as a model and his effectiveness as a reinforcer. If this interpretation were correct, we would predict that girls exposed to the same experimental manipulations would be positively responsive to the adult experimenter whether the modeled or reinforced behavior were congruous with sex gender or not.

Identification and Sex Role in Females: Their Relationships to Woman's-Role Attitudes and Susceptibility to Vicarious Reinforcement

The evidence reviewed to this point makes the case, we feel, for an important sex difference in the identification process for sons and daughters. Whereas the congruity between sex gender and sex-role behavior of the adult selected as the primary model for identification relates systematically to various performance outcomes for the male child, it seems to make little if any difference for the female child what the biological context of a model's sex-role behavior might be. At this point I would like to discuss the results of an investigation which was planned to accomplish two goals. First, the hope was not only to confirm the previous congruity findings for females but also to further our understanding of this sex difference. Our second goal was to establish that the congruity variable was not only of some significance to the social scientist in his quest for understanding the nature of sex-role development but, in addition, held some social significance as well. These rather ambitious goals led to a recent large-scale experiment (Heilbrun, 1972b) which I would like to describe in some detail.

During the fall quarter of 1972, 138 volunteer subjects were obtained from large undergraduate classes at Emory University. The subjects, largely freshmen, included 86 females (mean age = 18.2 years) and 52 males (mean age = 18.4 years). The investigation included two parts, with the first session devoted to the administration of a number of questionnaires. These included those necessary for deriving the identification and sex-role scores which have been used so extensively in our previous research. In addition, a questionnaire, developed by Fand (1955) and used more recently in Steinman's research (1963; Steinman & Fox, 1966), was used to elicit attitudes toward traditional and contemporary roles for women.

The Fand questionnaire includes two sets of statements with which the person can express varying degrees of agreement or disagreement. One set includes 17 statements of opinion stressing the importance of marriage, family, home, motherhood, selective employment, and conformity and deference to others' opinions. This set, which measures attitude toward the conventional woman's role, includes five items which relate to the importance of the husband's accomplishments and which imply the wife's ability to live vicariously through his achievements as a part of the conventional role. The second set of 17 statements is intended to convey the attitudes inherent in the contemporary women's "liberation" movement, such as the importance of personal achievement, autonomy, leadership, equal rights and freedoms (particularly in marriage), and personal fulfillment outside the home. A paired-comparison type of scoring procedure provides scores which can range from −68 (extreme endorsement of the conventional role) to +68 (extreme endorsement of the contemporary role).

Following completion of the questionnaires, subjects were asked to sign up for a subsequent small-group experimental session. Each of the 40 experimental groups contained at least one male and one female. However, group composition varied from two subjects (in 7.5% of the groups), to three subjects (in 35.0% of the groups), to four subjects (in 57.5% of the groups).

Upon arrival at the laboratory, the group was introduced to an experimental methodology devised to study the effects of vicarious reinforcement. The procedures, originally employed in an earlier experiment (Heilbrun, 1970b), were implemented by a female experimenter. Subjects were seated first around a large table and given a perceptual-motor task modeled after the digit-symbol subtest of the Wechsler Adult Intelligence Scale (1955). For those not familiar with this task, the person is asked to fill in as many symbols as possible in 90 seconds within boxes associated with randomly ordered numbers. Number-symbol pairings are keyed for the subject at the top of the page. The experimenter scored digit-symbol performance for all subjects in the group immediately upon their completion of the task.

The next procedural step was to choose one of the subjects from the group and inform him that he was going to receive special training which we had reason to believe could help him perform on the digit-symbol task just completed. While the selection of the "trainee" was made to appear spontaneous by the experimenter, the subject to be selected had been chosen prior to the arrival of the group and was always a male. The trainee was seated at one end of the experimental room in a chair facing the rear wall. Mounted on the wall were five disks, each bearing a different-size angle. The trainee was told that he would be given experience in making difficult angular discriminations, and if he could do well in this regard, there should result an improvement in his ability to perform on the digit-symbol task. If he could not learn to make these difficult discriminations, the instructions continued, no improvement in digit-symbol performance could be expected.

The trainee was then introduced to an angle-discrimination procedure devised by James (1957) within which he was given 20 chances to match test angles with the same-size standard angle on the wall. No correct matching was possible, however, since each test angle fell 5° between two of the standard angles. This discrimination is so difficult that the subject almost invariably fails to detect the absence of an identical match, opening the way to imposing preselected schedules of reinforcement upon performance. In the positive (success) condition the trainee was put on a 14-correct-6-incorrect schedule, with the experiment interposing positive statements about his performance after the tenth and twentieth choices. The negative (failure) condition involved a 6-correct-14-incorrect schedule and negative evaluative statements from the experimenter at the same two points. (The bona fide nature of this procedure was not questioned except in one group, and their data were excluded from the experimental part of the investigation.)

During the course of the angle discriminations, the remaining subjects were asked to sit in chairs, positioned so that they had a direct view of the trainee but could not see the standard angles. Thus, the observers were in a position to hear the reinforcement imposed upon the trainee and to view his responses; our interest was in determining the extent to which the individual was susceptible to experiencing that reinforcement vicariously.

Subjects were reassembled about the table as soon as the intervening reinforcement condition was completed and were administered an alternate form of the digit-symbol task. Prior to beginning, however, each subject was handed a slip of paper with the number correct from the first digit-symbol task printed upon it, and she was asked to write the number correct she thought she could achieve upon retest. The second digit-symbol task was then administered, which marked the end of the experiment.

Vicarious reinforcement was inferred when the subject's expectation of performance was influenced in a direction consistent with reinforcement imposed upon the male model. Given positive reinforcement of the trainee and the expectation that his success would facilitate digit-symbol performance, vicarious positive reinforcement would mediate the expectation of improved performance for the observer. Given negative reinforcement of the trainee and no expectation on his part of improved performance from the training, vicarious negative reinforcement would curtail the expectation of improved performance for the observer.

Identification, sex role, and attitudes toward the woman's role. If we begin the examination of these variables by looking at the relationship between sex-role status (MF Scale) and attitudes toward the woman's role, we can note first that the two questionnaire measures are positively correlated. The correlation for females ($r = .44$) was significant. Males, given the attitude scale under instructions to rate their preferences in how women should feel about the woman's role, generated a nonsignificant correlation of .21 between MF and woman's-role scores. Thus, we would conclude, from the female data at least, that masculine late adolescents more strongly favor the woman's life style of equal rights and freedom alongside men, and feminine late-adolescent girls are more in accord with traditional role expectancies for women.

Inspection of the data from which the correlations were generated led me to conclude that the correlational statistic was not telling the whole story, since there was the suggestion of a nonlinear relationship between masculinity-femininity and role attitudes in both the female and male data. This can be demonstrated if we compare the mean attitude scores for our subjects at the sex-role extremes and at more intermediate points. Four groups were constituted for both sexes using the same criteria: MF scores > 60 (more than one standard deviation above the college mean) = high masculine; MF scores 51–60 = masculine; MF scores 40–50 = feminine; MF scores < 40 = high feminine. Table 16 presents the woman's-role

TABLE 16

ATTITUDE TOWARD THE WOMAN'S ROLE FOR FEMALE AND MALE
LATE ADOLESCENTS VARYING IN MASCULINITY-FEMININITY

Sex of Adolescent	Sex-Role Status							
	High Masculine		Masculine		Feminine		High Feminine	
	N	Mean	N	Mean	N	Mean	N	Mean
Females	19	23.00	31	12.90	24	15.62	15	5.27
Males	6	15.17	11	7.64	26	8.27	9	4.78

NOTE: The higher the attitude scores represented in the body of the table, the stronger the support for the contemporary role for women; the lower the attitude scores, the stronger the support for the traditional woman's role.

attitude means for female and male groups constituted in this way. You can observe in this table of means that a clear relationship between sex role and attitudes exists only at the extremes of masculinity and femininity for both males and females. In fact, as far as we can tell from these means, woman's-role attitudes and sex role are unrelated in a broad middle range of the MF Scale covering two standard deviations (scores from 40 to 60). Despite this, analysis of variance confirmed that the differences among means were significant for both sexes ($p < .001$). The same analysis established that female endorsement of contemporary woman's-role values was generally higher than male preference for contemporary values in the female ($p < .025$).

Since the relationship between sex role and attitude toward the woman's role seemed most clearly depicted by using the format of Table 16, the same groupings representing extreme and moderate levels of masculinity and femininity were used to relate sex role to identification variables. This approach deployed both the parent-child similarity score and the parent-model score as covariates of MF status in order to establish whether either variable could be used to explain the attitudinal extremes of the high-masculine and high-feminine adolescents. What we see (Table 17), considering the similarity scores first, are two very different identification functions for females and males as far as these sex-role groupings are concerned. Male subjects demonstrate a significant ($p < .01$), and what appears to be a positive, linear relationship between similarity to the father and masculinity. Females deviate significantly ($p < .001$) in their similarity scores as a function of sex role, but the relationship looks decidedly curvilinear; deviation occurs almost exclusively at the high-masculine level, where girls show a strong similarity to the father. In contrast to these two significant similarity functions, no systematic relationship between parent-model scores and sex-role status was evidenced.

TABLE 17

PARENT-CHILD SIMILARITY AND PARENT MODEL ATTRIBUTES
FOR LATE ADOLESCENTS AT VARIOUS LEVELS OF
MASCULINITY-FEMININITY

Identification Variable	Sex-Role Status							
	High Masculine		Masculine		Feminine		High Feminine	
	N	Mean	N	Mean	N	Mean	N	Mean
Parent-Child Similarity								
Females	19	39.53	31	52.10	24	55.79	15	55.53
Males	6	57.83	11	50.54	26	48.58	9	46.44
Parent Model Attributes								
Females	19	6.26	31	6.39	24	6.00	15	6.27
Males	6	6.17	11	5.82	26	6.77	9	6.11

At this point, where we shall summarize our conclusions derived from the identification and sex-role data, let us narrow our concern to the female subjects only. As you shall see, it was with the female adolescent that this study was primarily concerned, and we included only enough male subjects to guarantee the availability of a rein- forced male model in the 40 experimental groups. Put simply, we found that the high-masculine girl who endorsed uniquely strong contemporary attitudes toward the woman's role differed also in terms of a uniquely strong identification with her father without regard to his sex-role attributes. Again we have found that con- gruity between biological sex and sex role of the parent model was unimportant for behavioral outcome of the identifying daughter. In this case, attitudinal outcome was a function only of strong modeling after a biological male and was not related to his sex-role attributes. Since this conclusion was reached without directly relating the identification and woman's-role scores, I would like to add one further bit of information. There were 19 girls in the high-masculine group, of whom 17 were identified with the male parent. The mean woman's-role attitude scores for the 17 girls was 24.30; the two exceptions, mother-identified high-masculine girls, had scores which averaged 12.00!

While the girl's strong identification with the male parent offers an interpretive lead in accounting for contemporary attitudes at the high-masculine extreme, it cannot be reversed to explain the more traditional attitudes found at the other sex-role extreme. High- feminine girls did not differ in either their parent-child similarity scores or their parent-model-attribute scores from girls who were classed as feminine or even masculine on Table 17. How, then, are we to account for the equally striking attitudinal deviation in the traditional direction for the high-feminine girls?

A possible answer to this question presented itself as we examined the employment status of the mothers as a moderating variable. Table 18 summarizes what happens to woman's-role attitudes as we consider the sex-role status of the primary-identification model and the mother's employment status jointly. Treatment of these means by analysis of variance revealed one significant ($p < .05$) effect of identification model; girls who identify with feminine mothers have more traditional attitudes toward the woman's role

TABLE 18

ATTITUDES TOWARD THE WOMAN'S ROLE FOR LATE-ADOLESCENT FEMALES
AS A FUNCTION OF SEX ROLE OF PARENT IDENTIFICATION MODEL
AND MATERNAL EMPLOYMENT STATUS

Employment Status	Sex Role of Identification Model							
	Feminine Mother		Masculine Mother		Feminine Father		Masculine Father	
	N	Mean	N	Mean	N	Mean	N	Mean
Working	9	1.67	10	19.90	9	22.00	10	16.80
Not Working	14	12.00	13	10.23	8	13.12	13	17.15
Total	23	7.96	23	14.43	17	17.82	23	17.00

than is the case for any other identification pattern. While this finding is both logical and of some interest, it fails to take cognizance of the most valuable information on the table, in my opinion. A near-significant interaction effect $(.05 > p < .10)$ suggests we might look further into the part played by the employment status of the identified parent in mediating woman's-role attitudes; analysis of simple effects rewarded this further inquiry.

Comparison of woman's-role attitudes for girls whose mothers were not employed failed to reveal any differences $(p > .10)$ among the four mean values; thus, girls whose mothers remained at home did not express differing attitudes concerning preferred life styles for women, no matter what their type of identification was. However, if the mother worked, the identification pattern was a significant $(p < .001)$ basis for differentiating woman's-role attitudes. In fact, I would go beyond this in interpreting the results for girls with working mothers. Identification with a feminine mother who worked resulted in extremely conventional attitudes $(\bar{X} = 1.67)$, but the involvement of a masculine mother in employment outside the home led to strong contemporary attitudes whether the mother was the primary identification model $(\bar{X} = 19.90)$ or not $(\bar{X} = 22.00)$.

The reason for pursuing this particular analysis was to identify a different basis for the conventional attitudes of the high-feminine girls on Table 16, since there was no way to apply the converse of the interpretation offered for the contemporary attitudes of the high-masculine girls. The uniquely strong identification with the male parent by high-masculine daughters was not matched by a uniquely strong identification with the female parent by their high-feminine counterparts. As it turned out, the conventionality of high-feminine girls in our study was attributable largely to the even more markedly conventional attitudes of 40% of the high-feminine group who identified with feminine *working* mothers.

While these findings regarding work status of the mother are not central to this paper, there is one further implication which is relevant. It would appear at first blush that we have in these data the first indication that sex gender-sex-role congruity in the identification model is important to a behavioral outcome in girls. We did find, after all, a set of attitudes systematically represented only in girls identified with feminine mothers. Yet this conclusion ignores the fact that these feminine mothers had to be working before the result obtained. Apparently, and I emphasize that this is simply an educated guess, the feminine mother had to demonstrate the viability of the conventional woman's role by extending herself beyond the boundaries of homemaking into the world of work before she could transmit conventional attitudes through the identification process. Finally, it should be pointed out that the other attitudinal extreme uncovered in the work-status analysis, the one associated with strong contemporary values, was evidenced without regard to congruity of the maternal model and, in fact, without regard to identification. If a masculine mother worked, her daughter tended to favor strongly the contemporary role. Reasoning backwards from the daughters' expressed attitudes, it would appear that the masculine mother's rejection of the conventional life style got through to the daughter whether she modeled after the mother or not.

Identification, sex role, and susceptibility to vicarious reinforcement. The conceptual linkage between woman's-role attitudes and susceptibility to vicarious reinforcement resides in the assumption that the woman who adopts the coventional life style should be able to live vicariously through the achievements of others, especially her husband. In contrast, the contemporary life style for a woman would orient her toward autonomy and the pursuit of her own achievements. If we assume that attitudes as important as these are likely to be compatible with other behavioral dispositions of the female, we would anticipate that under controlled laboratory conditions it would not be difficult to demonstrate that late-adolescent girls with traditional attitudes are more susceptible to vicarious reinforcement than similar girls with contemporary attitudes.

The first question we wished to answer was whether the girls' susceptibility to vicarious experience varied as a function of any of the three variables with which we have been concerned in this

TABLE 19

Sex Role, Parent Sex Role, and Identification Attributes
of Late-Adolescent Girls Varying in
Susceptibility to Vicarious Reinforcement

Sex Role or Identification Variable	Vicarious Reinforcement Condition			
	Positive		Negative	
	High Susceptible ($N = 26$)	Low Susceptible ($N = 22$)	High Susceptible ($N = 19$)	Low Susceptible ($N = 19$)
	Mean	Mean	Mean	Mean
Masculinity-Femininity of Daughter	53.19	51.18	52.42	51.24
Masculinity-Femininity of Parents	5.81	6.23	7.00	5.89
Parent Identification	49.03	55.09	47.68	53.16

paper—her own sex role, her parents' sex-role status, and her parent identification. To accomplish this, median discrepancy scores between anticipated achievement level and baseline performance were established independently for the positive-reinforcement and negative-reinforcement conditions and used to define high and low vicariously responsive groups under each condition. The resultant group attributes (Table 19) yielded only one reliable effect when exposed to analysis. Neither the daughter's masculinity-femininity nor that of her parent models was systematically related to her vicarious responsiveness, but the biological sex of the parent identification model was. Girls identified with their fathers were more influenced ($p < .025$) by the reinforcements imposed upon a male model than were girls identified with their mothers. As with woman's-role attitudes, we find the sex gender of the parent identification model revealed as the only variable related to the girl's susceptibility to vicarious experience, and again we find this to be so without regard for sex-gender-sex-role congruity of the parent.

We have established that extreme contemporary woman's-role attitudes in females were associated only with high masculinity, which, in turn, was contingent upon a strong identification with the

TABLE 20

ATTITUDES TOWARD THE WOMAN'S ROLE AS A FUNCTION
OF SUSCEPTIBILITY TO VICARIOUS REINFORCEMENT FOR
LATE-ADOLESCENT FEMALES

	Vicarious Reinforcement Condition			
	Positive		Negative	
	High Susceptible ($N = 26$)	Low Susceptible ($N = 22$)	High Susceptible ($N = 19$)	Low Susceptible ($N = 19$)
Mean Attitude Score	18.12	12.55	12.79	13.47

male parent. We found also that identification with the male parent was positively related to susceptibility to vicarious experience of reinforcement imposed upon a male model. Logically, it should follow that two things related to the same thing should be related to each other, but when we compared the woman's-role attitudes of vicarious responders and nonresponders (Table 20), the results were nonrevealing in a statistical sense. However, the one deviant mean on the table, for the high-positive vicarious responders, encouraged the belief that something was going on in these data which the foregoing analysis did not detect. Indeed, this was true, for by the simple expedient of introducing the sex gender of the identification model into the analysis (Table 21), a remarkably clear pattern of attitude scores emerged. Given identification with a biological male, there was a significant ($p < .025$) interaction involving susceptibility to vicarious experience and whether the experience was generated by positive or negative reinforcement administered to the male model. If the reinforcement was positive, strong contemporary values were expressed by those girls whose expectations were most influenced by what happened to the model. If the reinforcement was negative, strong contemporary values were found among those girls who were the least influenced by the model's reinforcements.

TABLE 21

ATTITUDES TOWARD THE WOMAN'S ROLE AS A FUNCTION OF
SUSCEPTIBILITY TO VICARIOUS REINFORCEMENT FOR LATE-ADOLESCENT
FEMALES IDENTIFIED WITH THEIR FATHERS AND THEIR MOTHERS

Sex Gender of Parent Identification Model	Vicarious Reinforcement Condition							
	Positive				Negative			
	High Susceptible		Low Susceptible		High Susceptible		Low Susceptible	
	N	Mean	N	Mean	N	Mean	N	Mean
Male	14	22.86	8	10.00	11	11.45	8	20.62
Female	12	12.58	15	13.27	8	14.62	11	8.27

On the other hand, it is clear from Table 21 that vicarious responding and preferred woman's life style are systematically linked only when the girl has primarily identified with the father. Analysis similar to that described above failed to identify any lawful ordering of woman's-role attitude scores and vicarious responding for girls whose primary identification was with the mother.

We shall reserve any major consideration of these results until the final section of this paper, where an attempt will be made to integrate them with earlier evidence as we try to assess the importance of the congruity factor for both sexes and to derive some hypotheses to account for the observed sex differences. I would only point out at this juncture that the unexpectedness of the findings regarding woman's role and vicarious experience has not eluded me. For those girls who have selected a woman as the primary identification model and who as a group would be considered to be on the feminine side, the stated preference for a more conventional or a more contemporary life style does not relate to vicarious experiencing. Our results, if generalized, suggest that acquiring feminine attributes through identification with a woman, which we might have thought to be an effective medium for entry into the conventional life style, does not systematically bring with it the capacity to experience the husband's reinforcements vicariously.

SUMMARY AND CONCLUSIONS

The thesis proposed for this paper and to which we have brought a considerable amount of evidence to bear is that the fit or congruity between biological and psychological sex of the parent identification model bears systematically upon behavioral outcomes for the son but not for the daughter. In the course of amplifying this position we have examined a variety of outcome behaviors which can be tied directly or indirectly to the identification process— personality traits, sex role, level of adjustment, attitudes toward the woman's role, and susceptibility to vicarious experience. In each case where evidence has been available for the son, the congruity between parent model attributes and the biological sex of the parent has been of functional significance to behavioral outcome. Conversely, the research findings for the female child consistently signal the absence of systematic outcome effects stemming from the congruity or incongruity of sex-gender-sex-role attributes of the parent identification model.

This empirical verdict for girls should prove to be embarrassing to someone (like myself) who expresses a strong commitment to modeling as the learning basis for identification. After all, if the girl comes to imitate the behavior of her primary model, how can the sex-role attributes of that model make so little difference? I shall point to three alternative explanations for this logical predicament, none of them exclusive of the others.

The Double-Standard Hypothesis

This line of reasoning includes two prongs. The first of these has already been presented as we discussed the finding that identification with a masculine father resulted in a feminine personality outcome in the daughter which was largely indistinguishable from the girl identified with a feminine mother. In the context of that discussion, evidence was presented suggesting that fathers do not differ in their nurturant behaviors directed toward the daughter as a function of their masculine or feminine sex-role status. This finding obtained despite the feminine qualities of nurturance and in contrast to the expected differentiation of nurturant behavior for masculine and feminine fathers vis-à-vis the son.

What if this failure of the father to behave in keeping with his usual sex-role attributes when interacting with the daughter were more the rule than the exception? Said another way, what if parents unintentionally employed a double standard of behavior depending upon the sex of the child, so that with sons the behavior of the father and the mother would be in keeping with their own sex roles, whereas behaviors directed toward the daughter more likely would be out of character with usual sex-role patterns? The consequence of this sex-differentiated behavior would be the availability to the daughter of a host of responses for imitation which fail to conform to the parents' standard repertories of sex-role responses. This could only have the effect of blurring relationships between the parent model's characteristic sex-role dispositions and the daughter's behavioral outcomes.

The second prong of the double-standard hypothesis directs attention to the rather dated (Brown, 1958) observation that our society is much more rigorous about sex-role conformity for the male than is the case for the female. While some might argue that these expectations for males have become less rigid, I doubt whether anyone would seriously contend that sex-role conformity pressures have approached equivalence. This particular double standard is especially relevant when we consider level of adjustment as a behavioral outcome, relating it to gender-role congruity in the parent. The point to be made is that the tie between adjustment and sex-role conformity for the male should be direct as systematic social reinforcement is delivered for conformity or nonconformity. However, since the reward systems for sex-role conformity of the girl are less systematic, even capricious, we would expect the conformity-adjustment linkage to be unclear. Looked at this way, it is not so much that the sex role of the parent identification model does not influence the daughter's sex role but that the daughter's sex role does not relate lawfully to adjustment.

The Transmutation Hypothesis

This hypothesis would account for the functional nonsignificance of sex-gender-sex-role fit in the parent identification history of the girl by her tendency to engage in a different brand of modeling behavior relative to the boy. It would assume that boys are much more literal in their imitative behavior than are girls; what he sees is what he does. The girl, on the other hand, transmutes the behavior of the model into another form, and it is this transformation of the model's behavior which becomes incorporated into her own behavior. Since imitative behavior is assumed to include a mediating stage involving implicit rehearsal, we have a reasonable nominee for the site of the transmutation.

The problem for me with this hypothesis is not with the assumption that behavioral transformation does occur between the observation of a model's behavior and the appearance of some facsimile of that response in the observer. The problem is why this should be more the case for the girl than the boy. Since I know of no evidence to bring to bear on the issue, I can only speculate as to the kind of thing we would look for to encourage this line of thought. Should we be able to demonstrate that girls' perceptions, fantasies, and recall are more responsive to their personal needs than are those of boys, the motivational basis for female transmutation would be laid.

As it stands now, this hypothesis should be considered only a logical way to explain why differences among identification models fail to register systematically in behavior differences among identifying girls. If the girl tends to impose her own idiosyncratic transmutation upon the model's behavior in the process of modeling, the dissipation of lawful relationships between model attributes and outcome behaviors follows.

The Group-Identification Hypothesis

Anyone conversant with the usage of the term *identification* will recognize that it has enjoyed two primary meanings applied to human behavior. We have used the term in only one of the two ways, to describe a learning process through which one person comes to take on the behavioral dispositions of another person, the model. In fact, our usage has been even narrower than this, since we have concerned ourselves only with the parent as model and the offspring as the person engaged in the identification process.

The second way in which identification has been conceptualized is to speak of identification with a group, a cause, a country, or an institution. Descriptively, identification is inferred when the person comes to adopt the values of the larger group and responds with appropriate affect when the group's ends are achieved or defeated. The intensity of behaviors generated by group identification can be documented by observing the crowds at college sporting events, the partisans during political campaigns, or the devout followers of some religious sects. While group identification may involve some homogeneity in behavior which symbolizes the common identity, the group-identification process does not in a strict sense involve imitative learning.

The group-identification hypothesis would propose that the effects of group identification interact with identification as model-ing in producing behavioral outcomes for girls. She responds both to the specific attributes of the father and mother which serve as cues for imitative behavior, but she also responds to the maleness or the femaleness of the model and may identify with the parent in terms of this group attribute.

Identification with a sex gender should be distinguished from sex-gender identity. The latter term has not enjoyed consistent usage but, as employed by investigators such as Kuhlman (1966), has come to mean a simple gender self-categorization as a boy or girl. This discriminative label comes to be learned upon the basis of physical (usually genital) differences by 3 to 4 years of age. In Kuhlman's view sex-gender identity organizes sex-role attitudes by determining the basic values to be attached to sex-role behaviors. Thus, a boy who identifies himself as a boy will value masculine behaviors be-cause they will allow him to behave in ways consistent with his identity. Mischel (1966) starts from the same point where the child establishes a sex-gender identity, but he emphasizes the importance of social reward and punishment in shaping the sex-role behaviors of the child.

However, sex-gender identification, as used in a group identification sense, refers to the sex gender from which the child or adolescent gains primary vicarious satisfaction. The distinction between Kuhlman's cognitive-developmental analysis and the group-identification hypothesis under consideration is his assumption that having a sex-gender identity brings with it an identification with that sex gender. We believe that this assumption is especially untenable for girls in our culture. From this point on, the term *sex-gender identification* shall be used to refer to that biological sex for which perceived values, prerogatives, and role expectations are more highly esteemed and from which the person obtains major vicarious experience.

Our investigation of vicarious reinforcement effects offers data which can be usefully applied to the group-identification hypothesis. Before we get to that, let me lay the groundwork by stating the assumption that maleness (being a boy) is often a fantasied preference for girls as they grow up, but femaleness (being a girl) rarely receives fantasied preference for boys. Empirical documentation for the preferential status accorded maleness in our culture can be found in the work of Brown (1957), Komarovsky (1946), Lynn (1959), McKee and Sherrifs (1960), and Wallin (1960).

We can assume, then, that many girls are in a position to gain vicarious satisfaction from observing the achievements (real or imagined) of boys and men. In short, they come to identify with maleness to the extent that they share the values of the group and vicariously experience the satisfactions which accompany group membership. The extent to which the girl's perceptions of her father contribute to her heightened evaluation of maleness will vary, of course, but it should be considerable. Our hypothesis would contend that the girl who identifies with her father is doing so both in a modeling sense and in a sex-gender identification sense because of his status as a male. Modeling should mediate some distinctions in behavior outcome, given masculine and feminine dispositions of the father. However, sex-gender identification involves the vicarious enjoyment of the rewards of maleness, not the imitation of behaviors by which these rewards are presumably achieved. The effect of this dual identification would be to divert some of the positive vicarious reinforcement necessary to imitative learning of specific behaviors of the father into the vicarious satisfactions of identifying with him as a male. This, in turn, should reduce the importance of the behavioral differences between male parent models, including their sex-role attributes, in mediating outcomes in daughters.

If you will recall the vicarious-reinforcement findings at this point, one major result found identification with the father, independent of his sex role, to be associated with greater vicarious responding, whether the male model succeeded or failed. This finding tells us that girls who are more vicariously responsive to what happens to a male peer are those who have identified with a male parent. Girls who have identified with the female parent tend to be unresponsive to the reinforcements imposed on a male model. I submit that the father-identified girls are those who care most about what happens to men in the sense that they are more likely to reap the vicarious harvest of the man's successes and failures. In other words, they have established a sex-gender identification with maleness. When you consider that the mean MF score of girls who were both father-identified and vicarious responders was a masculine 55.28 and that of girls who were mother-identified and vicarious nonresponders was a feminine 45.35, this adds even more doubt regarding the assumption that females who have assumed a feminine sex role are those who should accommodate most readily to the traditional marital role in which the wife lives through the husband's accomplishments.

The group-identification hypothesis places a great deal of explanatory weight upon the assumption that vicarious reinforcement for the girl may be generated as much by the achievements associated with maleness as by the specific behaviors (including sex-role behaviors) by which these ends are achieved. The result, as we have said, is proposed to be a reduction in modeling and in the strength of imitative learning. While the absence of evidence in the research literature which critically tests the group-identification hypothesis is not surprising, there are studies of imitative learning in children which bear upon its corollary. Given the observation of behaviors in a male model having the potential for eliciting vicarious satisfaction, girls' modeling behavior should be less than that of boys. Illustrative support for this corollary can be generated from an imaginative series of five experiments conducted by Bandura and his associates during the early 1960s.

When the methodologies of the Bandura experiments were such as to enhance the probability of vicarious satisfaction in the observer (Bandura, Ross, & Ross, 1961; Bandura, Ross, & Ross, 1963b), the absence of expected behavior-matching effects for the girl after observing a male model can be noted. In the 1961 Bandura, Ross, and Ross study, there was a deficit of imitative aggressive toy play for the girl following exposure to an adult male model relative to an adult female model. However, the incidence of generalized non-imitative aggression following exposure to the two models was about the same for girls. Boys demonstrated a consistent tendency to display more aggressive play of both types after viewing the male aggressive model.

The use of filmed boy models of aggression rather than live adult models distinguished the methodology of the Bandura, Ross, and Ross (1963b) study. This study also introduced differential consequences of aggression in the model to study vicarious reinforcement effects. Again we can note in the results that boys demonstrated an obvious vicarious reinforcement effect upon imitation; successful aggression was more readily imitated or elicited more generalized aggression in subsequent toy play than was the case for unsuccessful aggression. Girls, however, failed to show this effect, especially in generalized aggression. Thus, given a male model of aggression and the opportunity to experience vicarious satisfaction as an observer in these two Bandura, Ross, and Ross studies, girls failed to demonstrate the expected rise in incidence of aggressive behavior that was found in boys.

Two further experiments (Bandura & Huston, 1961; Bandura, Ross, & Ross, 1963a) included methodologies which make the contribution of sex-gender identification effects upon girls' modeling behavior extremely unlikely. They do serve to demonstrate, however, that the deficit in modeling for girls noted above is not to be found when the conditions required for sex-gender identification effects are not met. The Bandura and Huston study was concerned with the amount of imitative learning to be found *following* the occurrence of a nurturant or neutral interaction between an adult female model and nursery school children. The model's behavior included a series of novel verbal, motor, and aggressive responses embedded in the performance of a discrimination problem. Given a female model and behaviors unlikely to generate much vicarious satisfaction in the observer, no sex differences in imitative learning occurred. Bandura, Ross, and Ross (1963a) employed a similar methodology to test for imitation in boys and girls following a set of conditions designed to manipulate perceived social power of adult models. Using both male and female models and prescribed sets of novel responses of little seeming potential for stimulating vicarious satisfaction, no sex differences in imitation were observed whether the model was male or female or high or low in social power.

The final investigation we shall cite (Bandura & McDonald, 1963) is included because it provides evidence in support of the group-identification hypothesis as it might be applied to the opposite case. Girls who identify with femaleness should show less effective modeling in a situation where they experience vicarious satisfaction from observing the achievements of a female. Although this application of the hypothesis has not been discussed, it must be assumed that sex-gender identification with femaleness also could operate to reduce the effectiveness of sex-role modeling for those girls who identify with a female parent.

Bandura and McDonald studied the effects of modeling and reinforcement upon changes in objective and subjective moral judgments. Adult females served as models, so we can observe in this methodology the same congruity between sex of the model and modeling response as we had at the other extreme, when aggressive behaviors were linked with male models (as well as female). I make this observation since it is difficult to imagine that the girl could obtain much vicarious satisfaction from sex-gender identification if the male model performed some behavior out of keeping with maleness. Similarly, it should be difficult to elicit vicarious reinforcement from sex-gender identification with femaleness when a female model behaves out of keeping with her sex.

Analysis of the Bandura and McDonald data proceeded in terms of changes in subjective moral judgments and changes in objective moral judgments as a function of combinations of model reinforcement and child reinforcement. The child was always exposed to reinforcement conditions opposite to his demonstrated moral orientation, whether the reinforcement was applied to the moral responses of the female model or to the moral responses of the child. No difference in modeling behavior between boys and girls was found for those children who initially showed an objective orientation (generally speaking, the older children in the 5-to-11-year range of subject ages). For those (younger) children who began with a subjective orientation, however, they found evidence in the case of girls of weaker modeling after the moral responses of the female model. Boys were more responsive to modeling cues than girls when the model alone was reinforced. However, when the child was directly reinforced in addition to being given the opportunity for vicarious reinforcement, the girls were more responsive to changes than were the boys.

Consideration of one more set of data will bring this paper to a close. In order to relate vicarious responding to expressed attitudes toward the woman's role, it was necessary to consider parent identification as a moderating variable. It was only for father-identified girls that a significant relationship could be established, an interaction which found strong contemporary values among positive vicarious responders and negative vicarious nonresponders. This suggests to me, if I may go out on an already overburdened limb, that *one* explanation for strong contemporary values is a sex-gender identification with maleness but a selective capacity to experience only vicarious satisfactions. Given such a selective vicarious-reinforcement history, it is little wonder that the man's role in our society stands in such preferential contrast to that of the woman as traditionally conceived.

Whatever the empirical fate of the sex-gender-sex-role congruity issue or of the three hypotheses which have been generated to explain the absence of functional significance of model congruity for girls, I hope that this paper has accomplished one thing. Hopefully, it will have raised enough conceptual flak in exploring the complexities of identification and sex-role behavior that you will never again be comfortable with oversimplified explanations of these social phenomena.

REFERENCES

Ainsworth, M. D. S. *Infancy in Uganda.* Baltimore: Johns Hopkins Press, 1967.

Bandura, A. Social learning through imitation. In M. R. Jones (Ed.), *Nebraska symposium on motivation, 1962.* Lincoln: University of Nebraska Press, 1962. Pp. 211–269.

Bandura, A., & Huston, A. Identification as a process of incidental learning. *Journal of Abnormal and Social Psychology*, 1961, **63**, 311–318.

Bandura, A., & McDonald, F. The influence of social reinforcement and the behavior of models in shaping children's moral judgments. *Journal of Abnormal and Social Psychology*, 1963, **67**, 274–281.

Bandura, A.; Ross, D.; & Ross, S. A. Transmission of aggression through imitation of aggressive models. *Journal of Abnormal and Social Psychology*, 1961, **63**, 575–582.

Bandura, A.; Ross, D.; & Ross, S. A. A comparative test of the status envy, social power, and secondary reinforcement theories of identification learning. *Journal of Abnormal and Social Psychology*, 1963, **67**, 527–534. (a)

Bandura, A.; Ross, D.; & Ross, S. A. Vicarious reinforcement and imitation. *Journal of Abnormal and Social Psychology*, 1963, **67**, 601–607. (b)

Bronfenbrenner, U. The study of identification through interpersonal perception. In R. Tagiuri and L. Petrullo (Eds.), *Person perception and interpersonal behavior*. Stanford, Calif.: Stanford University Press, 1958. Pp. 110–130.

Brown, D. Masculinity-femininity development in children. *Journal of Consulting Psychology*, 1957, **21**, 197–202.

Brown, D. Sex-role development in a changing culture. *Psychological Bulletin*, 1958, **55**, 232–242.

Cosentino, F., & Heilbrun, A. B. Sex-role identity and aggression anxiety. *Psychological Reports*, 1964, **14**, 729–730.

DeLucia, L. The toy preference test: A measure of sex-role identification. *Child Development*, 1963, **34**, 107–117.

Edwards, A. L. *Manual for the Edwards Personal Preference Schedule*. New York: Psychological Corporation, 1957.

Fand, A. B. Sex role and self concept. Unpublished doctoral dissertation, Cornell University, 1955.

Gewirtz, J., & Stingle, K. Learning of generalized imitation as the basis for identification. *Psychological Review*, 1968, **75**, 374–397.

Gough, H. G. *Manual for the California Psychological Inventory*. Palo Alto, California: Consulting Psychologists Press, 1957.

Gough, H. G., & Heilbrun, A. B. *Joint Manual for the Adjective Check List and the Need Scales for the ACL*. Palo Alto, Calif.: Consulting Psychologists Press, 1965.

Grieser, M. A. The sex-role development and personal adjustment of late-adolescent females. Unpublished master's thesis, University of Nebraska, 1972.

Hathaway, S. R., & McKinley, J. C. *Manual for the Minnesota Multiphasic Personality Inventory*. (Rev. ed.) New York: Psychological Corporation, 1951.

Heilbrun, A. B. Personality differences between adjusted and maladjusted college students. *Journal of Applied Psychology*, 1960, **44**, 341–346.

Heilbrun, A. B. Parental identification and college adjustment. *Psychological Reports*, 1962, **10**, 853–854. (a)

Heilbrun, A. B. Prediction of first year college drop-out using ACL Need Scales. *Journal of Counseling Psychology*, 1962, **9**, 58–63. (b)

Heilbrun, A. B. Parent model attributes, nurturant reinforcement, and consistency of behavior in adolescents. *Child Development*, 1964, **35**, 151–167.

Heilbrun, A. B. The measurement of identification. *Child Development*, 1965, **36**, 111–127. (a)

Heilbrun, A. B. An empirical test of the modeling theory of sex-role learning. *Child Development*, 1965, **36**, 789–799. (b)

Heilbrun, A. B. Sex differences in identification learning. *Journal of Genetic Psychology*, 1965, **106**, 185–193. (c)

Heilbrun, A. B. Sex role, instrumental-expressive behavior, and psychopathology in females. *Journal of Abnormal Psychology*, 1968, **73**, 131–136.

Heilbrun, A. B. Parental identification and the patterning of vocational interests in college males and females. *Journal of Counseling Psychology*, 1969, **16**, 342–347.

Heilbrun, A. B. Identification and behavioral effectiveness during late adolescence. In E. D. Evans (Ed.), *Adolescents: Readings in behavior and development*. Hinsdale, Ill.: Dryden Press, 1970. Pp. 68–79. (a)

Heilbrun, A. B. Perceived maternal child-rearing experience and the effects of vicarious and direct reinforcement on males. *Child Development*, 1970, **41**, 253–262. (b)

Heilbrun, A. B. The secondary sex-role system in late adolescents and personality. Currently unpublished study, 1972. (a)

Heilbrun, A. B. Susceptibility to vicarious reinforcement effects and attitudes toward the role of women as related to identification and sex role in late-adolescent females. Currently unpublished study, 1972. (b)

Heilbrun, A. B., & Fromme, D. K. Parental identification of late adolescents and level of adjustment: The importance of parent model attributes, ordinal position, and sex of the child. *Journal of Genetic Psychology*, 1965, **107**, 49–59.

James, W. Internal versus external control of reinforcement as a basic variable in learning theory. Unpublished doctoral dissertation, Ohio State University, 1957.

Kagan, J. The concept of identification. *Psychological Review*, 1958, **65**, 296–305.

Kuhlman, L. A cognitive-developmental analysis of children's sex-role concepts and attitudes. In E. E. Maccoby (Ed.), *The development of sex differences*, Stanford, Calif.: Stanford University Press, 1966. Pp. 82–173.

Komarovsky, M. Cultural contradictions and sex roles. *American Journal of Sociology*, 1946, **52**, 184–189.

Lynn, D. B. A note on the sex differences in the development of masculine and feminine identification. *Psychological Review*, 1959, **66**, 126–135.

Lynn, D. B. *Parent and sex-role identification: A theoretical formulation.* Berkeley, Calif.: McCutchan Publishing Corporation, 1969.

McKee, J. P., & Sherrifs, A. C. Men's and women's beliefs, ideals, and self-concepts. In J. M. Seidman (Ed.), *The adolescent: A book of readings.* New York: Holt, Rinehart & Winston, 1960. Pp. 282–293.

Mischel, W. A social-learning view of sex differences in behavior. In E. E. Maccoby (Ed.), *The development of sex differences.* Stanford, Calif.: Stanford University Press, 1966. Pp. 56–81.

Murray, H. A. *Explorations in personality: A clinical and experimental study of fifty men of college age.* New York: Oxford University Press, 1938.

Parsons, T. Social structure and the development of personality: Freud's contribution to the integration of psychology and sociology. *Psychiatry*, 1958, **21**, 321–340.

Parsons, T., & Bales, R. F. *Family, socialization, and interaction process.* Glencoe, Ill.: Free Press, 1955.

Rosenberg, B. G., & Sutton-Smith, B. *Sex and identity.* New York: Holt, Rinehart & Winston, 1972.

Rosenthal, D. Concordance by sex in schizophrenia. *Psychological Bulletin*, 1962, **59**, 401–421.

Schaffer, H. R., & Emerson, P. E. The development of social attachments in infancy. *Monographs of the Society for Research in Child Development*, 1964, **29**(3), 1–77.

Sears, R. R. Identification as a form of behavioral development. In D. B. Harris (Ed.), *The concept of development.* Minneapolis: University of Minnesota Press, 1957. Pp. 149–161.

Steinman, A. G. A study of the concept of the feminine role of 51 middle-class American families. *Genetic Psychology Monographs*, 1963, **67**, 275–352.

Steinman, A. G., & Fox, D. J. Male-female perceptions of the female role in the United States. *Journal of Psychology*, 1966, **64**, 265–276.

Stoke, S. M. An inquiry into the concept of identification. *Journal of Genetic Psychology*, 1950, **76**, 163–189.

Strong, E. K., Jr. *Manual for the Strong Vocational Interest Blank.* Palo Alto, Calif.: Consulting Psychologists Press, 1959.

Terman, L. M., & Miles, C. C. *Sex and Personality.* New York: McGraw-Hill, 1936.

Wallin, P. Cultural contradictions and sex roles: A repeat study. In J. M. Seidman (Ed.), *The adolescent: A book of readings.* New York: Holt, Rinehart & Winston, 1960. Pp. 272–281.

Wechsler, D. *Wechsler Adult Intelligence Scale.* New York: Psychological Corporation, 1955.

Wismar, R. E. A comparison of the relative effects of modeling and reinforcement upon shaping sex-role behavior in preschool boys. Unpublished Master's thesis, Emory University, 1971.

Family Structure and Sex-Role Variations[1]

BENJAMIN G. ROSENBERG

Bowling Green State University

and

BRIAN SUTTON-SMITH

Columbia University

INTRODUCTION

The research program upon which we have been engaged for some years stands apart from the major foci of current interest in the field of sex-role development. There is at present an almost urgent debate over the respective roles of the biological and cultural factors in sex-role development. Are these sex differences present at birth or shortly thereafter? Is the evidence reliable? And even if there are such differences, are they of minimal importance or do they set in train developments which can only with difficulty be rerouted? If single individuals and whole cultures can be shown not to have done "what comes naturally," can there really be any important predeterminations? On the other hand, if most individuals and most cultures have been comfortable with traditional sex differences, doesn't that suggest there is some useful conspiracy between nature and culture to leave things the way they are? Or again, in less Olympian terms, are sex-role differences really established as early as has been argued? And how irrevocable are these differences, really? Isn't it just continued chauvinistic pressure that keeps women in their traditional place? Remove that pressure and

1. Much of the work cited herein was made possible by Grant #1R01 HD 067792–01 from NICHD.

much of the literature would surely begin to have a less deterministic ring.

In all this argument, important as it may be, historically considered, what tends to get lost in the battle is that there are not just men versus women, females versus males, but there are many varieties of both and some varieties in between. Psychologists have always fallen easy prey to the typological error that because there are usually basic physical differences between males and females, there would also be inevitable and clear-cut psychological differences between them. We have argued against this position more extensively in our recent book, *Sex and Identity* (Rosenberg & Sutton-Smith, 1972). It is an error which psychologists have managed to avoid in work in personality, where such typological thinking is regarded as at best a primitive tool, but an error which has persisted in thinking about sex differences, and an error which is heightened by the current controversies.

Men and women are more alike than they are different. And the similarities and differences run the gamut of many shades and intermixtures. It is to these subtleties that our own research has been directed. We have made our particular study the way in which the varieties of sex-role identity are affected by the family of origin. We have asked how the family structure has an effect on the sex-role identity of its child members. Even if there is a change historically in the cultural prescriptions for sex roles in the years to come, we assume that these cultural learnings will still continue to vary significantly as a result of their mediation through different family structural arrangements. Furthermore, it is our suspicion that the current arguments for female equality, as with those for gay liberation, etc., are, in the long run, arguments for cultural diversity. They are arguments for freedom to become different. This means that the issue of sex differences may, in the future, increasingly reduce itself to the issue of individual differences. In that case, contributions of the varied family structures to varieties of sex-role identity would be contributions to that broader subject matter of individual differences.

The rest of this paper is based on several data sources. First, there are our own studies of sex-role differences induced by sibling position as reviewed in our earlier book, *The Sibling* (Sutton-Smith

& Rosenberg, 1970). Secondly, we have undertaken a review of the subjects in the Berkeley Guidance and Oakland Growth Studies of the Institute of Human Development, University of California. With the kind assistance of Jack Block, Paul Mussen, and Marjorie Honzik, we have rescored this data in terms of sibling position, so that we have been able to compare the responses of these subjects to the California Q sort as described by Block (1971) at three different age levels: Junior High School, Senior High School, and 30 years of age. Thirdly, and more recently, we have drawn a pool of 1,000 college sophomores from Bowling Green State University, Ohio, and had them respond to an inventory reporting their own sibling position, number of offspring in the family, and the sibling positions of their own parents. These, then, are the major sources for the propositions advanced below.

PRIOR STUDIES IN FAMILY STRUCTURAL EFFECTS

We begin with a review of several of our earlier studies in which we sought to demonstrate the effects of family structure on various dependent variables. For example, in our work *The Sibling* (1970), we summed a considerable body of evidence which, to our mind, supports the view that firstborn children, because of hierarchical characteristics of their birth order position, continue to prefer roles of that sort. That is, because they are so closely associated with their parents in dependent roles (they receive twice the interaction as infants), and with their siblings in superior surrogate roles, in later life they prefer occupations that permit such hierarchical arrangements (Sutton-Smith, Roberts, & Rosenberg, 1964). Later-born, by contrast, with diluted power from parents and contestible power from older siblings, live in a more egalitarian world.

In support of this thesis about the way in which family structure leads to different role network expectancies, we cited the evidence that firstborn prefer nurturant and controlling adult roles (pp. 115–116), and that the later-born prefer more egalitarian gregariousness in their activities. Our best evidence comes from a study with Exner (Exner & Sutton-Smith, 1970) in which success in the Peace Corps was shown to be a product of both birth order and character of the job. In the relatively formal situation of teaching

English in the hierarchically ordered school structures of Southeast Asia, the firstborn were more successful than later-born. But, in the open-ended situations of establishing new elementary village schools in the isolated islands of Micronesia, the latter-born were more successful.

Again, even with the birth order literature on *achievement, affiliation,* and *anxiety,* we were able to demonstrate that most studies were insufficiently precise with respect to the sibling structures that were, in fact, relevant to these variables. That literature supposedly has shown that the early-born, particularly the only, is more achieving and affiliative than the later-born. And this has been explained in various ways, namely, as the result of the greater inter-action between the early-born and the parents, which leads to more modeling of parents; or as a result of parental inconsistencies in treatment of the first-born; or as a result of sibling rivalries. We have shown with the Berkeley longitudinal material on two-child families that these predictions do not hold for all family structures, but hold for the same-sex boys (M1MM v. M2), although not for the same-sex girls (F1F v. FF2); and they work for one cross-sex pair (F1M v. FM2), but not for the other (M1F v. MF2).[2] We have gone into the multiple family-structural reasons at length in our book (chapter 9) and will not repeat them. But these differences in the two-child family and in age spacing (which only operates at the intermediate gap of 2 to 4 years) help to explain the inconsistencies in that literature.

More important, from our present viewpoint, is the emphasis once again that such factors strongly vary the type of person and therefore the type of psychosexual animal you are. In all our data, for example, the older girl with a younger brother from the two-child family is *both* highly achieving and highly dependent through-out her first 20 years of development. She has the classic sex-role contradiction, and the data across many studies is very consistent. The major reason probably is the stimulating and rivalrous effect of her younger brother, given the usual preference for him in sex-

---

2. The notation system employed throughout this paper refers to sibling sex, sex of the subject, and birth order. The number following the letter refers to the subject, e.g., M1M indicates a firstborn male with a younger brother, MF2 refers to a second-born girl with an older brother, and so on.

role stereotypes. For this woman, the call to sexual liberation is much more powerful than to a woman who presumably has a much less conflicting call to achievement in her life record, such as the second-born with an older sister who is a relatively affiliative, depressive later-born female. We could add many more illustrations of this sort, all showing the effect of family-structural variables on sex-role learning.

In order to point up the relative paucity of our knowledge of structural effects on sex role and the many ways in which it may be influential, we move next to several of our studies in which we discovered that the father's responses to a sex-role inventory are significantly affected by the sex of his children. In one study, the sample

TABLE 1

FATHER'S FEMININITY SCORES AS A FUNCTION OF SIBLING
CONSTELLATION IN TWO-CHILD FAMILIES

Family Structure	N	Scores
All-girl families (F1F and FF2)	90	16.55
Boy-girl families reported by females (F1M and MF2)	70	17.46
Boy-girl families reported by males (M1F and FM2)	49	17.00
All-male families (M1M and MM2)	40	18.55

NOTE: Adapted from Rosenberg and Sutton-Smith, 1968, and Rosenberg and Sutton-Smith, 1971b.

was composed of 160 college sophomore females and 89 males, their actual siblings (males and females), and their mothers and fathers. The *Gough Scale of Psychological Femininity* (1952) was administered directly to the subject's own siblings, mother, and father. All of the subjects were members of the two-child family. While many results are reported in detail elsewhere, the most interesting outcome for the present purposes is revealed by Table 1 (Rosenberg & Sutton-Smith, 1968, 1971b). In this table, the higher the score, the higher the acknowledged femininity on the part of the father respondents.

These results indicate that the more males there are in the family, the more feminine is the father's score; alternatively, the more females in the family, the more masculine is his score. That is, fathers of the male dyads are relatively more willing, on the Gough scale, to admit to anxiety, discomfort, sensitivity, emotional disturbances, and so on, which are admissions about behaviors traditionally regarded as feminine. The difference is both significant and most striking between fathers of the all-girl dyad and fathers of the all-boy dyad. Others have shown that such sibling patterns can have an effect on parents' femininity scores, working with 5-year-old children, so that we may assume these influences persist throughout development.

In the earlier Rosenberg and Sutton-Smith study (1968), the mothers' femininity scores showed no such relationship to sibling composition. We can gain some understanding of this phenomenon by a study of the patterns of correlations of mothers, fathers, and two siblings in this study. In the all-girl-group family, the girls' scores correlated with each other and with those of the mother, but the fathers' scores did not. The father's femininity score showed no significant correlations with any of his other family members. But in the boy-girl and the boy-boy dyad, by contrast, the scores of all family members intercorrelated in a variety of ways with each other. From these various findings, it may be inferred that males with "too much feminine" influence may indeed have been resisting or counteracting it, or were in some way in conflict with it.

We have a number of other examples of a similar effect. For example, while males with one sister show a more-than-typical interest in female activities, males with two sisters showed a reversal of this pattern and accentuated their masculine interests, both as reported on inventories and as observed in classrooms (Rosenberg & Sutton-Smith, 1964). Similarly, some of the age transformation data fits the same thesis. The boy with the older sister who appears very feminine throughout childhood reverses this situation at college and shows an above-average masculine pattern. While other males are demonstrating more interest in entrepreneurial activities, he is showing heightened concern to be a rugged outdoors person. We have suggested that this is somewhat like a delayed preadolescence.

Naturally there are various ways of explaining this counteridentification phenomena. What we believe we see here are instances of one set of norms (family structure expectancies) coming into conflict with another set of norms (sex-role stereotypes) which, though mediated by the family, are also represented very strongly outside of it in peer activity and mass media. When the two conflict, some adaptation to both has to be made.

Another illustration of these complexities is provided by a comparison of two-child families of the same sex, that is, a girl with a younger sister and a boy with a younger brother. In a large number of studies we have noted a cross-sex effect (*The Sibling*, p. 31). That is, the firstborn female with the younger sister and the second-born male with the older brother are somewhat alike, and in turn, the other pair are somewhat alike (F1F & MM2 v. M1M & FF2). The first pair have shown up in a number of studies as less conforming, more Machiavellian, less uncertain under conditions of threat, and less often gregarious, where the other pair have been the reverse, more tender rather than tough minded.

Our interpretation here is that sex-role norms make it preferable for a girl to be like a mother and have charge of the younger ones. That is a favorable position for her (even though she gets more rivalry from her mother). The younger sister who gets mothered has relatively less experience nurturing other children. (We have wondered earlier whether she compensates by having more children!) Similarly, it is easier for a male if he has a male model and if he is allowed to be independent and is not expected to act out the nurturing older-sibling role. Children's preferences are for being the older female or the younger male. Mother's preferences, however, are the reverse—for the younger female and the older male. Here we have a conflict of emphasis between what peers see as most suitable from a sex-role point of view (to be the nurturing older female, F1F, or the independent younger male, MM2) and what mothers want for themselves, a nonrivalrous baby (FF2), or a close leading man (M1M).

So what we inject here, one might say, along with the sex-stereotype norms, are the oedipal norms, which themselves sometimes conflict with other features of family structure and sometimes coincide with it. They work most remarkably in the only-child family where the daughter identifies very strongly with the father and the son with the mother, in each case apparently substituting identification with the member of the opposite sex in place of rivalry with their same-sex parent.

CONCLUSION

This summary of our earlier studies shows that, generally, family-structural effects combine in various ways with sex-role stereotypes and with intimate family relations and rivalries (oedipal effects) to produce various outcomes. They raise, too, the question of whether family-structural effects are usually *replicated* in subsequent relationships (as in the Peace Corps data) or *counteracted* (as in the father femininity data). In the new study which we present below in which family structure and its effects on number of offspring and spouse characteristics are involved, a major issue is this one of replication.

THE FAMILY SYSTEMIC EFFECT

We begin with the general proposition that the major general effect in the data to be reported is that whether we are discussing number of offspring, the characteristics of the spouse, the personality characteristics of the subject, or the sex-role preferences of the subject, these tend to replicate those which are characteristic of the subject within his original family structure. It is as though the subject, in his subsequent life relationships, seeks to reproduce those conditions with which he was familiar in his family of origin. Elsewhere, Walter Toman (1971) has termed this the *duplication* theorem of social relationships: "New social relationships tend to have more chances of permanence and success the closer they resemble earlier and earliest (intrafamilial) social relationships [p. 47]." While we were earlier of a skeptical mind with respect to this theorem (Sutton-Smith & Rosenberg, 1970, p. 7), our present review adds considerable support to the evidence Toman has already adduced. To a significant degree, statistically speaking, the sex-role identity that a subject manifests in subsequent life is the identity he learned in his family. While this is not a surprising formulation in terms of either learning or psychoanalytic theory, the finding of a matching between family structure and later proclivities is of novel impact.

FAMILY SIZE AND NUMBER OF OFFSPRING

In our earlier efforts, it had been possible to demonstrate the continuing influence of one's sibling condition (sex, sex of sibling, birth order, and family size) on the development of his sex-role identity, cognitive activities, and a variety of other personological measures. We were increasingly convinced by these outcomes that no matter how few our variables, we could not conceptualize a multisignificant trait as the consequent of one causal system or variable. That is to say, covarying four or five variables allowed prediction as no one or two variables might. And more important, on an intuitive or common-sense basis, the genesis of a plurisignificant trait such as sex-role identity must be based in a configuration of causal sources.

Having moved from demonstrating the coerciveness of family-construct variables on personality formation to a series of studies on cognitive (or, if you will, "harder") activities, we asked ourselves the basic question: How predictive are these outcomes in some of the major life decisions made by the individual? No more stringent test presumably exists than the prediction of complex life decisions which remain, to this day, poorly understood by psychology. Thus, we set ourselves the task of investigating such "knowables" as numbers of offspring and spouse selection, phenomena all-important in the understanding of adult personality, having profound implications for total life style, sex role, economics, etc., and yet, to this point, best "understood" in romantic or folklorist terms.

In particular, we were looking at the influence of family size, ordinal position, and sibling sex status on the number of offspring and on mate selection. The way we defined mate selection was on the basis of mate's family size, mate's birth order, and mate's sibling status.

In a recently completed study, we examined the interrelationships among 1,000 intact families and their sex, sex of sibling, family size, and ordinal position.[3] These four-way interactions reflect the relationship of these variables to the numbers of offspring. Keep in mind our awareness that these are only four of a host of variables which presumably are of importance in determining the complex outcomes we are predicting.

For brevity, let us summarize the findings on the family-size variable. Mother's family size is significantly ($p < .0001$) related to

3. The authors are indebted to Don Robertson for his invaluable assistance in the above study.

the number of offspring. Less so, but in the predicted directions, father's family size is positively related ($p = .22$) to the number of offspring. The obvious holds: large family size of the parent predicts to large numbers of offspring; small predicts to small. Indeed, the best predictor of the number of offspring lies with the mothers from large families. When we introduce sibling status, later-born mothers in large families who have immediately older sisters are prone to many offspring, as contrasted with later-born mothers in large families with older brothers ($p = .08$).

Though the status of the father is, as we have noted, a less adequate predictor of number of offspring ($p = .22$), some interesting parallels exist. In general, firstborn fathers from large families have large numbers of children, while later-born fathers have fewer ($p = .28$). That same father who is an early-born (second) with an older brother in a large family tends to have many offspring ($p = .12$).

Summarizing to this point: family size is remarkably coercive in

TABLE 2

MOTHER-FATHER FAMILY SIZES AND NUMBERS OF OFFSPRING

Family Size of Parents	Offspring			Total N
	2	3	4	
MoSFS-FaSFS[a]				
N	111	100	102	313
%	35.5	31.9	32.6	
MoLFS-FaLFS				
N	84	51	66	201
%	41.8	25.4	32.8	
MoSFS-FaLFS				
N	77	70	82	229
%	33.6	30.6	35.8	
MoLFS-FaSFS				
N	69	62	126	257
%	26.8	24.1	49.0	
Total				
N	341	283	376	1000
%	34.1	28.3	27.6	

NOTE: $X^2 = 24.1418$; $p = .005$

[a] Mo = Mother; Fa = Father; SFS = small family size; LFS = large family size.

predicting the numbers of offspring, mother's family size being the best predictor, while early or firstborn children in large families have more offspring than later-borns, and possession of an older, like-sex sibling is predictive of large numbers of offspring. Aptly, we might describe the phenomena as a *replication strategy*. That is to say, across all variables, humans appear to recreate, in their adult lives and the major decisions they make as adults (offspring, marriage, etc.), the social-psychological community in which they have developed.

The next question to ask is what the reciprocals in the mother-father dyad tell us about numbers of offspring. Combining small family-sized mothers and fathers, large-family-sized mothers and fathers, and small-large and large-small, as in Table 2, evidence clearly indicates that small-small leads to few offspring, while large-large leads to many offspring ($p = .005$). For those parental dyads in which the family size of one is disparate from the other, regardless of who comes from a small family, mother or father, it leads to small numbers of offspring. That is, the parent from a small family of origin is most influential in determining the number of offspring. Birth order combined with the parental family size provides little, except that birth order is a better additive in prediction for fathers than mothers. Sibling status adds little.

In summary, family size is a powerful predictor of offspring, sibling influences (i.e., the interaction of family size, birth order, and sibling status) are clearest in large-family members, one's sibling community replicates itself in great measure in adulthood, birth order is a relatively nonpredictive variable once family size is known, and unquestionably, mothers are the primary determiners of population. It is rewarding that this outcome fits well with folklore and intuitive, common-sense expectations. Fathers *do* play a role, but it appears that mothers determine the numbers of offspring in the typical parental dyad.

FAMILY SIZE AND CHOICE OF SPOUSE

The next question addresses itself to the *selection of spouse*. In brief, women and men are prone to marry a spouse from a family size resembling their own ($p = .0001$). That is, if mother or father is from a small family, it is highly likely that he or she will marry a person from a small family. Though the addition of birth order and sibling status add little, birth order does again seem more influential for fathers and mothers.

Another question of interest has to do with spouse's birth order. Generally, it appears very powerful for both mothers ($p = .0005$) and for fathers ($p = .007$). Women from a small family of origin marry early-born males; women from a large family of origin marry later-born males. This may be contaminated by family size, of course. Father's family size is a good predictor of mother's birth order, with early-born fathers in large families with an older brother marrying later-born mothers, and early-born fathers with an older sister marrying early-born mothers ($p = .06$). One might speculate on the latter finding: the early-born male with an older brother (and little direct influence of females in development) appears to select a more feminine spouse (one who has an older sister), while the early-born father presumably dominated by an older sister (mother surrogate, more powerful) selects an early-born spouse (more dominant) who continues the surrogation. But, alas, the latter speculation, and that is all it is, requires much more intensive study in order to be believed.

We might add that in Toman's data, drawn from large Swiss and German samples, the number of children did not simply *replicate* the number in the family of origin, as we have found here and as Altus (1970) has found. In addition, Toman found that the compatibility of spouses also affected the number of children. That is, if the spouses reproduced their sibling relationships in the family of origin, they were more likely to have children. Spouses were said to be more compatible if they had opposite-sex siblings, and if they were of reciprocal rank-order sibling positions (higher to lower).[4]

Conclusion. While it may not seem as if family size and number of offspring are, directly speaking, a matter of sex-role identity, we would argue, contrarily, that this is very potent evidence that family structure has contributed to subsequent decisions about genera-

4. Our borderline finding that girls in larger families are more likely to have more children if they have older sisters (rather than older brothers) gives some evidence as well of modeling tendencies.

tivity (how many children one wants, etc.). It can be argued, as Erikson has done, that such decisions are the essence of a mature identity. The mother who decides to have children is making a declaration about her own compatibility with children. And judging by our results, this is a compatibility learned through early experience. It probably has implications also for competence in handling other children in teaching or coaching capacities, or in any nurturance capacity.

THE TWO-CHILD FAMILY

A somewhat more precise way of examining the complexity in which we find ourselves is to look at the two-child family, for which sex, sex of sibling, birth order, and family size are well controlled.

In the two-child family (well investigated in the literature) with family size constant, one can readily examine the effects of birth order and sibling status, in addition to the fact that only eight basic categories of individuals comprising these several statuses exist (M1M, M1F, MM2, FM2, F1F, F1M, FF2, MF2). The results of the present analysis in Table 3 reveal that birth order and same-opposite sex of sibling are highly predictive. For *males*, same sex (M1M, MM2) predicts to numbers of children, firstborn having many, second-borns having few. Birth order, alone, is highly predictive of spouse selection, firstborns marrying women from large families, second-borns marrying women from small families. In addition, firstborns marry later-borns, second-borns marry early-borns. And finally, same-sex males marry feminine wives (women with sisters), males with an opposite-sex sibling (M1F, FM2) marry more masculine wives (i.e., a woman with a brother).

One fact seems clear: second-born males insist on reifying roles of their own childhood in the number of their offspring (few) and in spouse selections (early-born or small-family women); that is, they replicate their own siblife.

Having a like-sex sibling (reinforcing one's masculinity) is of equal import; like-sex males (M1M, MM2) marry feminine women (i.e., girls with sisters). Again, one might speculate that possessing an all-male developmental life results in little knowledge of the

TABLE 3

EFFECTS OF BIRTH ORDER AND SIBLING STATUS OF MOTHERS AND
FATHERS FROM TWO-CHILD FAMILIES ON CHOICE OF MATE

Subjects	Mothers			
	Offspring	FFS	FBO	FSS
F1F	Have large families	Trend to marry SFS man	Marry early-born	Marry man with male sibling
FF2	Have small families	Marry only or SFS man	Marry early-born	
F1M		Marry LFS man	Marry late-born	Marry man with female sibling
MF2		Trend to marry LFS man		

Subjects	Fathers			
	Offspring	MFS	MBO	MSS
M1M	Trend to have large families	Marry LFS woman	Marry late-born	
MM2	Trend to have small families	Marry SFS woman	Marry early-born	Marry woman with female sibling
M1F			Marry late-born	Marry woman with male sibling
FM2		Marry SFS woman	Marry early-born	Marry woman with male sibling

NOTE: FS refers to family size, BO to birth order, and SS to sibling status. Thus, FFS refers to father's family size, MFS to mother's family size, FBO to father's birth order, etc.

feminine role, and consequently an "idealized" image of woman-hood (as though women were "little princesses"). Opposite-sex males (M1F, FM2) marry women who have had brothers, and presumably are more masculine, or masculine-aware. Thus, throughout their lives they recapitulate roles learned from their own family developmental history and marry women who have shared both sex roles.

For *females* in the two-child families, the outcomes are quite similar, like-sex females being highly predictive of numbers of offspring: firstborn girls with younger sisters (F1F) have many, second-born girls with older sisters (FF2) have few offspring. Again, as we have seen for the males in the two-child family, for like-sex siblings, the second-born girls marry only children or small-family-sized males, while the opposite-sex females (F1M, MF2) marry males from large families. F1Fs marry feminine husbands, F1Ms marry masculine husbands.

Thus, for the sex-sibling influences on women, firstborn girls with a younger sister play out the generalized surrogate role, as we noted in our 1964 "role taking" paper. They appear to recapitulate, with a less-powerful male whom they marry, the powerful, nurturant mother role in which they are so well trained. The second-born girl, however, recapitulates her early sibship life by retaining a small family.

To sum the individual positions in terms of spouse selection and their presumed masculinity-femininity, FF2s prefer only children or early-born males; F1Ms prefer males from large families, or later-born males, or males with a brother. F1F prefers a spouse with an older sister; and MF2s prefer husbands with an older brother. The transparency of sex-sibship predictions are clear. For men, FM2s marry only girls, M1Ms marry later-borns with sisters, MM2s marry early-borns with sisters, and M1F marries a later-born girl with an older brother.

One cannot avoid the conclusion that sibling sex status is remarkably predictive of such profound life decisions as mate selection and offspring dictates. The data outcomes make clear that the sibling community in which the organism develops replicates itself in the adult world. One would never assume that such predictive outcomes were in the conscious possession of the developing individual, but look carefully: firstborn like-sex males *and* females recapitulate *parent surrogation* in numbers of offspring and power-nurture roles with their spouses; second-borns of both sexes demonstrate clearly their need to replicate their sibling roles (early, small, few offspring) —that is, they retain with vigor their collectivity, their passions, their individual identities, and the role changes and flexibility in the small family. The results indicate greater statistical significance for males, suggesting that they account for more of the variance in spouse selection, just as mothers appeared more influential in determining the number of offspring. And finally, like-sex females prefer a mate with a sister; opposite-sex females prefer a mate with a brother, continuing the notion that role awareness and role sharing in sex-sibships is a powerful predictor of what spouse selection is likely to occur.

In some sense the present data modifies the Toman findings, insofar as it indicates that there is a significant tendency for subjects to choose similar rather than *reciprocal* spouses. However, his data has to do with the *success* of the relationship rather than simply its character. It could be that early marriage choices are dictated more often by similarity, and later, more often by complementarity. Toman found that later marriages (over 27 years) showed more such complementary parallelism.

In the data presented, the early-born boy from a large family who has an older sister and then marries an "early born mother" (*sic*), can be assumed to be reaching for a complementary relationship. However, the boy in the same position, but with an older brother, who marries a later-born sister with older sisters does not fit the complementarity prediction. What interests us about this situation is that he is typically one of the most masculine of boys, having older brothers to model after, and he marries one of the most feminine of girls, who has older sisters to model after. Her femininity as female and his masculinity as male provides us with an example of the type of complementarity described in the romantic literature. This is the marriage which the typological error predicts, but which, our data suggest, occurs amongst subjects who have been prevented by family structure from learning that there are more comfortable role supports for a successful marriage. They are both later-borns with same-sex older siblings. So they marry rank-order similarity, buttressed, perhaps, as we argue, by romantic complementarity.

In the research that we have been citing here, predictions from birth order or sex status of siblings alone were relatively minor as compared with those of family size, thus supporting Schooler's recent fairly negative conclusion about birth order effects alone (1972), although we would hasten to add that most of the data to which Schooler refers does not institute the controls necessary for particular sibling composition and sibling spacing that are necessary (Jones, 1933; Sutton-Smith & Rosenberg, 1970).

THE FAMILY OF THREE VERSUS THE FAMILY OF FOUR

There is perhaps no better way of bringing home the impact of family size than by comparing the family of the only child with families of two children. We have reviewed this evidence in detail elsewhere, so we will present it here only briefly (Rosenberg & Sutton-Smith, 1971a). The subjects in this study, from the longitudinal data of the Institute of Human Development, University of California, Berkeley,[5] were 14 only females and 18 firstborn females from two-child families, the latter including 13 F1F and 5 F1M. The differences between these females are presented in Table 4.

The table indicates that there are marked differences in Q-sort-derived characteristics of these two groups from these different family structures. The greatest differences in the 94 possible comparisons occurred in the earlier JHS comparisons (30), fewer at SHS (19), and still fewer at 30 years of age (12). Judging by this personality-trait study, family-structure effects attenuate with age. However, we must keep in mind the prior evidence that they continue to affect number of offspring and the characteristics of one's spouse, which are fairly weighty outcomes.

When the only girls are compared with the firstborn, they turn out to be very different on the characteristics of this Q sort. At JHS the onlies are significantly higher than the F1s on talkativeness, self-dramatizing expressiveness, rebelliousness, inability to delay gratification, pushing limits, self-indulgence, emotional involvement with the opposite sex, and the direct expression of hostility.

5. These important studies have been in progress for some 40 years under the careful guidance of Jean Macfarlane, Nancy Bayley, and Marjorie Honzik. The authors of the paper are deeply indebted to Marjorie Honzik, Jack Block, and Paul Mussen for making these data available. For extended description of the basic sample and rich outcomes of the Berkeley Guidance and the Oakland Growth Studies, the reader is referred to Jones, Bayley, Macfarlane, and Honzik (1971).

They are also high on assertiveness, responsiveness to humor, and extrapunitiveness. At adulthood they are still self-indulgent, have difficulty in delaying gratification, push limits, judge self by popularity, etc. In sum, at 30 years of age, these only girls are still very

TABLE 4

PERSONALITY TRAITS OF FIRSTBORN VERSUS
ONLY FEMALES

Firstborn Females (N = 18)					Only Females (N = 14)		
JHS	SHS	Adult	#	Item	JHS	SHS	Adult
4.48	5.03	6.42	4	talkative	6.61****	6.26	6.32
5.61***	4.85	5.18	14	submissive	3.97	4.07	4.56
5.72	4.97	5.47	10	bodily symptoms	5.43	6.26***	6.37
5.11	5.09	4.32	23	extrapunitive	5.59	6.47**	4.66
4.50***	4.53	4.50	24	rational, objective	3.30	3.83	4.39
6.85****	5.52	5.91***	25	overcontrolled	4.02	4.45	4.51
3.76	3.94	3.46	27	condescending	4.42	5.35**	4.40
4.96***	4.89*	4.75	40	fearful	3.31	3.85	4.18
4.38**	4.48	3.72	42	delay, avoid action	3.40	3.76	3.57
4.89	4.92	5.85	43	expressive	6.09***	5.62	6.16
6.29****	5.50***	6.42	47	readiness to feel guilty	4.54	4.19	6.02
5.07***	4.85	4.17	48	aloofness	3.02	3.92	3.81
4.55	4.07	5.48***	51	values intellectual	3.93	3.73	3.88
4.35	4.42	4.83	52	assertive	5.95**	5.81**	5.98
3.63	4.09	3.22	53	can't delay gratification	5.31***	5.40*	4.83***
5.11	5.14	5.79	56	responds to humor	5.95**	5.57	5.51
3.37	3.31	5.14**	60	self insight	3.89	3.00	3.90
3.03	3.94	3.14	62	rebellious	4.76***	4.59	3.37
6.50	5.94	4.55	63	judges self conventionally	6.90	7.00*	6.10**
2.65	3.68	2.74	65	pushes limits	4.23***	4.85*	3.96**
4.24	5.26	3.77	67	self-indulgent	5.88***	6.71**	5.31***
5.53**	5.20	4.67	69	sensitive to demand	4.57	5.90	4.37
4.65	5.59	5.32	80	emotionally invested in opposite sex	6.19***	6.07	5.53
3.33	3.75	3.80	94	expresses hostility directly	4.73***	4.52	4.52
3.61	4.37	4.71	99	self-dramatizing	5.35****	5.66*	5.27
5.37***	5.05	4.39	100	doesn't vary roles	4.19	4.69	4.26

SOURCE: Institute of Human Development, longitudinal data derived from the California Q Sort.

**** p < .001
*** p < .01–.02
** p < .05
* p < .10

much displaying certain personality characteristics originally also displayed during late childhood. Their identity has a distinctly narcissistic, assertive quality, although given the other evidence of the successfulness of only children in the literature, their demanding characteristics apparently pay off in terms of life outcomes (Rosenberg, 1966).

Firstborn girls are, by contrast, much more traditionally feminine. They exceed the onlies at JHS on submissiveness, on fearfulness, in a tendency to delay commitment, in a readiness to feel guilty, in a touchiness regarding demands made upon them, in possessing insight, in arousing nurturance in others, and in being rational, objective, overcontrolled, etc. By adulthood, only a few of these differences remain, but the F1F are still overcontrolled, dependable, submissive, and possessing insight. The contrary traditional female characteristics of dependency and empathy seem reflected here.

Here, then, are two sets of girls, from different family sizes, who have markedly different characteristics and, presumably, remarkably different sex-role identities at age 30 years.[6] One could argue from these data that the small one-child family is much more potent in its influence than the larger family. We have shown elsewhere that the only child does indeed see the parents as more powerful than children in the two-child family (Sutton-Smith & Rosenberg, 1970, chapter 4).

When the only males $(N = 11)$ are contrasted with the firstborn males $(N = 22)$ in the same study there are only two significant relationships, although, as an examination of Table 5 will show, once again onlies tend to be more outgoing and firstborn males more overcontrolled. Still, the finding of little influence is like the rest of the literature in indicating that the family of origin is more potent with females than with males in all respects. The usual argument is that males' greater independence brings them into contact with many alternative sources of learning and, as a result, attenuates the influence of the family. The girls' comparative stability could be held to be supporting evidence for such a proposition.

Our assumption would be that family structure effects on personality would decrease (for such personality traits) as a function of family size, this being less true the higher the proportion of female siblings. Our speculation

6. We would argue against the randomness of these 30-year-old characteristics because of their general consistency on all three measures over the age span. Such consistency compares most favorably with predictions made from parental treatments alone in other longitudinal research.

TABLE 5

PERSONALITY TRAITS OF FIRSTBORN VERSUS
ONLY MALES

Firstborn Males ($N = 22$)					Only Males ($N = 11$)		
JHS	SHS	Adult	#	Item	JHS	SHS	Adult
5.38	4.36	5.98	4	talkative	4.97	5.66*	5.73
6.13	5.36	5.80*	13	thin-skinned; sensitive	5.91	5.42	4.95
6.19	5.71*	5.46	25	overcontolled	5.75	4.15	5.47
3.87	3.83	4.29	36	negativistic	4.09	4.90*	4.04
2.94	2.79	3.23	37	guileful; manipulative	3.24	4.09*	3.57
3.74	3.98	3.96	60	insight into motives	3.07	3.57	5.32*
3.03	3.65	3.04	65	pushes limits	3.76	4.60	4.24*
4.98	5.15***	5.35	79	ruminative; persistent	5.39	3.69	4.73
3.75	3.54	4.58*	87	makes the simple comp.	4.72**	3.75	3.56
3.80	4.25	4.24	94	expresses hostility directly	4.24	5.18*	4.85

SOURCE: Institute of Human Development, longitudinal data derived from the California *Q* Sort.

  *** $p < .01-.02$
  ** $p < .05$
  * $p < .10$

about the source of these different predictive capacities is as follows:
In the small family, and in the family in which home influences are
relatively powerful (as with girls) and in which the parents are
practically all-powerful (as with the only girl), then interpersonal
relationships are more intense. The indulgent and unsuppressed
narcissistic character of the only girl speaks to such an intensity.
The firstborn, by contrast, with their overcontrolled status, suggest
that already, even with two children, there has been a relative
victory of role socialization over emotionality. That is, the older
have been forced to be nurturant and controlled with respect to the
younger, despite sibling rivalry. Extending the same line of comparisons, we could argue that the larger family is more of a collective in which there is a more impersonal division of roles and duties,
which is the point of view taken by Bossard and Boll in their studies
of the large family (1956). Parental involvement, availability, time,
monies, and energies decrease as a function of increase in family
size. In the small family with the least division of resources, a life is
more intense, interactions are freer, with less rules and structures;
there is more conflict, more coalitional activity (oedipal rivalry)

than in large families. Since the resources are so little divided, narcissistic conflict can predominate.

All of which is to say that when small-family members, by and large, choose spouses from small families and have few children, and when large-family members do the contrary, this is not mere replication. It is choosing *a particular emotional climate* in which to live.

THE PREDICTIVE POWER OF FAMILY-STRUCTURAL EFFECTS

Naturally, throughout all this data we are looking for structural variables which will have a powerful predictive effect. Family size is clearly such a variable. What we would like to emphasize now is that this effect is really quite remarkable in the literature on sex-role development. Such durable effects are a rarity in that literature. For example, in the case of the three- and four-member families just dealt with, the reader will note that with few exceptions, none of the variables differentiate between the groups involved at every age level (junior high school, senior high school, and 30 years of age). The only variables that do differentiate across these age levels are the following characteristics of the only girls: unable to delay gratification, self-indulgent, and pushing limits. Their sex role is predictable across all age groups in these ways. None of the other groups are.

If we move out of birth order into general personality characteristics associated with sex role, the permanency of effects is even less remarkable. One example is most striking: looking at the longitudinal data on 57 females and 58 males from the Berkeley Guidance Study and examining 35 behavioral ratings for each subject from ages 4 through 16 via yearly assessments, we found that out of 442 tests of significance of male-female differences, only 31, or 7%, achieved the .05 level of significance. And no variable differentiates between the sexes at all age levels, though a couple of variables distinguish across about 4 out of the 12 age levels (boys have more speech problems and night restlessness). If there are permanent differences between the sexes, we may ask, where are they?

On the basis of such data, it seems safer to argue that there are not really very substantial, permanent, universal, enduring differences between the sexes. There are differences, but they come and go, and the bulk of data shows similarity between the sexes rather than differences.

However, if we take such a viewpoint, we have to explain first our own coercive data above, and also, why it is that most of the thinking about sex-role development assumes that there are such fairly permanent differences.

With respect to our own data, frankly, we are not sure why the effects are so powerful. Our current speculation is that the variable of family size is working for us as some sort of *carrier* for the network of relatively enduring relationships and interactions of modeling and complementation that exist in their various permutations amongst all the members. Perhaps family size is a multivariate nexus, a consistent environment over many years, which its members grow to find rewarding and which they seek to perpetuate with their children and spouses. At least, that is our speculation.

On the Absence of Sex-Role Differences

Our position in this paper has been that sex-role stereotypes have been overemphasized, that there are innumerable differences within the sexes and between the sexes in varieties and shades of sex-role development, and that our attention should be focused upon these. We have interpreted some of our data above to suggest that there are very few enduring and universal differences between the sexes. We need first to explain, therefore, why most psychologists have imagined that there are such permanent differences.

Based on our early cross-cultural work (Sutton-Smith, 1973b), we suggest that the postneolithic drift of human cultures toward warlike societies has led to a maximization of the importance of *two*, rather than the more customary multiple sex roles (Mead, 1961). In warlike societies it is viable to stress the males into the inhibition of emotionality so that their ego development becomes bound up with aggressive service to the tribal unit on the basis of a quite infantile tie to the mothering person. Complementarily, the female, while adopting a role of abasement and inferiority, continues to succour (because her own emotional development is not equally arrested) the infantile warrior. The male is given power without emotional maturity, and the female is given emotional maturity without power. Undoubtedly, this brief sketch oversimplifies the picture, but we believe it is the strength of some such dyadic role relationships which has ideologically forced most of us into oversimplified views of sex-role differences. We have expected to find universal and enduring sex-role differences, when the evidence shows only minimal and fluctuating sex-role differences in both cognitive and personality dimensions. The mass of data over any multivariate assessment does not show sex differences, though it shows vast individual differences. Incidentally, we would add that, in fairness, critics of this traditional position should, if they so insist, speak of the "chauvinist dyad," not the "chauvinist male pig." The demure, downtrodden female "mothers" her "pig" and keeps him in sway to her emotional dominance. Perhaps it is wiser to avoid epithets altogether and endeavor to discover who is calling whom what and for what reason.

Given the ideological emphasis on the importance of male warriors, it becomes understandable why many comparative psychologists and biologists give a great emphasis to the universality of sex differences across species and to the similarity between animal and human sex differences. We do not find the evidence, however, so overwhelming. It is not that there are not differences of a basic biological sort (the core of Money's 1973 quadrad of women gestating, lactating, and menstruating, versus men impregnating; see pp. 225–226), and not that these are not usually elaborated in many coercive ways by human societies; but there is clearly no inevitability that these basic biological differences *must* be elaborated into extensive patterns of psychological sex differences. Money has shown with his many cases just how important is the learned identity, even when it clashes with, or rather, is not based on, an homologous genetic identity. The paradox in Money's work, we feel, is that it does tend to overemphasize the importance of early determination. The disadvantage in working with extreme cases as he does is that he is dealing with subjects whose identity is felt to be in jeopardy, and the parents and counselor put a great deal of effort into avoiding or resolving any dissonance between body biology and role identity. This means that sex-role identity is stamped in as soon as possible and with as little ambiguity as possible. It is our suspicion that in the more normal case, the child only gradually confirms his identity over a somewhat longer period, arriving at a fairly firm destination by the beginning of childhood, but even then showing considerable lability until adolescent norms take over. Alongside Money's clear evidence that infant identity can be shifted and boys made into girls or girls made into boys, we need to add the older evidence of Whiting and co-workers (1958) that adolescents also can be given basic shifts in sex-role identity through initiation rites. In the Whiting cases, boys with a substantially female role identification were shifted to masculinity by very severe initiation ceremonies. We may sum this argument by pointing to the quite different developmental consequences that follow in *traumatic,* as compared with *optimal,* cases. In the traumatic case (human or animal), the outcome is indeed predictable, given the early circumstances. In the optimal case, however, *the animal or human undamaged by early circumstances goes on learning and is open to subsequent influences.* We have detailed this argument elsewhere (Sutton-Smith, 1973; Rosenberg & Sutton-Smith, 1972).

In the normal course of sex-role development, therefore, we see a gradual acquisition of the individual sex-role character which continues throughout many years and is much less fixed than is usually argued, although like the rest of personality, the adopted role becomes increasingly stable from age 4 onward.

On the Acquisition of Individual Sex-Role Patterns

While we are fully aware that in dealing with family-structural effects we are only touching a fragment of the contributions to sex-role identity, we can at least claim, given our data above, that those effects are multiple. It seems doubtful to us that there can be much power to explanations which concentrate on unidimensional explanations, for example, on "identification" with the parent. Explanations of that sort hark to the philosophical "essentialism" to be found in unitary trait theories, recently so soundly criticized by Mischel (1969, 1971). What seems to us more likely to occur is that the original biological differences are overlaid by many response systems which are sustained according to their appropriateness with other family members, peers, teachers, etc., and with the opposite sex. At different ages, new facets of biological sex—for example, hormones, body size, and strength—feed into these other systems and are either amplified or ignored, according to cultural habit. In these terms, the study of sex-role "identity" becomes a study of the development of that identity as responsive to age norms and settings. Family structure provides a series of such settings as it changes itself, just as do neighborhoods, schools, and so on. Sex-role stereotypes permeate these age differences and settings in various ways, but as yet we do not know if their effects are as extensive or powerful as they seem to have been on the sex-role researchers who have emphasized such differences.

CONCLUSION

It has been demonstrated that family-structural effects can be a powerful influence on an individual's sex-role development. Furthermore, it has been shown that these effects are numerous and diverse. The data of this paper have been interpreted to support the notion that human sex roles are much more diversified than sex-role stereotypes seem to indicate. In fact, we have argued that sex similarities are overwhelmingly greater than sex differences, and that what is needed is a more subtle psychology of the way in which particular age and context pressures sometimes give rise to those empirical differences of which we have made so much. We would take the point of view that the study of sex-role differences is a contribution to the psychology of individual differences, a contribution to those individuals who prefer, in their own way, to be different.

REFERENCES

Altus, W. D. Marriage and order of birth. *Proceedings of the American Psychological Association*, 78th Convention, 1970. Pp. 361–362.

Block, J. *Lives through time*. Berkeley: Bancroft Press, 1971.

Bossard, J. H. S., & Boll, Eleanor, S. *The large family system: An original study in the sociology of family behavior*. Philadelphia: University of Pennsylvania Press, 1956.

Exner, J., & Sutton-Smith, B. Birth order and hierarchical v. innovative role requirements. *Journal of Personality*, 1970, **38**, 581–587.

Gough, H. G. Identifying psychological femininity. *Educational and Psychological Measurement*, 1952, **12**, 427–439.

Jones, H. E. Order of birth in relation to the development of the child. In C. Murchison (Ed.), *A handbook of child psychology*. Worcester: Clark University Press, 1933. Pp. 204–241.

Jones, M. C.; Bayley, N.; Macfarlane, J. W.; & Honzik, M. P. (Eds.), *The course of human development*. Waltham, Mass.: Xerox College Publishers, 1971.

Mead, Margaret. Cultural determinants of sexual behavior. In W. C. Young (Ed.), *Sex and internal secretions*. Vol. 2. Baltimore: Williams & Wilkins, 1961. Pp. 1,433–1480.

Mischel, W. *On continuity and change in personality*. Society for Research in Child Development, Santa Monica, Calif., March, 1969.

Mischel, W. *Introduction to personality*. New York: Holt, Rinehart & Winston, 1971.

Rosenberg, B. G. Siblings' effects on siblings—and parents: The search for a representative design in research on sex role identification. Paper presented at the meeting of the American Orthopsychiatric Association, San Francisco, April, 1966.

Rosenberg, B. G., & Sutton-Smith, B. Ordinal position and sex role identification. *Genetic Psychology Monographs*, 1964, **70**, 297–328.

Rosenberg, B. G., & Sutton-Smith, B. Family interaction effects on masculinity-femininity. *Journal of Personality and Social Psychology*, 1968, **8**, 117–120.

Rosenberg, B. G., & Sutton-Smith, B. Do siblings really count? A longitudinal analysis. Paper presented at the meeting of the Society for Research in Child Development, Minneapolis, April, 1971. (a)

Rosenberg, B. G., & Sutton-Smith, B. Sex role identification and sibling composition. *Journal of Genetic Psychology*, 1971, **118**, 29–32. (b)

Rosenberg, B. G., & Sutton-Smith, B. *Sex and identity*. New York: Holt, Rinehart & Winston, 1972.

Schooler, C. Birth order effects: Not here, not now! *Psychological Bulletin*, 1972, **78**, 161–175.

Sutton-Smith, B. *Child Psychology*. New York: Appleton-Century-Crofts, 1973. (a)

Sutton-Smith, B. *The folkgames of children*. Austin: University of Texas Press, 1973. (b)

Sutton-Smith, B.; Roberts, J. R.; & Rosenberg, B. G. Sibling associations and role involvement. *Merrill-Palmer Quarterly*, 1964, **10**, 25–38.

Sutton-Smith, B., & Rosenberg, B. G. *The Sibling*. New York: Holt, Rinehart & Winston, 1970.

Toman, W. *Family constellation*. New York: Springer, 1971.

Whiting, J. W. M.; Kluckhohn, R.; & Anthony, A. The function of male initiation ceremonies at puberty. In E. E. Maccoby, T. Newcomb, & E. Hartley (Eds.), *Readings in social psychology*. New York: Holt, Rinehart & Winston, 1958. Pp. 61–64.

Prenatal Hormones and Postnatal Socialization in Gender Identity Differentiation[1]

JOHN MONEY

Johns Hopkins University School of Medicine

FOREWORD[2]

This is the Nebraska Symposium on Motivation. Therefore, I think it fair and appropriate for me to tell you at the outset that I don't subscribe to the doctrine of motivation! In general, and in the study and theory of sex in particular, drives, instincts, needs, or motivations are impossible concepts for me to handle empirically and operationally. For me, they belong in history's storage closet along with teleology, phlogiston, vital forces, and demoniac possessions. Of course, I am able to converse with patients and other people whose idioms they are, and in fact, I may even reciprocate their use in interviewing for a sexual history. But an idiom is not an organizing

1. Supported by USPHS Grant HD00325, and by funds from The Grant Foundation.

The publisher regrets that the schedule for this volume did not permit use of the author's preferred spelling *transexual* throughout the paper.

2. I have edited this chapter from a taped transcript of the two lectures delivered at the University of Nebraska on the occasion of the symposium. I have retained the narrative style of talking, for I have written formally on the same subject matter on other occasions, and want to have it now told as a story, informally. The storyteller's style is easier to understand and remember. There is no sacrifice of accuracy. Those who need the paraphernalia of scholarship, especially full bibliographic documentation, will find it in *Man and Woman, Boy and Girl* (Money & Ehrhardt, 1972).

principle or concept of science. And it is as an organizing principle that I reject a sexual drive, an instinct, a need, or motivation.

That is not to say, however, that I would substitute a mechanistic stimulus-response principle whereby sexual man and woman become scientistic robots—not at all. I accept as a first principle sexual behavior, like all of man's behavior, as a kinetic or dynamic system by definition. I do not need to put drive into it. Like the solar system, it goes; that is the scheme of things. My job and yours as scientists is to figure out the principles of the system's going. Here I can be a little facetious and say that we're figuring out its "go-itivity" or its "go-ationality," if you can tolerate these bastard graftings of Latin suffixes. I am being more than a little facetious here because it is, in fact, true that without Latin and Greek suffixes most of motivation theory would have had no vehicle for its existence.

Some years ago I wrote a short paper on linguistic resources and psychodynamic theory. It is fascinating to see that we are victims of language when it comes to basic principles. For example, one always has to use some other psychic force or drive to explain dreams, because you can't have a word like "dreamivity" or "dreamuance" that explains something else. Anything that is known to us by an Anglo-Saxon or Nordic root is something that has to be explained by something else which has a Latin or Greek root.

I've found it possible to make headway if I substitute for motivation the concept of *threshold*—threshold for the release or inhibition of behavior. Then I can classify the types of behavior released or inhibited, the primary types being lexical versus gestural. In another way one might say imagistic versus signalistic or, in simplest English, voice talk versus body talk. The concept of threshold is really an extraordinarily useful one and it conveys a great advantage of continuity and unity to what would otherwise be disparate and divided. Thus I—and you too—may look for threshold differences in the release or the inhibition of sexual behavior. The threshold may apply to behavior attributable to genetic programming, or to prenatal hormonal programming, or to toxic programming, or to circulating hormonal programming at puberty, or after puberty to pheromonal programming—pheromones being stimulating odors, recently under investigation for the first time in primate sexuality.

You and I may also look for differences of threshold with regard to visual image programming of erotic arousal. There is an implication for sex differences here, in that men are much more girl watchers than women are boy watchers. Men have at puberty nature's own presentation of a pornography show to them in their wet dreams and their masturbation fantasies, in a way that women are not so programmed for visual imagery. One could go on, one step further up the ladder, and say that thresholds can be studied with regard to activation or inhibition in social history programming. The top of the ladder would represent traumatic or deteriorative change in the central nervous system—change in the threshold for release or inhibition of sexual behavior. In that respect the temporal lobe of the brain is particularly important. A lesion of the temporal lobe is very likely to change sexual behavior thresholds in some way or another. But the deteriorative process could also be a matter of disease in the genitalia themselves and not simply of sexual pathways in the brain.

You see then that the concept of threshold does indeed have great value because of the great spectrum that it applies to. It helps to tie what would otherwise be a lot of loose ends together. It allows me to think developmentally or longitudinally also in terms of stages or experiences that are programmed serially, or hierarchically or cybernetically.

No longer do I need to be enslaved to such worn-out platitudes of dichotomy as nature versus nurture, the biological versus the social, the innate versus the acquired, or the physiological versus the psychological. All these dichotomies capitalize on the very ancient, pre-Platonic, pre-Biblical dichotomy of the body versus the mind, or the physical versus the spiritual. This body-mind dichotomy is now so ingrained a principle of our vernacular or folk metaphysics that it is something very difficult for us to get rid of. Yet as scientists I believe we have to find our way around it. Otherwise it spells total disaster to the development of sexual science today, and tomorrow, and in the future.

I've found at least one escape from what I call here the disaster of false dichotomies by replacing it with a hexotomy—a $2 \times 2 \times 2$

schema in which the phyletic is juxtaposed against the biographic, the imperative against the optional, and the nativistic against the cultural (Table 1).

In the cells of Table 1 you see entries that are pertinent to my topic, gender role and identity. You could take aggression, if you wanted, and fill the cells with appropriate examples. As a matter

TABLE 1

EXAMPLES OF GENDER IDENTITY/ROLE DETERMINANTS
CLASSIFIED ACCORDING TO A 2 × 2 × 2 SCHEMA

	Nativistic	Cultural
Species-shared, or PHYLETIC		
Imperative	Menstruation, gestation, lactation (women) vs. impregnation (men)	Social models for identification and complementation in gender identity differentiation
Optional	Population size, fertility rate, and sex ratio	Population birth-death ratio. Diminishing age of puberty
Individually unique, or BIOGRAPHIC		
Imperative	Chromosome anomalies, e.g., 45,X; 47,XXY; 47,XYY. Vestigial penis. Vestigial uterus. Vaginal atresia	Sex announcement and rearing as male, female, or ambiguous
Optional	Getting pregnant. Breast feeding. Anorexic amenorrhea. Castration	Gender-divergent work. Gender-divergent cosmetics and grooming. Gender-divergent child care

of fact, you can play an intellectual game with a table like this and, beginning with cells empty, fill them in according to what your topic of interest is.

You can see on the left of the table that there are some aspects of behavior with respect to gender identity that are *phyletic*, which means that they are shared by all members of our species. In fact, they may even be shared by members of other primate species too.

And there are others that are idiosyncratic or individually unique, for which I think the best word is *biographic*. Of course we are used to thinking of biography as something that happened to us after we were born, but in fact we have, each one of us, a prenatal biography, too, and it may not be phyletically shared by other members of the species. It may be unique. For example (if I take something that is nativistic rather than culturally determined, and that's individually unique and also imperative), I could say that if you have an extra Y chromosome in your cells, and you're a man, then that's a unique part of your own biography. Yet it's certainly very biological in the usual sense of that term, and it is an imperative, since you can't get rid of that extra Y chromosome under any circumstances whatsoever. I might say you have to learn to live with it.

For people with whom I've worked who have an extra Y chromosome, it is in fact very true that they have to learn to live with it, or at least with its consequences. One of the chief consequences is that it is much too easy for them to release behavior—they are very impulsive and they get into a lot of trouble that way. They are not in fact aggressive people, as you've heard in the headlines of the newspapers; they're impulsive people. They're just as likely to impulsively cry out or impulsively eat or impulsively give things away—or impulsively steal—as they are to be impulsively destructive or violent. And, in fact, they're really not very violent at all as a group.

Below the biographic-imperative-nativistic cell is the biographic-optional-nativistic cell. Here an example would be getting pregnant. Another example would be deciding to breast feed, and yet another, anorexic amenorrhea—anorexic meaning as a sequel to not eating. Finally, there is the example of castration, which could be done by yourself, if a male, or by somebody else if either a male or a female.

I'm particularly interested in the phyletically shared, imperative nativistic elements, because here one comes across some of the inescapable or imperative ascriptions of dimorphic gender behavior. Menstruation, gestation, and lactation for women are imperatives that cannot be escaped—even when they do not occur, even if they're suppressed, they still have to be reckoned with. For men it's impregnation that is the sexually dimorphic imperative. Even in a case of sterility, it has to be reckoned with as a something that should have been present.

Among the phyletically shared, optional nativistic elements is the matter of population size—for example, fertility rate and sex ratio. We heard yesterday from Dr. Rosenberg and Dr. Sutton-Smith some fascinating things about family size for which there is yet no complete story and explanation as to how the size is regulated, under the circumstances that they presented of people copying, from their own childhood experience, the image of what a family is. One doesn't know much yet about anything that regulates population size. Thus, it's an optional sort of thing.

Perhaps one of the most unexpected discoveries from reading a table like Table 1 is that some cultural determinants can be phyletically shared and imperative. We've tended to always look upon cultural things and psychological things as *only* cultural and psychological: such things are learned, and if something can be learned it can be unlearned, people assume. Well, I think that sells our science too cheaply. That kind of attitude toward so basic a phenomenon as learning does not, in fact, really apply. It is a species necessity, a species imperative, that some cultural phenomena occur if the individual is going to be able to develop. You can't develop your native language unless you have a social language model around at the right age. And so, in the matter of gender identity, you can't develop your gender identity unless you have models around at the right age. The right age for developing your gender identity is not quite from birth onwards I think, but in many instances with bright children from about 6 months onward and certainly from 18 months onward. I would say that the crucial period is from 18 months to 3 or 4 years.

I've had that dramatically illustrated for me in the last month because of the article in *Time* magazine on January 8, 1973, about the twin pair which I'm going to mention to you toward the end of today's talk, where the one child had a sex reassignment because of the total ablation of the penis by accident. This piece of news in the public media brought letters from two couples who were in distress because they had a young baby that had been born with a micropenis and they had not been given directions that fully satisfied them in their local medical centers. One couple had a baby 18 months old, just beginning to talk and use the pronouns and nouns that differentiate sex in language, and just beginning to embed the dimorphism of gender identity that is so essential and imperative to all of us, something that we seem to be totally unable to live without. This family is now in the state of extreme contentment at having resolved what seemed to be an absolutely impossible problem by having had their baby officially and surgically sex-reassigned on Monday last.

Another family, a very serious-thinking, concerned, and wise young couple, graduate students, have a baby who is $2\frac{1}{2}$ years old and has been allowed to slip through the sieve of indecision up to this point. They're going through a terrible agony about whether they should dare make the decision of sex reassignment or not. At $2\frac{1}{2}$ this little boy is completely aware of the fact that he is a little boy even though he really has no penis at all, only an empty foreskin. If the decision for reassignment is made, it is going to be necessary to do a tremendous amount of psychological work with him to help him to grow his way into the idea of the change. The only way that I think it can be done will be to present it to him, in a fairy-tale sort of way, with stories of people who are allowed to change their sex in the same way that princesses are allowed to turn into toads and otherwise transmogrify in fairy stories. One simply cannot take this youngster at $2\frac{1}{2}$, as young as that is, and impose by edict a change of sex. These two cases illustrate very nicely the idea that there are some phyletic cultural imperatives, and they are not optional in any way whatsoever.

There are also, of course, some phyletic cultural options too, one of which strikes me as most extraordinary, since nobody has been able to explain it: the fact that the age of puberty is going systematically down, down every 10 years by 4 months (Tanner, 1962). Records have been retrieved dating back to 1830, beginning with early records from Sweden and supplemented with subsequent statistics found in various countries and institutions of Europe and America. Possibly the phenomenon is culturally related to changes in food supply after the Napoleonic wars, but people have done such weird hypothesis making as in suggesting that it was related to the invention of the bicycle in the low countries of Europe, so that people got out of genetically pooled village groups and crossbred with one another—which is a nice, fanciful idea but it doesn't seem like it holds much water to me.

The whole business of population, birth, and death ratio is another one of the phyletic cultural options. Obviously, man can play around with the death ratio by having wars, or, as the Australian aborigines did, by getting rid of each other in an official feuding system, or, as the New Guinea people did, with the headhunting institution.

I can't resist the temptation to digress here and say that I was really confronted with the challenges of why the Australian aboriginal people have never proliferated on the monsoonal north coast of Australia, which (I discovered when I went there) is no desert at all but is as lush a place to live as any part of the monsoonal Philippines, Southeast Asia, or Indonesia. I can come up with only one explanation which makes perfectly good sense to me, and that is that the aborigines institutionalized the relationship of falling in love with the relationship of killing each other. Since every human death had to be avenged by the death of another, killing turned out to be a very effective method of zero population growth. In love vengeance, it works this way. You are assigned to a promise man or promise girl on a kind of cultural chess board, even before you are conceived. Yet, when you get to adolescence and young adulthood you are also supposed to have a relationship, a love relationship. The girl, who is promised to another man, is supposed to initiate it illicitly with a boy who is also promised elsewhere, and who is supposed to respond to it. There is a chance that they may be able to escape from the vengeance of the promised man, who has the right to kill them both or to get his promise girl back by killing the boy she is in love with. Though the couple may escape into the bush or onto a remote island and not be immediately discovered, vengeance can be sought even 20 years later. Usually it used to mean that if the affair was not settled peaceably by some exchange of goods, the man would be killed. That is not true today, since the European legal system is beginning to take over in the twentieth century, but the feuds still go on, and some of them have to be settled by an exchange of money. Financial settlements create a very difficult cultural problem for the aboriginal people of the north coast, in Arnhem Land, at the present time, because they do indeed have a great surplus of young men for whom there are no promise girls, since they haven't yet abolished their age-old polygamous system. Well, so much for a phyletic cultural option that relates death to sex and population growth.

Now for a consideration of the biographic imperatives that are not nativistic but cultural, yet imperative nonetheless. For the most part, one never thinks that it's an imperative, personal, and idiosyncratic piece of one's biography to have one's sex entered on the birth certificate. One doesn't think of that because it seems to be just one of those things that one never thinks about. If you have a baby born with indeterminate appearance of the sex organs, then you suddenly realize how imperative is that first announcement: "It's a boy!" "It's a girl!" It has to be definite—you can't dial the telephone and say: "We don't know what sex it is, and we're going to leave it undecided forever."

Biographically unique, culturally prescribed, and optional elements of gender difference pertain mostly to gender-dimorphic work, gender-dimorphic play, gender-dimorphic cosmetics, clothing styles, and grooming care, and gender-dimorphic differences in child care. Of all the cells on Table 1, this one is the most important for contemporary discussion with regard to liberation—the liberation, I'd like to emphasize, not only of women but of men. Men are still losing out by not yet being liberated enough.

Let me remind you, by reverting for a moment to the old terminology on which we have all been raised, that Table 1 brings to your attention the fact that biological determinants need not be innate, but they may originate culturally. Castration is a biological determinant of certain behavior that follows, yet that behavior is not necessarily innate. Also, biological determinants may be individually unique. They don't need to be species-shared. They may be optional instead of imperative. By contrast, psychological determinants, contrary to our common assumptions, may be innate; they may originate in heredity or in hormonal chemistries. They may be imperative and not optional. A resolution of these apparent paradoxes is illustrated in Figure 1.

Prenatal and Postnatal Components of Gender Identity Differentiation

The purpose of Figure 1 is to show the sequential and cumulative components of gender identity differentiation. At the outset, when

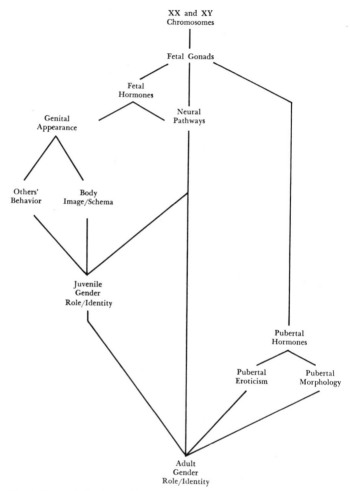

FIG. 1. Sequential and cumulative components of gender identity differentiation.

the sperm joins the egg, chromosomal sex is determined. Though typically XX for the female and XY for the male, chromosomal sex may be atypical, as when one X is missing in a morphologic female (45,X, Turner's syndrome) or when there is a supernumerary X (47,XXY, Klinefelter's syndrome) or Y (47,XYY syndrome) in a morphologic male.

Contrary to what a lot of, shall I say, our folkloristic feel of things leads us to believe, the chromosomes are tremendously unimportant as direct determinants of the program of gender identity differentiation after their little moment of glory in controlling the future by programming the differentiation of the gonads. From then on, the program becomes the responsibility of the gonads and their hormones. One doesn't hear from the X and Y chromosomes directly again, ever. That's with respect to gender identity itself. I'll allow a peripheral modification, should you press me very hard with regard to the sex chromosomes. For example, a man with an extra X chromosome in every cell is typically relatively apathetic sexually. His cells do not take up and utilize male hormones very well in puberty and adulthood. In addition, he possibly is at much higher risk for the development of some form of behavior disability. Apart from such special modifications, the general rule does hold that chromosomal genetics themselves are not particularly important in the differentiation of gender identity after what I called their brief moment of glory.

To get the correct image in your mind, think of runners in a relay race. Each one of the entries on Figure 1 then becomes a runner carrying the program and handing it over to the next runner, who will carry it on to the next, and so on. As you see, there's a certain amount of crossover and joining, rather than simply running in parallel streams. The fetal gonads have a very brief time in which they are the responsible runners. A most important thing then happens, namely, hormones from the fetal testes appear. The basic rule here, of which you will hear more as I go on in my talk, is this: add some male factor to get a male; do nothing and get a female. To say it in an easy way to remember, God created Eve first and then added something to get Adam. You have to revise the story of Genesis, which is very nice for the proponents of the women's liberation movement. Mary Jane Sherfey, in her new book (1972), makes a great deal of this particular new reversal of doctrine based on the study of embryonic differentiation. However, male chauvinistic pigs can hit right back at her with the same ammunition and say, "Aha, but men are so much better because they have something added." So you're right back where you started anyway!

The fetal testicular hormones with their additive principal to differentiate a male do two things. One is that they program what the external sex organs will look like—whether the little tubercle will develop into a penis by protruding outward or whether it will stay small, shrink back, and develop into a clitoris, for example. But even more important, so far as new knowledge is concerned, fetal gonadal hormones also have an influence on neural pathways in the brain. If I had said that even as recently as 10 years ago, people would be wanting to put me away. To imagine that fetal gonadal hormones could have anything to do with brain pathways! Yet they shouldn't have been so ready to discredit such an idea, since for many decades now it's been known that if you don't have enough thyroid hormone as a fetus, you will not develop enough cortical cells and you will be mentally retarded, even severely retarded, and will be diagnosed as a cretin.

The whole idea that sex hormones will be able to influence the central nervous system is one that is only beginning to be appreciated and to be understood, as a result of experimental studies on animals which began around the late 1950s. I could spend the entire remainder of my time talking about fetal hormones and their influence on brain pathways, but I do not propose to do that. I propose simply to make this statement: it is a new field of inquiry, and there's a great reservoir of information from animal studies which clearly establishes without any shadow of a doubt that fetal gonadal hormones do influence pathways in the central nervous system. Particularly they influence pathways in the region of the hypothalamus in connection with the pituitary and in connection with the newly discovered releasing hormones that are released themselves from cells in the hypothalamus. Releasing hormones influence the pituitary gland in its hormonal functioning. Now I'll leave the pituitary and its hypothalamic control by saying that for those who are particularly interested, it's rather comprehensively summarized in two chapters in the book *Man and Woman, Boy and Girl*, chapters 4 and 5 (Money & Ehrhardt, 1972).

The matter of the influence of sex hormone on neural pathways I will not totally leave, for I'm going to have something more to say about the behavioral effects of androgen, the male sex hormone, in connection with the concept of *tomboyism*, with illustrations of genetic female patients who got an excess amount of male hormone in fetal life. They ended up with tomboyish behavior regardless of whether they were raised up as boys or girls.

Genital appearance, on the left of Figure 1, bifurcates in its influence as it transmits the program onward. It does so by influencing the behavior of others, first of all with that headline announcement "It's a boy," or "It's a girl," which, although only four words, actually influences billions of pieces of behavior of several thousands of people toward that individual throughout life—not without continued reinforcement, since the dimorphic appearance of the sex organs normally never changes, and so reiterates the message. Genital appearance reiterates the message also to the growing child himself or herself when, after the early period of infancy, the child is able to get the image of the sex organ in through the eyes as well as through the touch and feel. A child is then able to make comparisons with other people who use the same gender-differentiating nouns and pronouns as does the child himself or herself. In brief, the appearance of the sex organs has a self-influence by way of the body image or the body schema.

Put all of those influences together—the behavior of others, the body schema, and neural pathways. Then you have developing the juvenile gender identity which I have already identified as beginning to be on display, so to speak, somewhere between the age of 18 months and a year later, and then continuing from there on. The juvenile gender identity may differentiate as conforming to the stereotype of male or female or it may be ambiguous. Usually it is not ambiguous, of course, although cases of ambiguity are those that one needs to study more, in order to learn more about differentiation according to the norms.

The juvenile gender identity finally develops into the adult gender role or identity; I prefer to say both together—gender identity/role. The sex hormones from the gonads awakening at puberty feed in their new influence which—and this is obvious to everyone—exerts itself first by changing the body shape into that of an adolescent girl or an adolescent boy. They also have a very important influence that still needs a lot more investigation to be understood in its entirety—an influence on the subjective experience of eroticism. The sex hormones at puberty do not determine anything at all about the gender identity as masculine or feminine;

they simply activate what is already there by changing the threshold for the release of sexual behavior and the subjective feeling of eroticism. To illustrate this point: if a person is destined to live under the handicap of being a sadist, let's say, and to be erotically arousable by imagery only if it includes some sadistic element in it, the laying down of the sadistic tendency will have already been accomplished in childhood. It will not be a result of the effects of the pubertal hormones.

Another example, which is not so self-evident and creates a lot of controversy at the present time, is the phenomenon of homosexuality. There are many who would like to believe that homosexual people—one should talk about them mostly as bisexual people—are somehow hormonally different from so-called normal people. Well, in actual fact, there is no conclusive evidence, in spite of two or three recent reports in the medical literature to the contrary, that homosexual people in general are different in the quantities or ratios of sex hormones circulating in the bloodstream. Even in the few who may be hormonally different, it cannot be said that hormonal factors are directly responsible for homosexuality of gender orientation. The problems that issue in ambiguous gender identity or bisexual gender identity, or even in the unambiguous reversal of the expected direction of gender identity into complete homosexuality or complete lesbianism, are all established during the period of juvenile gender identity differentiation. At the time of puberty, they simply come into fruition.

Here is a comment about the conjunction of role/identity or identity/role. I would like only one word. When I originally used the words *gender role* for the first paper that I published on the psychology of hermaphroditism (Money, Hampson, & Hampson, 1955), I defined it as follows: "We mean all those things that a person says or does to disclose himself or herself as having the status of boy or man, girl or woman, respectively. It includes, but is not restricted to, sexuality in the sense of eroticism. Gender role is appraised in relation to the following: general mannerisms, deportment and demeanor; play preferences and recreational interests; spontaneous topics of talk in unprompted conversation and casual comment; content of dreams, daydreams, and fantasies; replies to oblique inquiries and projective tests; evidence of erotic practices and, finally, the person's own replies to direct inquiry." It doesn't mean just the way a person conforms or fails to conform to a role formulated by others or handed down by society. The ideal definition of *role* would be one that comprises the subjective part of it that a person self-reports and the objective part of it which other people observe. With both parts together being a unity, one would escape the mind-body problem. But our society cannot escape thinking in terms of mind and body. So, no sooner was gender role accepted as the useful concept it is—and it was accepted with great rapidity—than also the term *gender identity* was put alongside it. Once again one had the split between mind and body, or body and mind. The best way to overcome that split at the present time, I think, is simply to talk about role/identity and try to make it a single unity.

ADRENOGENITAL SYNDROME: MATCHED PAIRS

Now I come to some clinical material. I'm dealing here with a particular subspecialty of hermaphroditism, namely, the female hermaphrodite with the adrenogenital syndrome. A female hermaphrodite is one with ambiguous or contradictory sex organs externally, and with two ovaries internally and a uterus and fallopian tubes. In the adrenogenital syndrome, the ambiguity is produced by an abnormal functioning of the fetal adrenocortical glands, that abnormality itself being genetically recessively determined. The mechanism of the error is that the fetus itself makes too much of—I'll say it in an easy way to remember—a funky hormone. Instead of making the cortisol that it is supposed to be programmed to make, it releases an unfinished synthesis of cortisol which turns out to be a male sex hormone in biological action. The excessive flood of male hormone in the bloodstream turns Eve into Adam, if you want the allegorical way to remember it.

Here you have a picture (Figure 2) of two genetic females with two ovaries and a uterus and fallopian tubes, internally, and with a penis and a fused empty scrotum, externally. Metaphorically, you are in the Land of the Midnight Sun, with your concept of the eternal verity of day and night destroyed. This picture is put here to disturb and destroy your concept of the eternal verity of male and female. Later there are pictures that show you a genetic male with

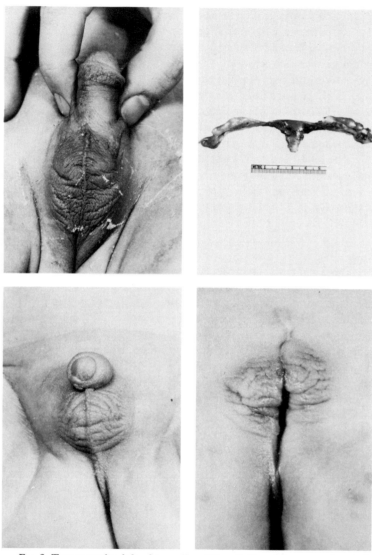

Fig. 2. Two examples, left, of masculine differentiation of the external genitals in genetic and gonadal females with the adrenogenital syndrome. Top right, the internal female organs were removed as the child had been assigned and reared as a boy. Bottom right, the child was diagnosed neonatally, reannounced as a girl, and surgically corrected, with the vaginal orifice exteriorized.

236

an XY chromosome pattern and a perfectly normal set of female external genitalia—which also takes you into the Land of the Midnight Sun of sex.

The other point about Figure 2 is that one of the babies remained undiagnosed at the time of birth and so was reared as a boy. The other one was diagnosed and reared as a girl. She had nearly died through a complication occurring in some cases of the adrenogenital syndrome, namely, lack of ability to retain salt in the bloodstream. She became dehydrated, which led to the complete diagnosis with regard to sexual status. The decision was made to institute corrective hormonal therapy with cortisone, reannounce the sex, and feminize the external sex organs surgically in order to allow the baby to grow up with the option of having her own pregnancy, if life would so ordain. This baby you are going to hear more of, shortly.

Figure 3 demonstrates embryologically how it's possible for nature to allow a genetic female with two ovaries to have a penis. The theme here is that the anlagen of the sex organs are the same for the male and female. The tubercle at the top can turn into the glans of the penis or the glans of the clitoris. The shaft behind it can elongate and become the spongy tissue of the corpora cavernosa of the penis or remain small as the main body of the clitoris. The two strips of skin underneath the tubercle, the urethrolabial folds, can wrap themselves around the protruding penis and fuse, as can be seen on the underside of any penis, to make the urethral tube of the penis; or else they can stay separated to form the labia minora and the hood of the clitoris. The external labioscrotal swellings can stay separated to become the labia majora of the female; or they also can fuse together to make the sac of the scrotum. When a baby is born at the halfway or unfinished stage, as you see at the center of Figure 3, you have no chance of deciding what the internal organs will prove to be, nor the genetic sex, by inspection of the external organs alone. The appearance may be exactly the same in a genetic male or a genetic female when the sex organs are incompletely differentiated.

Figure 4 shows the surgically reconstructed genitals of the baby in the lower half of Figure 2. Here the child is 8 years of age. There is no clitoris or clitoral structure left, because it had turned into a penis which needed to be removed. The opening of the vagina was

EXTERNAL GENITAL DIFFERENTIATION IN THE HUMAN FETUS

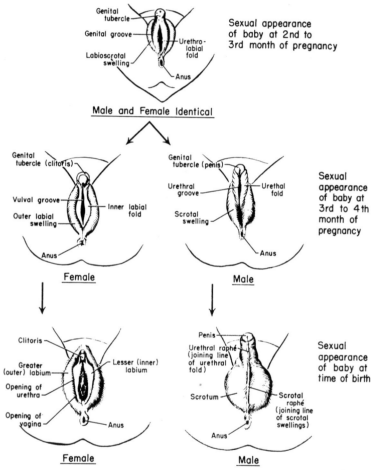

Fig. 3. The external sex organs of male and female differentiate from the same anlagen and cannot be distinguished if a baby is born with differentiation not finished.

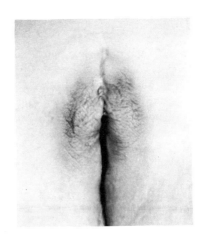

FIG. 4. Genitalia of the baby in the lower half of Figure 2, at the age of 8 years.

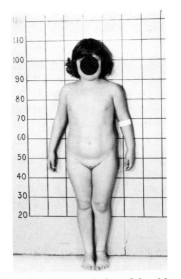

FIG. 5. Frontal view of the girl represented in Figure 4, showing femininity of genital appearance, age 8.

FIG. 6. The same girl as in Figure 5, age 8. Her choice of clothing happens to match her tomboyism, on this occasion.

freed from its internal position near the neck of the bladder and exteriorized. As one studies older patients, women who are already embarked on their sex lives after a history of this kind of surgery, one learns that they do not lose the capacity for sexual feeling and pleasure and they do not lose the capacity for sexual climax either. Nature is so intent on associating good feelings with the reproduction of the species that she is able to allow ablation of large amounts of genital tissue without destroying the good feeling and the feeling of climax.

Figure 5 shows that you really have to have a look as in a gynecologist's examination before you can see that this little girl is genetically atypical. She can go in the pool naked; she can go in the tub at home, and nobody needs to pay any particular attention to her genital configuration and make her feel different by reason of their responses. In Figure 6, you see her some years ago in her brand new pantsuit for her annual checkup at the hospital. It's not exactly an accident that she is wearing the pantsuit, because she was allowed to help choose her clothes. It was highly fashionable for her to have it; but it does happen to underline the fact that she is, like other prenatally androgenized girls, a tomboy in her behavior.

I'll have more to say about tomboyism. In the meantime, Figure 7 shows a parallel case, reared as a boy. My plan is to present pairs, matched pairs of hermaphroditic children, the one raised as a girl and the other raised as a boy, but both having the same identical diagnosis. The boy of Figure 7 first came to my attention at the age of 13. He was born with an almost perfect penis—there had been no surgery and no need for it (Figure 8). The urethral opening was only just a millimeter or two displaced from where you would expect, and the foreskin is not quite wrapped around at the very tip, but he had no problems urinating in the standing position. Figure 9 shows you this boy at age 13 looking like a boy except for breast feminization. Thereby hangs a very important tale which, in association with Figure 10, demonstrates how foolish it was to think of this person as a girl. In infancy, this child was regarded as a boy with undescended testes. The diagnosis of adrenogenital syndrome in a genetic female was not established until age 12. Earlier, beginning with pubic hair at age 3, he had become pubertally masculinized; puberty is always early and always masculinizing in

 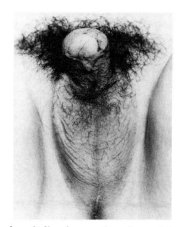

FIGS. 7 and 8. Two views of the unaltered genitalia of a genetic and gonadal female with the adrenogenital syndrome, age 13. No surgery was required, as the child was assigned at birth as a boy and has remained living as one.

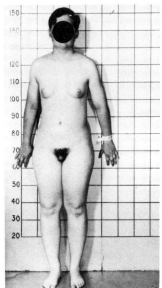 

FIG. 9. Frontal appearance at age 13 of the case represented in Figures 7 and 8. The breasts grew as a result of treatment inappropriate for a boy, and were surgically removed, to his great satisfaction.

FIG. 10. The same boy as in Figure 9, aged 13. He forms a matched pair with the girl of Figure 6, concordant for diagnosis, but discordant for gender identity and role.

241

the hormonally untreated adrenogenital syndrome, regardless of whether the genetic sex is male or female. The local physician decided to institute the standard therapy for children with the adrenogenital syndrome, giving cortisone to correct the masculinizing hormonal malfunction of the adrenal cortices. In a genetic female, this treatment eventually releases the ovaries to function normally, and so to induce somatic feminization and the onset of menstruation. The psychologically uninformed might assume that hormonal feminization of the body would, ipso facto, be paralleled by hormonal feminization of the mind. There are those in biology and medicine who metaphorically believe in the tablets of the stones—cod and stones being the old terms for scrotum and testicles —and believe that the testicles or ovaries determine everything about gender identity. Not so! This boy's gender identity as a boy was so firmly implanted by age 13 that nothing could uproot it. He wanted only one thing of the medical profession—that it rid him of the breasts he hated so much, and then never bother him again.

His parents were respectful of medical opinion and they tried to accept the advice that, because their son had ovaries, he should be a girl. But they couldn't make any sense out of it. They could not see any correspondence in behavior between their son and their other child, his older sister. The mother told me that her decision finally came when she found a love letter that the boy had written to his girl friend. At that point, it didn't make any sense to her to make him live as a girl, if he was going to be falling in love with a girl. There are times when common sense prevails over professional sense, and so these people did seek a second consultation. At Johns Hopkins it was decided, on the basis of experience accumulated in cases like this, that the child should indeed be allowed to live as a boy and given appropriate surgical and hormonal therapy, including ovariectomy and hysterectomy. If he had been changed by force to live as a girl, the only advantage he could have gotten from it would have been to be able to procreate as a female; but if you're going to be a total lesbian you don't procreate anyway!

Unchanged, he will be able to avoid a major psychological disruption of his life, which he's very happy about. He will not be required to try to live something which to him is a lie. He will be able to live a normal sexual life as a man. He will have only one disability, which is shared by many other males in our society, namely, that he will have his fatherhood by adoption or by recourse to the sperm bank. Now in mid-teenage, he has already discovered that his penis performs adequately in sexual intercourse and that his romantic attractions are exclusively toward girls. His interests, pastimes, and pursuits are traditionally masculine. Through a local youth-career organization, he is well on his way to establishing himself as an independent cattle rancher.

In this first pair of cases, by a rare chance the boy had a history of being allowed to commence a feminizing puberty and develop breasts. The girl will soon do the same, in keeping with her feminine, albeit tomboyish, mentality. The boy's mentality remained masculine. His case thus demonstrates and emphasizes the point that even when the hormones of puberty are completely reversed, as in this boy, to make his breasts grow and his periods nearly begin, there is no change whatsoever in the gender identity to correspond with the physiological changes in endocrine functioning.

Now I have two more cases (Figure 11) that show the story in reverse, in that the girl as well as the boy grew up hormonally untreated and somatically masculinized. At birth the external sex organs had the hermaphroditic, ambiguous appearance of a clitorine penis or a penile clitoris, of which a quite typical example is shown in Figure 12. This picture illustrates to you the commonest appearance of hermaphroditism when it comes into the clinic for the newborn, irrespective of genetic sex. It's really quite rare to see the complete fusion that provides a penis on the genetic female, as in the two preceding cases.

At birth the two patients of Figure 11 had unfinished sex organs resembling those of Figure 12. Both have a diagnosis of genetic female with the adrenogenital syndrome. Both grew up all during childhood with masculinizing hormones, as they were born before corrective therapy with cortisone was discovered in 1950. In this case it was the one living as a girl who got the wrong body shape. They're both masculinized, let me remind you at the cost of being repetitive, because the adrenogenital syndrome is one in which the cortices of the adrenal glands release a masculinizing hormone instead of their proper product, which is cortisol. At the time of

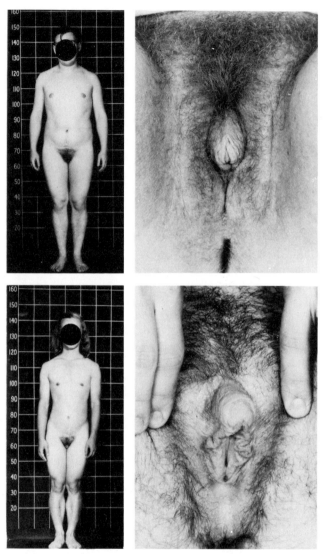

Fig. 11. A matched pair of genetic and gonadal females, born hermaphroditic with the untreated adrenogenital syndrome, concordant for diagnosis, but discordant for gender identity and role. In this example, the remarkable feature is the untreated hormonal virilization. Virilization of the girl (lower), contrasts with the feminization of the boy of Figure 9; in both instances the incongruous hormonal sex failed to alter the basic gender identity.

photography both were young, about 12, and, as you see, very well masculinized for 12-year-olds, by reason of the fact that their adrenal cortical glands continued to malfunction postnatally as they had prenatally, allowing the onset of masculinizing puberty very early. The pubic hair can begin to show as early as age 3, and a few strands even earlier. The timing as well as the dimorphism of puberty is wrong.

The didactic point of Figure 11 is, once again, that the differentiation of the gender identity, the self-feeling, the self-conviction, and the behavior—all of the elements of gender role—in these children swung in the direction of the sex of their assignment and rearing. Yet once again, as with the other two people of Figures 6 and 10, there was a strong element of tomboyism. The boy of Figure 10 had as his favorite activity rough-riding on motorcycles out in the desert and going in the mountains fishing and hunting with his dad. He had a good and close relationship with his dad. The boy of Figure 11 gave conclusive evidence of his gender identity by getting married; and when after some years the marriage didn't work, presumably because of the difficulty of the sexual relationship, he didn't give up in despair but got married again. The girl of Figure 11 went through quite a difficult period of escaping from the years of feeling a freak. A history of extraordinarily neurotic parents also was of no help. It took her until her late twenties to build up self-confidence enough as a woman to get married, which she had long wanted to do. Until then she used to say that her standards were so high that she couldn't find a boyfriend to match them. But in fact, she was scared. It took me a long time to find out what she and other people like her were scared about, even though they looked very attractive in physical appearance by the time their treatment had been completed. What prevents them from developing a romantic life seems to be that, in an almost magical way, they are afraid that their first boyfriend, married or not, with whom they get into bed for a complete sexual relationship will be able to read the secret of their body image—not the secret of their body, but the secret of their body image. It requires a tremendous amount of courage to consummate the first experience of exposing oneself naked, in toto. Then almost overnight the awful hangup melts

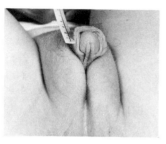

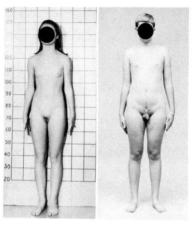

Fig. 12. This unfinished sex organ could be the penile clitoris of a genetic female or the clitorine penis of a genetic male. Actually it is the former. The case is one of the untreated, female, hermaphroditic adrenogenital syndrome. Note the premature appearance of pubic hair at age 18 months, due to lack of regulatory cortisone therapy. There is one external urogenital opening hidden from view, which subdivides into urethra and vagina internally.

Fig. 13. Another matched pair of genetic and gonadal females, born hermaphroditic with the adrenogenital syndrome, concordant for diagnosis, but discordant for gender identity and role. In this example, the special feature is that each was thought to be a boy at birth but became discordant for assigned sex and surgical treatment program owing to discordant diagnostic histories. Both had their childhood growth correctly regulated by means of cortisone therapy. Pubertal hormonal development was therapeutically controlled to be concordant with gender identity. The boy had prosthetic testes implanted.

Fig. 14. Genetic female monkey with the external appearance of a normal male due to experimental injection of the pregnant mother with male sex hormone. The internal organs are female. The behavior is tomboyish. (Photo courtesy of Robert Goy and Charles Phoenix.)

246

away and they are able to get on with the regular business of living, which is what happened with this young woman too.

The didactic point of Figure 11, to reiterate, is that the girl's female gender identity was able to survive so extraordinary a degree of the disfigurement of masculinization. The next pair of cases (Figure 13) illustrates something that's a little closer to the ideal in the way of case management in that both children were born just around 1950, and both got the developmental benefits of cortisone treatment to suppress the abnormal functioning of the adrenal glands. The one living as a boy was already $3\frac{1}{2}$ years old when he came to the hospital for the first time and had undergone three operations elsewhere by a urologist who had simply assumed the case to be one of undescended testicles in a male with an unfinished hypospadiac penis. The operations failed because the urine would back up into the feminine structures internally and there create infections. That led to the final discovery of what the complete diagnosis was.

This boy at the time, then $3\frac{1}{2}$ years old, was as terror stricken as any child I have ever seen. In the hospital he would repeatedly say, "Choo-choo train, mommy, go home." He also had a story about how the nurses were going to cut off his wee-wee and that he had a little sister, Kathy, and that the nurses had already cut off her wee-wee and had thrown it away, but his big brother in the Air Force was going to bring him a big, new wee-wee. I think you scarcely need more in order to arrive at the conclusion that it would have been malpractice to cut off his wee-wee and throw it away. He was allowed to continue living as the boy that he believed himself to be. He did not get feminization at puberty because his internal organs had been surgically removed and there were no ovaries there to secrete female hormones. His own adrenal cortices would have masculinized him, had he been taken off cortisone therapy. However, the treatment of choice was to continue cortisone and add male-hormone therapy with an injection once a month of long-acting testosterone enanthate. Artificial testes were surgically implanted in the repaired scrotum.

Both children of this matched pair had been born with equally large hypertrophy of the clitoris. Each was mistaken for a boy at birth. In the case of the girl, the diagnosis of adrenogenital syndrome in a genetic female was established at 2 months of age after emergency hospitalization for salt-losing. The baby's sex was then reannounced as female. Cortisone therapy was subsequently maintained continuously. Masculinization was prevented, and at teenage, puberty was normally feminizing, except for delay in the onset of menstruation until age 20.

The boy had very severe family problems which I can epitomize by saying that his chronically ill father was tormented by his mother when she got in a rage with him; her method of tormenting him was to say that he was a weakling because he tolerated her and this child when he knew perfectly well that this one of the children was not his own, and that she had illegitimately conceived him. The boy survived that kind of morale destroying environment and managed to establish himself as a boy, even to the extent of being a bit of a hoodlum. He found a degree of self-esteem in being accepted by kids who were themselves social rebels. He did not himself get into any serious trouble. He has developed a masculine appearance, as expected on the basis of the endocrine therapy he receives.

TOMBOYISM

List 1 gives the variables of tomboyism as it is all but universally encountered in children with a history of prenatal androgenization, as in the adrenogenital syndrome.

List 1: Variables of Tomboyism

1. Kinetic energy expenditure
2. Dominance assertion
3. Toy and sports preferences
4. Preferred styles in clothes, cosmetics, and grooming
5. Parentalism in play
6. Career ambition
7. Body image
8. Arousal by visual and narrative erotic imagery

I got some lead as to what the basic elements of tomboyism might be from the studies of hermaphroditic female monkeys that were experimentally produced at the Oregon Regional Primate Center by Goy, Phoenix, and others working there. One reads reports from them of rough-and-tumble play in these female monkeys that were androgenized and given a penis before they were born. The equivalent of rough-and-tumble play in human beings is a great enthusiasm for outdoor, athletic energy expenditure. It's not just cavorting around on a bicycle or climbing trees. It's also getting into the organized, group-competitive sports of childhood, so that even those children who are growing up as girls like to be accepted by the local football group on the neighborhood lot, or the baseball group, or the basketball group. They like the competitiveness of it. But a fascinating thing emerges here with regard to tomboy girls; they don't really assert their dominance for a high place in the dominance hierarchy against boys to the point where boys won't tolerate it. After all, they do have a girl's name, even if they are wearing blue jeans. They're perfectly clearly girls, not boys. They seem somehow to estimate that they had better not, if they are to be accepted in a boys' group, push their luck too far by trying to take over the domain of leadership of the group.

Tomboyish play in childhood favors toys that do something or fit in with the active games of childhood—guns for cops-and-robbers or cowboys-and-Indians, for instance, and wheeled carts and vehicles. These are the toys conventionally designed for boys.

I have a digressive reminiscence here. Among the aboriginal people of Arnhem Land on Australia's north coast, I visited the children of the nursery school. It was at the time of the morning when the 4-year-olds had the choice of which corner they would go to, to choose playthings for a 15-minute play period. A bunch of exuberant little boys headed for the dolls' corner, each one grabbing a doll carriage. The girls who headed for that corner gathered together a blanket, dolls, and food utensils. They made a nest for the doll babies, gave them food, put them to sleep, and generally did their maternal thing. The boys jammed dolls helter-skelter into their carriages and cavorted around, using them as cars and trucks. No effeminate boys, these!

Clothing preference runs along with recreational and play preference in tomboyish girls. Shirts, shorts, blue jeans, and plain utilitarian styles are preferred over dresses and ornamentation. The same applies to haircuts and jewelry. Perfume is acceptable—I'm not at all sure what to make of that. There's no aversion to getting dressed up in the conventional feminine way for special occasions like birthday parties, going to church, or going to visit grandmother. A tomboyish girl is not like a transvestite child who has an obsessive and abiding hatred of the clothes she's supposed to be dressed in. For the tomboy it's a matter of preference, not of obsession.

Maternalism is the next item. I prefer to speak of parentalism as practiced by girls, for parentalism is seen in boys too. I tend to think of parentalism as being the obverse of kinetic energy expenditure and dominance assertion. Children with a history of the adrenogenital syndrome, those reared as girls as well as those reared as boys, really don't have any interest in dolls and playing with dolls. One hears from the mothers that dolls as birthday or Christmas gifts get put on the shelf or in the closet, and there they stay. The following conversation with the girl of Figure 6 was transcribed from her interview on play:

YOU HAVEN'T MENTIONED ANYTHING ABOUT PLAYING WITH DOLLS. Well, sometime in the summer when we get our new room fixed up I think I'm going to get a different doll—something like a smaller one. My mom won't let me get a smaller one yet. Mine was too big, so I gave it to my sister, because I don't like big dolls. I like little dolls. Big ones are too big to carry around and stuff. I like little ones better. SOME GIRLS ARE CRAZY ABOUT PLAYING DOLLS AND PLAYING MOTHER. Yeah, sometimes me and Cindy do that too. HOW DO YOU PLAY THAT? Well, up at Cindy's—she had a play crib and stuff, and she had a little tractor, and I would ride it, and go out and mow the lawn and stuff. And she'd stay in the house and cook and stuff on her play stove that she has. WERE YOU PLAYING THE FATHER OR THE BROTHER OR WHAT? I'd play the father and she plays the mother. DO YOU SOMETIMES PLAY THE MOTHER AND LET HER PLAY THE FATHER? Yeah. WHICH DO YOU LIKE TO PLAY BEST? I don't know. WHICH DOES SHE LIKE TO PLAY BEST? I guess the mother. I don't know which one she does.

Work—a career other than housewife—is important in the ambitions and play rehearsals of adrenogenital children. The girls are all quite dedicated to an extradomestic career, not because they rule out the possibility of romance and marriage, but because they would like eventually to have both a job and a husband. If pushed to choose, I think they would for the most part give priority to the extradomestic rather than the domestic career. They are almost without exception high achievers in school. In spite of the negative implications of persistent medical supervision and daily medication, and in some instances in spite of even the pressures of a broken home or divorce, they manage to maintain a high level of accomplishment. Usually the school record is in keeping with career ambition.

As teenage progresses, achievement and career tend to take first place over romance, dating, and boyfriends. Adrenogenital girls are not particularly different from their brothers with the same diagnosis, in their relative lateness in reaching the romantic age, and in having their first experience of falling in love. The girls, as already mentioned, are also about one year late in getting their first menstrual period and may be several years late. Thus, I am willing to entertain the hypothesis that the early flood of androgens in the bloodstream before birth may do something to the biological clock of falling in love. This clock undoubtedly has its locus in pathways of the brain, probably in the old cortex, the limbic system. There are those who think that to be scientific about falling in love is a joke. In fact, it is necessary for scientists to take the phenomenon seriously and to do something about studying it. The opportunity for scientific study expands if falling in love is recognized as a form of pair bonding.

The establishment of pair bonding can be studied in animals. Did you know that chimpanzees and gorillas show a form of falling in love and have favorite partners? Among monkeys also, as you may learn from people who work in primate labs, a female may fall in love with a male keeper, establishing a permanent pair bond to the exclusion of any male monkey.

Frank Beach once told me a story about pair bonding in the beagle dog. Years ago he did an experiment in which he tethered males far apart in an open field and allowed a free-ranging bitch in heat to pick the partner of her choice. It serendipitously occurred to him 7 years later to repeat the experiment, the animals meanwhile not having had contact with one another, to see what happened to partner choice. Lo and behold, the females directed their attention to the same partner, even after 7 years. That's pair bonding for you!

In human beings, falling in love is related to, but not perfectly correlated with, hormonal puberty. I have followed boys with somatically precocious puberty who were fully developed-looking by the age of 8 or 9, and the earliest I have seen the genuine experience of a love affair was age 12. Apparently there is a dyssynchrony between the biological clocks of somatic puberty and of falling in love.

The entry *body image* in List 1 is a reminder of the fact that tomboyish girls typically have a feminine body image, as represented by the sex of first choice in the Draw-A-Person test. If the tomboyish girl was born with ambiguous, hermaphroditic external genitalia, then to guarantee femininity of body image, corrective feminizing surgery should be effected as soon after birth as possible. In those cases of a genetic female assigned, reared, and surgically corrected as a male, the body image differentiates as male.

I want to be cautious and tentative about the final entry of List 1, visual and narrative erotic imagery. I think there is a difference in the function of the visual and narrative erotic image in the typical male as compared with the typical female. As already mentioned, the boy at puberty gets confronted with the sexual imagery of a wet dream in a way that a girl doesn't. Kinsey's conclusion appears still to hold, namely, that women have their first truly erotic dreams with orgasm not in puberty, when boys have theirs, but much later in life. I think that tomboyish adrenogenital girls, once they reach the romantic stage, are more responsive to the visual and narrative erotic image with respect to sexual arousal than a random sample of women would be. However, I'm leaving that as an optional rather than a dogmatic statement at the present time.

I have a somewhat speculative point to add about IQ, relative to career ambition and achievement in children exposed to a prenatal excess of steroidal hormone, androgen included. Such children, it appears, tend to have a higher IQ than would otherwise be expected (Money, 1971). This finding in the adrenogenital syndrome is reinforced by a similar finding in a group of 10 girls born with hermaphroditic sex organs because their mothers were given a synthetic progestinic hormone—a pregnancy hormone—to prevent threatened miscarriage. Six of these 10 girls turned out to have an IQ above 130, a finding difficult to attribute to sampling bias or chance alone. The most likely explanation is that the hormone had an IQ-elevating effect. I make this mention specifically because a member of the audience, Miss June Reinisch, is planning a confirmatory study. She has access to a suitably large sample of subjects and her research, when it is completed, will let us know for sure, I think, whether prenatal steroidal hormones have some beneficial effect on IQ or not.

Figure 14 is a reminder that tomboyism has its counterpart in the rhesus monkey in which hermaphroditic daughters can be produced experimentally by injecting the pregnant mother with testosterone, thereby masculinizing the genetic female fetus. The monkey thus provides an experimental model for the study of prenatal hormonal influences on subsequent behavior, as for example in the increased frequency of rough-and-tumble play in the juvenile behavior of hermaphroditized females.

AMBIVALENCE AND REASSIGNMENT

With the next group of illustrations, I want to move on and show you yet two more examples of the adrenogenital syndrome in a genetic female—two people who decided to change their sexual status at the age of 11. The one on the left in Figure 15 was in the process of changing to live as a girl and was developing breasts under the influence of cortisone therapy prior to undergoing feminizing surgical repair of the genitalia. The one on the right, who had lived hormonally untreated, had just had his hair cut to live as a boy.

There is a long story here which I shall abbreviate by saying simply that the common factor in each child's life—one that I have learned to be attentive to in any child requesting sex reassignment— was that the sex of original assignment was never clearly and unequivocally settled. The parents were allowed to go home with their new infant, insecure in their knowledge of the child's sex and uncertain whether or not it might eventually need to be changed. For example, the child on the right of Figure 15 was sent home—

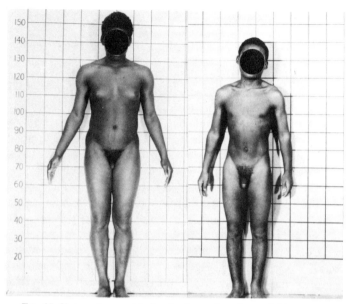

FIG. 15. Yet another matched pair of genetic and gonadal females, born hermaphroditic with the adrenogenital syndrome, concordant for diagnosis but discordant for biographic history and reassigned sex at age 12. The reassignment was boy-to-girl, left, and girl-to-boy, right. Both reassignments were self-initiated. The breasts on the girl are the result of 3 months of hormonal therapy on cortisone, prior to feminizing genital surgery. In both cases there was a history of ambiguity in the sex of assignment and rearing.

FIG. 16. Preoperative appearance of the external genitalia of the girl in Figure 15, left.

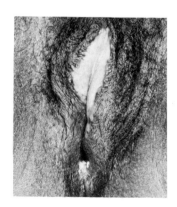

FIG. 17. Postoperative appearance of the genitalia of Figure 16.

254

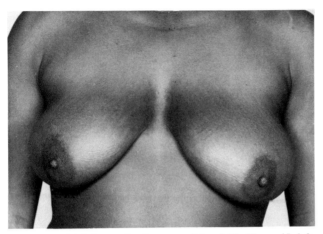

Fig. 18. Adult breast development of the girl in Figure 15, left, after several years of corrective cortisone therapy.

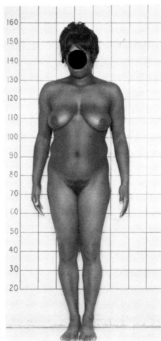

Fig. 19. Frontal view at age 24 of the girl in Figure 15, left.

255

remarkably enough, from one of the nation's major research centers —ostensibly as a girl, but with a birth certificate that still said Jimmy and with a huge sex organ that looked like a penis. No wonder that the barely literate parents wondered whether anyone in the medical profession really knew what they were doing.

It is, when you think of it, quite sensible and logical for a child who has differentiated an ambiguous gender identity to come up with the hypothesis that the only way to straighten things out is to try the other way—the way of the other sex. There are only three alternatives. One is to stay ambiguous and confused, belonging to neither sex. One is to try to be a boy (or girl); and the third is to try the other option, to see if that makes life better. In both of the present instances, the children have indeed, after 14 and 8 years, respectively, found that life has been much better for them.

The next illustrations will show you what can be effected, Pygmalion-like, with hormonal and surgical intervention. Figure 16 shows the preoperative appearance of the external genitalia of the patient who elected to change to live as a girl. There is an extremely enlarged clitoral-looking organ and no external opening of the vagina. The opening of the vagina is internal, near the neck of the bladder. Figure 17 shows the postoperative appearance of the genitalia many years later, at which time the patient was a married woman with a history of having no difficulty in coitus and in achieving climax. In Figure 18, you see the end product of breast growth after the girl had been on therapy with cortisone to allow her own ovaries to come into action, following the changeover from living as a boy. The overall appearance of the adult body form is seen in Figure 19. Note the hips. Their relative narrowness is explained by reason of the fact that bone growth had been completed prematurely under the influence of adrenocortical androgens, before somatic feminization began under the influence of cortisone therapy.

The next sequence of illustrations shows the transformation of the patient who changed to live as a boy, beginning with the pre- and postoperative appearance of the external genitalia (Figures 20, 21). The internal sex organs were surgically removed. After the final stage of plastic surgery of the penis, the boy could stand up to urinate. Figure 22 shows a different body configuration as com-

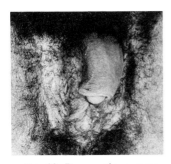

FIG. 20. Preoperative appearance of the external genitalia of the boy in Figure 15, right.

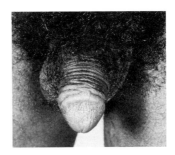

FIG. 21. Postoperative appearance of the genitalia of Figure 20.

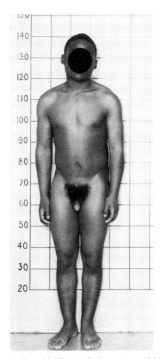

FIG. 22. Frontal view at age 14 of the boy in Figure 15, right. Lack of feminized physique is due to the program of hormonal regulation, plus ovariectomy.

FIG. 23. The same boy as in Figure 22 at age 15, showing stereotypic masculine stance and expression.

pared with Figure 19 and demonstrates what happens when estrogen is not permitted to take its effect, but is replaced by androgen instead. Initially the boy was masculinized by his own adrenal androgens. Then, after removal of the ovaries, he was put on cortisone therapy for regulation of adrenocortical function. He then needed once-a-month injections of male sex hormone, long-acting testosterone enanthate. Should he forget his medications or drop out from follow-up, then his own adrenal cortices will resume secreting their masculinizing hormone. The value of continuing cortisone therapy is that it improves general health status. Figure 23 is another of those pictures which capture enough of the language of the body posture to tell a good deal about gender identity. How many are the acquired positions and postures of the body that are sexually dimorphic! In adulthood, this patient is very short, 4 ft. 8 in., which is explained by the fact that, untreated hormonally in childhood, he grew too rapidly and the epiphyses of the bones fused too soon, thus bringing statural growth to a premature halt. As a young adult, the boy does not like being so short, but for him it is a trivial disability as compared with having been formerly trapped in the assigned role of a female.

At the time he first appeared in the hospital, as a girl, this boy was unable to talk about his sexual dilemma. The girl also, when first in the clinic as a boy, Stanley, was electively mute for all matters pertaining to sex, even clothing preference. On such a touchy subject, vocal communication with me, parents, friends, or anyone was impossible. For Stanley the issue was resolved after five sessions of counseling, two of them with the mother present, in which I did the talking when elective mutism forbade a dialogue. One morning, following a late afternoon appointment, I found the message (Figure 24) on a scrap of paper, folded into a tight little wad, on the floor. Six years later I used this note, with the second patient, as the focus of a parable about the use of written messages to break the barrier of elective mutism. Eventually, on the eve of becoming he, the patient wrote his own message, separately in the presence of his mother, then of the father (Figure 25). It was a highly dramatic session, with the child not being sure whether the parents would give their consent or not. Written by a child who was to all intents and purposes illiterate, it is a message that strikes me as having the

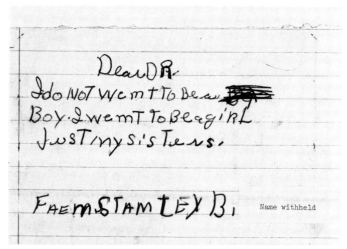

Name withheld

FIG. 24. The message, unsolicited, which broke the elective mutism of the girl in Figure 15, left. "Dear Dr. I do not want to be a boy. I want to be a girl just (like) my sisters."

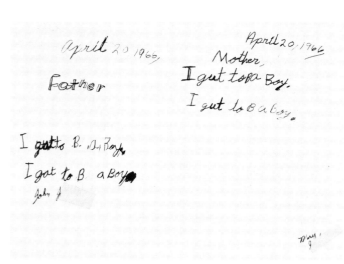

FIG. 25. The message from the boy of Figure 15, right, written twice, once in the presence of the father, and later in the presence of the mother. Each parent accepted the child's decision by signing his or her paper. The content of the message was original, in response to a request to break elective mutism by writing something.

259

greatest power of any three-letter-word sentence I have ever read—
"I got to be a boy."

Let me remind you once again that these two children who elected sex reassignment, one to be a girl, the other to be a boy, had the same diagnosis, namely, genetic female with the adrenogenital syndrome, and that this diagnosis applied also to the other preceding three matched pairs. Thus, you have four different pairs of people with the same diagnostic status but with four different hormonal and behavioral histories. I think these eight people are important on two counts. One is that they show beautifully the prenatal components of gender dimorphic behavior which, in this particular prenatally masculinizing syndrome, is tomboyishness in the genetic female. The other is that they show, even more spectacularly, the extraordinary power of the postnatal components of gender dimorphic behavior.

Since you have pairs of individuals who spend the major part of their lives thinking and acting like boys or girls, respectively, perhaps the most important point to see as a principle here is that the prenatal components of gender dimorphic behavior do not automatically dictate the final story of what your total gender identity will be. Yet, the prenatal component can be incorporated into the postnatally determined part of the gender identity. Fortunately for all the girls in this story that I have presented, there's no problem for a girl to be a tomboyish girl or a tomboyish woman in our society today. It's a perfectly acceptable variant of the feminine pattern in our particular era of cultural history. It's extraordinarily much more difficult for a boy who is not completely conforming to the masculine idealized stereotype. It's so difficult that there isn't even a word for him—unless you call him a sissy or an artistic and sensitive boy, and you've damned him either way. There's a great deal more pressure to make boys conform to the rigid stereotype. More variability is permissible to the female.

Again now, the principle that strikes me as extremely important is that the prenatal component can be woven into and incorporated into the postnatal component in gender identity differentiation. From an ethical point of view, I believe that the inference to make here is that one needs to ease up on the stereotypes and to allow more leeway for individual variation to find its own expression.

And in that respect, you hear that Dr. Sutton-Smith, Dr. Rosenberg, and I are all saying the same thing. Right? I get nods of acquiesence and that makes me feel very good.

DEANDROGENIZATION OF THE MALE

God created Eve first. I've already said that once in my talk. The cartoon of Figure 26, given me by Dr. Friedmund Neumann of West Berlin, epitomizes the new knowledge of prenatal hormones and sexual differentiation of the male by reason of something added —just as the angels are flying around with a big testosterone needle, and shooting up Eve into Adam. I suspect that psychosexual differentiation of the male, the differentiation of the basic dimorphism of gender identity, also requires something added. I wouldn't be surprised if the something added is, yet again, a prenatal hormonal influence on the nervous system that allows the eyes, the vision, to be sexually responsive to the erotic image. I refer again to the fact that there does seem to be a basic sex difference in the way in which nature uses the eye to initiate an erotic turn-on. The female is not by any means incapable of responding to, say, a sexy movie. But she is more dependent, so far as I have been able to ascertain, directly or indirectly, on the buildup of the sentiment of the relationship and on, above all else, the tactile feelings of close embrace.

Everything I have told you about masculinization of the genetic female in the adrenogenital syndrome has its counterpart in the demasculinization of the genetic male, as in the androgen-insensitivity syndrome. The rat of Figure 27 is a genetic male that was born with female external sex organs because, as a fetus, it was deandrogenized because its mother was injected with antiandrogen. In this instance, the antiandrogen was cyproterone acetate. Under the influence of that medication, the fetus was unable to secrete androgen from its own testicles. Minus the Adam principle, it turned into a morphologic female externally. Internally, it is male. In human beings a similar thing happens spontaneously in the syndrome which is known as the testicular-feminizing or androgen-insensitivity syndrome.

Figure 28 is a reminder that the androgen-insensitivity syndrome

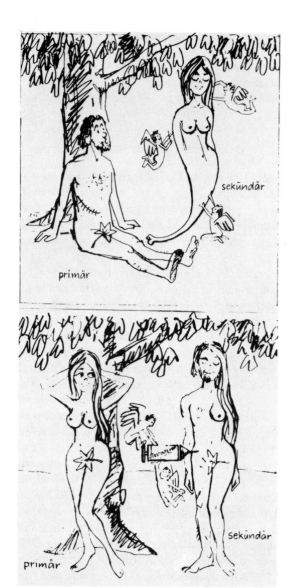

FIG. 26. Cartoon representation of two versions of sexual differentiation, the Biblical (top) and embryogenetic (lower). In embryogenesis, Nature's plan is to create a female, regardless of genetic sex, unless something masculinizing is added. Normally, the masculinizing principle is added from the developing testes, represented as an angelic injection of testosterone, the male sex hormone, in the lower drawing. (Courtesy of Friedmund Neumann, West Berlin.)

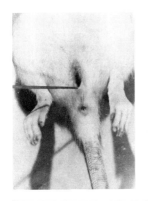

FIG. 27. Female external genitalia in a genetic and gonadal male rat, deandrogenized in utero by injections of the antiandrogen, cyproterone acetate, injected into the pregnant mother. (Photo courtesy of Friedmund Neumann, West Berlin.)

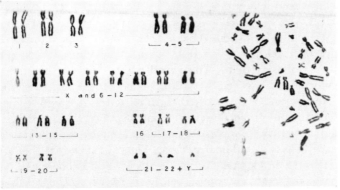

FIG. 28. Chromosomal spread (right) and karyotype (left) of a genetic male with an X and a Y chromosome (46,XY).

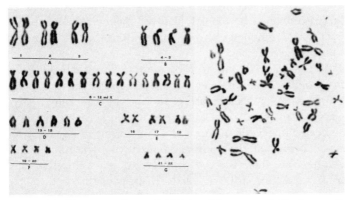

FIG. 29. Chromosomal spread (right) and karyotype (left) of a genetic female with two XX chromosomes (46,XX).

263

occurs in a genetic male with the 46,XY chromosome pattern, and not the 46,XX chromosome pattern of the female (Figure 29).

Figure 30 shows the female external sex organs of a child of 10 with a 46,XY chromosome pattern. In this case the degree of androgen insensitivity was complete, thus allowing perfect feminine differentiation of the external genitalia in fetal life. In the delivery room, the baby was pronounced a girl. The obstetrician correctly surmised that the lump in each groin was a gonad which would prove to be testicular in structure. He knew that the baby should, nonetheless, be assigned and reared as a girl. At 2 days of age the baby was seen by a urologist who, on the basis of a test of chromosomal sex, advised changing the sex to male, saying that a penis might eventually be constructed. A few weeks later, after further study, the urologist reversed his recommendation, referring the child to Johns Hopkins. The gonad on the left side became too prominent and was removed. The gonad on the right remained unobtrusive and was preserved. Like all testes, it would secrete a certain amount of female sex hormone at puberty. Since the body would be sensitive to this estrogen, but not to the androgen it would secrete, puberty would be feminizing. Figure 31 shows the spontaneous feminine development of the breasts at age 13. There had been no hormonal treatment whatsoever. Every male has enough estrogen secreted by his testes to make breasts like that, if only the estrogen effect would not be suppressed by the much larger amount of androgen that is being made. There is indeed not a complete day-and-night difference hormonally between the sexes. Each sex makes some of both hormones, estrogen and androgen, and it is the ratio that makes the difference.

It is time now for me to show you another matched pair of hermaphrodites, this time genetic males, concordant for diagnosis and discordant for sex of rearing, so that you will know that the lessons from matched pairs of genetic female hermaphrodites can be replicated in genetic males. Both of the people in Figure 32 have a partial degree of the androgen-insensitivity syndrome—partial in the sense that there was a slight degree of masculinization of the external sex organs visible at birth. It happens that both of these people were considered to be girls on the day of birth. In one case no question of sex ever arose. She grew up as a girl and had a

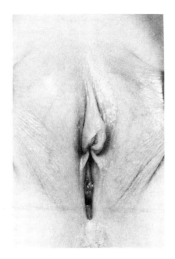

Fig. 30. Normal female appearance of the external genitalia in a child, age 10 years, a genetic male with the androgen-insensitivity (testicular feminizing) syndrome.

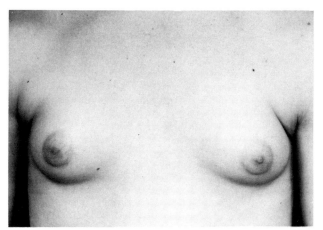

Fig. 31. Breasts developing in the same case as represented in Figure 30, at age 13, stimulated by the female hormone, estrogen, secreted in amounts normal for the male from the testis. Cellular insensitivity to androgen throughout the body in this case allows only testicular estrogen to take effect. Insensitive to androgen, the testes are sterile.

265

spontaneous, feminizing puberty. It was failure to have a first menstrual period that brought her to medical attention. The diagnosis was established, and it was discovered that she needed surgery to lengthen the vaginal canal so as to permit effective coitus.

In the case of the other baby, at the age of $3\frac{1}{2}$ months a physician recognized that the clitoris was a little enlarged and that the vaginal canal was not normally developed. An extensive diagnostic work-up was thereupon undertaken. The finding of a small, imperfect testis undescended on each side led to a decision to require the parents to reassign their child as a boy. The change was made at age $4\frac{1}{2}$ months. As a boy, the patient had many admissions for attempted masculine reconstruction of the external genitals. At 13 he began to grow breasts, which required surgical removal. He is now adult in age and has been married for some years. Behaviorally and psychologically he did very well as a boy in childhood and early adolescence. Within the last 3 years, however, he underwent a great crisis of very severe depression—a crisis which, I think, hinges on the fact of having finally reached the day of reckoning in which he had to admit to himself: "There's no hope, I'm never going to be normal." There had always been the medical promise of success, until finally the day of reckoning arrived. For this man, the account to be settled was not whether he could or could not have some kind of a sex life, as is so often the case. He had already established that he could. His unsettled account was whether he could ever look old enough. At 25 he got a job as an insurance salesman. Clients ridiculed and belittled him as though he were a boy of 16 or 17 pretending to be a salesman and had no business trying to con them. He had to quit. There was nothing he could do to look more mature. Because his system was unable to use androgen, his face could not grow a beard, he could not get a masculine, adult-looking skin texture, his voice did not deepen fully, and his body shape remained too youthful. He would look like a kid forever. As a point in case management, it's a tragedy to allow a baby of this type to be assigned and reared as a boy simply because the child is a genetic male and has two testes. It happens that the testes are hormonally inadequate, are not fertile, and should be removed to avoid the risk of early cancer. But all that is beside the point. The point is—and Figure 32 allows

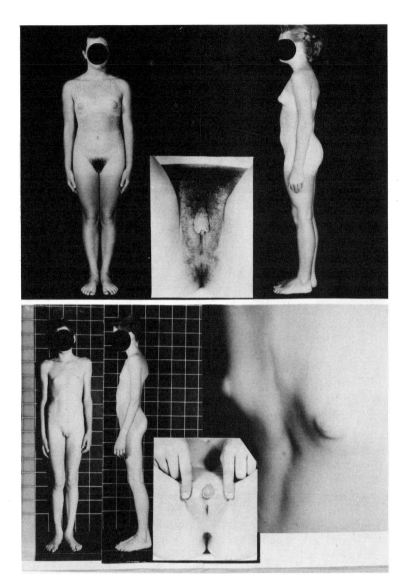

FIG. 32. Matched pair of genetic and gonadal male hermaphrodites, concordant for diagnosis, but discordant for assigned sex, rearing, and gender identity. Both have the partial androgen-insensitivity syndrome, which accounts for adolescent breast development. The boy underwent surgery to flatten his chest.

267

me to reiterate my thesis yet once again—that whatever the prenatal contribution to gender identity differentiation, the postnatal contribution is remarkable and profound in its importance and scope.

Thus, here you have two people who could both have been living as women or both as men. Instead, one is living as a man with a male gender identity in spite of all the hurdles. The other is living as a woman with a female gender identity and without the hurdles of the man. She has to admit that she is sterile and cannot have her own pregnancies. It so happens in this case that the wife and husband have both decided, for their own various reasons, that they want to live without children. They are making a very satisfactory and happy home life. I have seen them together, alone, and in the company of friends and relatives. I assure you that if you met this couple in your home, in your church, in your school, or in this room right here, it would never occur to you to suspect an XY chromosome constitution. There you have an example of how complete and total the contradiction of genetic sex can be in the differentiation of gender identity, especially in its postnatal phase.

The growth of breasts at puberty favors the one of a matched pair of hermaphrodites reared and living as a girl. By contrast, it is the one living as a boy who is favored when puberty in a matched pair is masculinizing. Figures 33 and 34 exemplify the latter, namely, two genetic male hermaphrodites born with ambiguous genitalia who did not have the androgen-insensitivity syndrome and who began to masculinize at puberty. The boy had several operations for repair of his penis in childhood. Now, in adulthood, it is small but able to function coitally. He has no particular problems in appearing and being accepted as a man and in accepting himself as a man. Likewise, the girl has no particular problem either, as a result of hormonal and surgical feminizing treatment. You can see that she has a pretty good figure and also that the surgically repaired sex organs give her complete adequacy for copulation. The sequence of her hormonal feminization under treatment with estrogen is shown in Figure 34. When this girl first came into the clinic at age 11, she was already advancing into a completely masculinizing puberty. Developmentally she was still sufficiently immature for

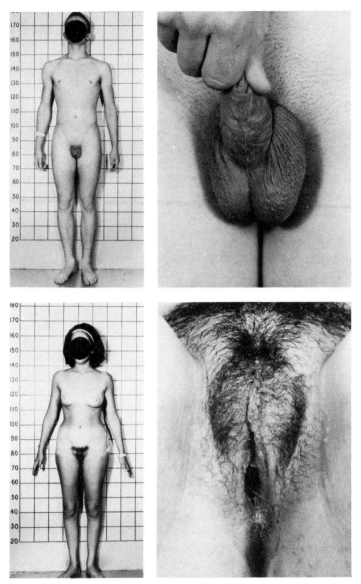

FIG. 33. Matched pair of genetic and gonadal male hermaphrodites, concordant for diagnosis, but discordant for assigned sex, rearing, and gender identity. At puberty both began masculinizing. In the girl, at teenage, the surgical and hormonal program was effectively aimed at feminization and in the boy, at masculinization, to be congruous with the gender identity.

269

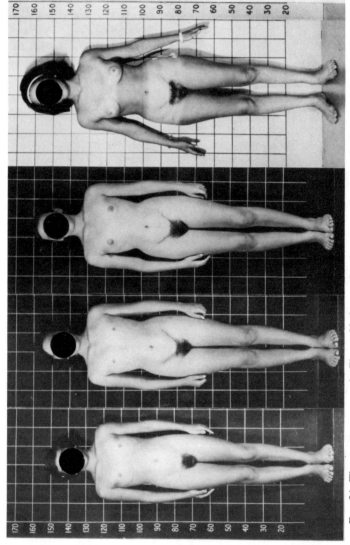

FIG. 34. The same person as in Figure 33, lower, showing progressive stages in hormonal feminization under treatment with estrogen. The pictures are taken at ages 11, 12, 13 and 19. The genetic and gonadal sex are male.

feminization to take the place of masculinization, after the masculinizing influence of the testicles was removed and replaced with estrogen substitution therapy. The progressive ages shown in Figure 34 are 11, 12, 13, and 19. At age 19 her rehabilitation was completed with surgery for construction of the vaginal canal, in anticipation of marriage.

IDENTIFICATION AND COMPLEMENTATION: PAIRED GENDER SCHEMAS

Identification and complementation: I particularly want to draw your attention to complementation, because I am aware of the fact that in the literature of psychology, especially social psychology and child development, there has been too much emphasis—in fact, almost an exclusive emphasis—on the idea of identification as the mechanism whereby gender identity is established. I became aware that there is another principle, complementation, particularly in studying children who were obliged to undergo sex reassignment around or after the age of 18 months, which is the critical upper age-limit for making a change.

Figures 35 and 36 show you just such a case—a genetic male with a malformed, ambiguous-looking micropenis, who was reassigned to live as a girl at the age of 17 months. The penis was practically nonexistent, just a little nubbin of skin, and there was no urinary canal through the organ itself, the urinary opening being in the feminine position. The decision regarding the sex of rearing should have been settled much earlier. I think there was more than a little foot dragging on the part of people who didn't want to commit themselves professionally to the decision that the baby, although a genetic male, would be better off in life as a female.

After the reassignment had been completed, I requested the parents, who are good observers, to give me some comments about how they themselves changed to be the parents of a daughter after having been the parents of a son for 17 months, using the pronoun *he* and other masculine nouns and pronouns. The father told me a story which proved important to my own intellectual development in recognizing and understanding the business of complementation.

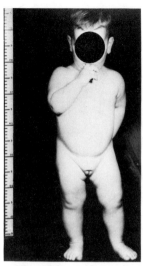

FIG. 35. Preoperative frontal appearance of a genetic and gonadal male child with ambiguous external genitalia, who was reassigned to live as a girl at age 17 months.

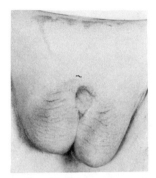

FIG. 36. Preoperative genital appearance of the child in Figure 35. The hypospadiac microphallus looked more like a clitoris than a penis. It had no urinary tube, and the urinary orifice was in a feminine position.

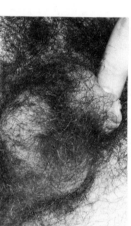

FIGS. 37 and 38. Two views of the external genitals in a case of micropenis.

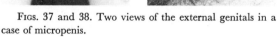

FIG. 39. Adolescent virilization of physique in the same case as in Figures 37 and 38.

272

It was a family tradition that when the father arrived home from work in the evening, the first 10 or 15 minutes was family time: the baby, her brother, two years older, and mother and father joined in fun together in the living room before they ate supper. Some months after the reassignment, the older brother developed a boisterous game of dancing to rock-and-roll music on his record player. His little sister, wanting to be a big shot like her brother, copied him. The father found himself quite spontaneously with an impulse to hold his daughter in close person-to-person dancing. At first she resisted, in favor of what her brother was doing. Soon she recognized a real payoff in being her daddy's favorite and began to catch on to the proverbial wrapping of her father around her little finger. The brother didn't like to be left out. He wanted some of the same favoritism. But his father couldn't see himself in the role of dancing with his son, whom he directed to his mother. So the boy and his mother danced together, while the father danced with his daughter. Here, in a simple way, you have an example of complementation. The father was teaching his daughter how to be a little girl, complementing his masculine behavior with her own feminine response. The mother approved and also gave her son a corresponding example of complementary behavior.

To avoid ambiguity of gender identity in favor of its unity as either masculine or feminine, a developing child is benefited if the mother and father, or any other important representatives of the schemas of femininity and masculinity in a child's life, agree with one another concerning the boundaries of the two schemas. It is difficult and confusing if a mother transmits one set of messages to her son concerning what she approves of as masculine and if his father transmits a discrepant set. It is common to encounter such discrepancy in the case of young boys with the gender identity problem of sissiness. These are boys who insist on playing with girls and girls' toys, dressing up in feminine attire, and wishing to be a girl so that, as young as age 7, they may overtly request to change sex. The father of such a boy usually does not resent the fact that his child has a penis, but the mother is ambivalent about it or repulsed by it. She does not reject the child and may even dote on him to the point of excessive ownership of her own wondrous creation, but with a covert reservation about "that thing—like the one your father is always bothering me with." The mother does not want a girl and does not consistently treat her son as though he were a girl. It is rather that she puts a blackout on that awful appendage and pretends it isn't there. From the point of view of the child, you have in such a case an example of what I mean by fuzzy boundaries as to what constitutes masculine and feminine.

Now, of course, I'm opening myself to the criticism of being chauvinistic as to what's masculine and what's feminine. But I am not chauvinistic, because the fact is that it really doesn't too much matter what is enclosed within the boundaries of masculine and feminine, so long as the important males and females in a child's life are in agreement about them.

Ideally, it is preferable if the parents are able to convey much the same information about boundaries as do the parents of their child's playmates, his school teachers, and the people he watches on television. Yet, there is indeed a good deal of latitude available here. It is more important that the parents agree with one another than that together they agree with other people. Or when a child has close relationships in infancy with more people than his parents, then the group should be in agreement.

Agreement needs to be about basic, not trivial, aspects of sex difference. It is of trivial consequence that mother drives the tractor and daddy makes the pancakes, because these are trivial things with respect to the boundaries of gender identity differentiation. The basic things are that you've got a penis or a vagina and you're proud of it. Vaginas are marvelous because they're for making babies, and there's a baby nest up there, beyond them. Penises, too, are marvelous.

For all the blurring of sex differences in occupation and recreation that are being discussed these days, I don't see any evidence whatsoever that people want to change the sexually dimorphic pronouns or nouns. We are still making exactly the same clear distinction between mother and father, brother and sister, he and she, him and her, and so on through all the sexually dimorphic part of the language as we always have done. So I don't see that we are going to have a problem by blurring deliberately, if that's the way it's going to be, some of the other boundaries of the masculine and the feminine stereotypes. As a matter of fact, should it come to voting, I'd vote in favor of blurring some boundaries, because I think it gives much better freedom of individual opportunity to members of both sexes.

I like to take note that this day and age of blurring vocational and avocational boundaries of sex also happens to be an era in which people are taking off their clothes in public. That leaves no question about whether you have a sex insignia hanging on the end of your belly or a baby nest safely tucked inside. The more that nudity is an easy-going thing among young children, the better, so far as their sense of gender identity as male or female is concerned. I don't think that one needs to worry about the day that might come, the day of surgical implants, when males might elect to have a uterus implanted in which to carry a donor pregnancy. Science fiction always allows for everything to happen, and anything that's been written in science fiction is quite likely to happen in science sometime later. I'll face that music when it starts to play!

Another fact that I observe in today's changes in the mores as to what constitutes the stereotypes of male and female behavioral dimorphism is that it is difficult to find a man with the new style of long hair and the new style of unisex clothing who doesn't make it pretty obvious that he is still a man. I refer to the fact that beards and mustaches are coming back in fashion at the same time that some of the other sexually dimorphic signals have been changed or blurred. The voice, too, can seldom be disguised.

In this matter of clear boundaries, dimorphic behavior, and identification and complementation, I like to see an analogy with native language. Perhaps you actually know cases of children who come of parents who migrated from "the old country" and who, in the new place of living in this country, resent the language of the old people. It's not uncommon to find in such a case that the children will know how to listen to the language of the old people, but they won't use it. They won't speak it at all. These children actually have the two language schemas built into the brain. One is for listening with, and the other is for listening and talking with. Of course, I know that there are many bilingual children who listen and talk in both languages. I'm picking the other example because of the analogy to be found with gender identity. What happens in gender identity differentiation is that most children find that one of the gender schemas is the equivalent of the language schema for listening with, the other being the equivalent of the one for listening and talking with.

There are a few children who become, shall I say, ambisexuous in their gender identity. They are the ones who worry most people, like many of us who run counseling clinics. The ordinary boy and the ordinary girl differentiate a monosexuous gender identity. For the boy this means that the schema that governs output as well as intake, the identification schema, is the one assimilated from father, big brother, and other males, including television heroes. The complementation schema for this boy is the input schema of knowing how females will react and behave, so that he can complement their behavior with his own masculinely identified output.

Almost anyone reading this page could try to utilize his or her complementation schema for output as well as input, as people often do for a charade on New Year's Eve or Halloween at a masked ball. But in playacting the role of the other sex, most people look awkward and goofy. A few people find themselves extremely fluent in their ability to playact that way. The majority have only one gender schema, the one that's based on identification, in which they can act fluently, spontaneously, and naturally. For them this schema is more highly elaborated than the other—I almost want to say, stronger than the schema based on complementation—and for a very good reason. One gets a good deal more reinforcement from other people for behaving according to the schema that they consider the correct one, namely, the identification schema.

I learned this lesson concerning reinforcement from the study of transsexual people who undergo a sex reassignment in adulthood. These people have for a long time, if not always, felt that they were somewhow masquerading in the wrong body. A male transsexual— either sex can provide the example—gives body signals as a male; he does this regardless of what he feels, however, and despite feminine demeanor, unless he is able to give a complete impersonation. People therefore respond to him as a male. Even when he doesn't behave in a properly masculine way, he is responded to negatively as a sissy or an effeminate male, a homosexual or a transvestite. The police in particular respond to him in a very negative way if he masquerades on the street in female clothes, while at the same time he emits body signals of being a male by reason of body shape, for example, or the appearance of a beard or a deep voice.

When a male transsexual gets a sex reassignment, when he has a more feminine appearance from treatment with female hormone, and when he behaves 24 hours a day in a feminine way, he gets responded to as females do. Car doors are opened for him in his role as her; men stand back at elevators for her to enter or leave first, and so on with dozens of other aspects of etiquette.

After a few months, and more remarkably so after a period of a few years of reassignment, male transsexuals wear their femininity comfortably. If not first nature, it has certainly become second nature. The awkwardness perceived on their first visit is gone. Many of these people so awkwardly exaggerate femininity when they first appear to inquire about sex reassignment that I have sometimes described them as looking like midnight whores dressed up at 8:00 A.M., in a hospital waiting room. Five years later they look like women whom even astute elevator operators can't distinguish from other women who come in and out of the building. There you have a beautiful example of how extraordinarily important are the responses of other people in building up the greater elaborateness of the gender identity which is that of your identification and not of your complementation.

With that, let me repeat what you've already heard earlier, namely, that the imperatives of sexually dimorphic behavior are few, and they hinge around hormonal functions which can best be aphoristically stated as governing the fact that women are the ones who menstruate, gestate, and lactate, and men are the ones who impregnate. If we somehow manage to get that basic sex difference clearly across to our children, then they are at liberty to be optional about almost any other of the sexual behavior differences and need not have a problem with their basic gender identity.

A CASE OF AMBIGUITY

I'd like now to discuss the case of a boy who did have a difficulty in establishing his basic gender identity, which is male, secondary to the problem of having a micropenis. He is in his twenties now and his penis is full grown. It is not erect in Figure 37, but you can estimate that it is only just big enough for intercourse. It requires something over 2½ inches of erectile length for the penis to penetrate far enough into the vagina for a man to feel satisfied with what he can do for his partner. A short penis works well enough for a man to get good erotic feeling and orgasm. Even with his penis amputated, a man can get sexual arousal, feeling, and climax. His terror lies not in the loss of his own climax, but in the loss of his ability to reciprocate. It's an ego wound that's involved. The young man represented in Figure 37 is ego wounded. It's a serious problem for him and a problem for me in the sense that he is harassed with imagery of suicide.

In the next picture (Figure 38), you see the smallness of the penis and how narrow it is, as well as short. The general body build shows excellent virilization (Figure 39). There is no androgen insensitivity here. It is necessary for a long-acting androgen injection to be given once a month, for the testes have atrophied.

I have a special story to tell you about this man with regard to gender identity differentiation in boyhood. At age 10, he began to show some changes from a unified, boyish direction of gender identity differentiation. Reports from school indicated that he was not joining with boys' groups anymore, but at recess and lunch time he was going out to play in the girls' playground area where only a few boys joined with the girls. On that year's visit to the hospital, he did not indicate on his own initiative that he thought anything was going wrong, though he had specifically requested the appointment to talk with me. He liked to come down once a year, which was his prerogative.

I used the technique which I discovered some years ago and have become very fond of. It's an excellent one for eliciting information. I've called it the parable technique. I told him about another patient of mine, a boy like himself. It was in fact a composite and not a specific case reference. This other boy, I related, had once told me that he sometimes wondered whether God had really intended for him to be a girl, since he didn't have a decent-sized penis to be a boy with. And, in fact, he had had a dream—I intentionally utilized the remoteness of a dream—that he had really decided to change his sex and be a girl.

With that, it was I who was surprised, for the boy answered

very coolly that he had thought about that sometimes. It turned out that he had read various follow-up reports of the Christine Jorgensen case in the media and so had gotten the idea of sex reassignment as a possibility in life. At age 10, he also had worked out the idea that he would not want to bother with a sex reassignment unless the medical profession could guarantee his own pregnancy as a female. Then the change would be worth the effort. Since no such guarantee was possible, he decided to remain living as a boy. I recalled an almost forgotten practice in our clinic, namely, the use of an ointment with male sex hormone in it—testosterone ointment. Applied locally to the penis, this ointment makes it grow as if at puberty, while the remainder of the body is left immature. This juvenile enlargement of the penis is not of much help once the age of puberty is reached, but it makes a boy feel a lot better while he is still a 10-year-old. That's because he gets a penis twice as big as it was. The change in his genital appearance gave this boy a boost of morale.

We referred to this conversation about sex reassignment a couple of times in follow-up meetings in the next year or so. Then I decided not to flog dead horses and allowed the idea to go into remission, so to speak. I figured he would bring it up again, if need be. He did not, so by the time he was 19 I decided it was time to find out whether the idea of sex reassignment had completely gone away or whether it was still present in his mind. I learned that in his masturbation fantasies, according to his own estimate, about 25% of the time the content of the fantasy that appeared—I deliberately say appeared, because he did not evoke it; it had an autonomy of its own—was of himself as a girl having sex with a boy. On those particular occasions he could not, without the fantasy, masturbate to ejaculation. On other occasions, about 75% of the time, the fantasy that appeared was one of his being a boy with a normal-sized penis having normal sexual intercourse with a girl.

Another manifestation of gender ambiguity became evident after a problem at home was resolved when the boy left home to complete the final 2 years of his secondary education at a boarding school. He suddenly began to pick up from his serious underachievement at school. One of the signs of his picking up was that, with unusual rapidity, he began to learn French and then began writing

French verse. At the same time, he wrote English short stories, also. It dawned on me one day that the French verse was very lyrical and feminine, and the English short stories were rough and rugged and had a lot of masculine, assertive imagery in them. In a subsequent follow-up interview, I told the writer of my impressions and of my hypothesis that he was laying the foundation for a possibility that if he ever changed to be a girl, he would go to France to live and speak French. If he made the grade living as a boy, he would stay living in America, speaking English. He told me that I was right and that he had in fact already laid plans to be able to go for a year of study leave in a French institution.

This is a rather neat example of how sex and achievement, or underachievement and dropoutism, may tie together. I suspect there are a lot more stories that we could learn about sex and dropping out of college if we became more attuned and sensitive to what to look for.

Here, then, is a case in which one has the rare opportunity of having a kind of transparency, or window, through which to see ambiguity of gender identity differentiation taking place, and of having some sense of understanding where the ambiguity comes from. I don't know too much about the contribution of family factors that I'd care to be dogmatic about, but I do know that from as far back as the boy can remember, he and his mother were deadlocked in a feud. My interpretation of the feud could be correct, though I am diffident about it. It is that here one had a case of a mother who was saying, "Well, if you've got only a little penis, you'd better have a big brain." The boy had no other active form of ammunition with which to fight his mother whenever he needed to assert himself. So he used the ready-made ammunition of not using his brain for academic achievement.

Transvestite Disexuous Identity

I now turn to another series of illustrations (Figures 40–48) that have to do with the imperfect differentiation of a unitary or mono-sexuous gender identity—one in which the resolution of ambiguity is to be both masculine and feminine, alternatively. This is the resolution that one finds in the transvestite, especially in the transvestite man who is erotically interested in the genetic female and who does not get particularly turned on—in fact, gets turned off, even—by the idea of himself as one of two males, each with a penis, in a sexual relationship. If you are lucky enough to be able to retrieve the life story of a male transvestite, you can get at least some clues as to where the deviation in monosexuous gender identity differentiation took place. However, I wish to focus on phenomenology, not psychodynamics, at this point. The series of illustrations demonstrates the phenomenon of the seesaw swing of male to female in the typical male transvestite.

You see the person sitting at a temporary boudoir table, so to speak, as a kind of trancelike thing happens, and Bill becomes Jennifer. To go with the two names, there are two wardrobes and two personalities, as once referred to already. These illustrations are selected from a much larger collection. Every conceivable posture of female life is represented, including pregnancy. You can hardly believe that the person who comes into your office as Bill is the same one who also comes in as Jennifer.

TRANSSEXUAL REASSIGNMENT

In the next illustration (Figure 49) you have a picture of normal male sex organs. Here the story is different than in the transvestite. The illustration and those that follow (Figures 50–54) are of a transsexual male. He has been reassigned to live as a female for some 6 or 7 years now. At the time of first appearance in the clinic, the social presentation was that of a woman. He had lived as an impersonator and so, in effect, had made the social reassignment in advance of the hormonal and surgical reassignment. In the transsexual person, the conviction of masquerading in the wrong anatomy has its origin extremely early in life, according to available evidence, as most of you are well aware by now. Sometimes the person has given up fighting the impossible from childhood on. There are, in some cases, stories of transsexual boys going to school dressed in girls' clothes and being sent home on that account. They then perhaps compromise by dressing in unisex clothes for school. There are other stories of transsexuals who fought against their compulsion

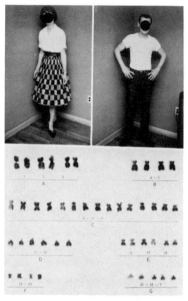

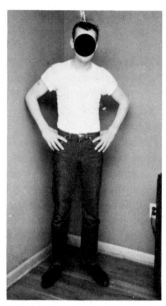

FIG. 40. Karyotype, below, of a genetic male transvestite, and his appearance, above, with two names, two wardrobes, and two personalities.

FIG. 41.

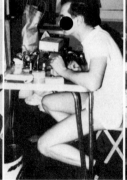

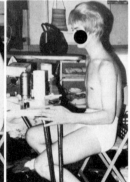

FIG. 42.   FIG. 43.   FIG. 44.

Fig. 45.

Fig. 46.

Fig. 47.

Fig. 48.

Figs. 41–48. A sequence of eight views of the metamorphosis of a male transvestite into his feminine alter ego.

283

and tried to live as men, until finally they surrendered. They couldn't make the grade any more.

It's not a question of either-or when it comes to the differential diagnosis of transsexualism from transvestism. It's a question, rather, of distribution on a continuum, for there are various intermediate grades and forms of disexuous gender identity. Sex reassignment raises its own special problem of differential diagnosis. For that, the best answer that I've found is this: if a person requests a sex reassignment as the solution to his or her otherwise intolerable gender problem, then that person should always go through the social reassignment first. Thus I require all patients whom I evaluate to have lived and rehabilitated themselves in the new sex for 2 years prior to irreversible surgery. They may have the help of hormones of which the effects are reversible, save for deepening of the voice in the female-to-male transsexual on androgen. Surgery then is a confirmation of what's already been achieved. I may make one exception for the female-to-male transsexual in allowing removal of the breasts during the rehabilitative period, for it adds a great deal of freedom in the type of clothes worn and the type of job held and, therefore, the degree of economic rehabilitation that can be achieved. Moreover, it is possible to insert breast implants, should the need ever arise.

To return to the male-to-female illustrations, you see the form being worn in the newly constructed vaginal canal, to keep it open while healing. You see, later, the appearance of a serviceable vaginal cavity. I say serviceable advisedly, because this girl had plenty of experience sexually, even before surgery. Some people raise their eyebrows at promiscuity. My policy is that, in psychology and medicine, it's none of our business to legislate a person's sex life. That holds even for people who use or enjoy their sex lives as a way of earning a living. We are not required to make a decision of a moral type on that particular issue.

In the full view, nude, you see first an early picture showing a little breast growth under the influence of female hormone treatment. Impatient, the patient went off to another hospital where she could more easily and rapidly get breast implants. In some cases, breast enlargement in the genetic male on estrogen therapy equals that of the genetic female with large breasts. In other cases, it leaves less

FIG. 49.

FIG. 50.

FIG. 51.

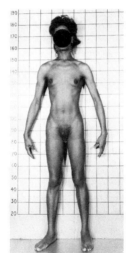

FIG. 52.

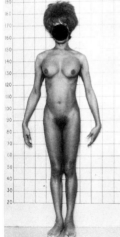

FIG. 53.

FIG. 54.

FIGS. 49–54. The surgical and hormonal metamorphosis of a male-to-female transsexual.

285

than desired, just as in some genetic females the breasts are smaller than they desire. One does not ask for a pose, as in the final illustration of the series. It is spontaneous. Many male-to-female transsexuals are expert at *Vogue* magazine posing. It's as if they manage the exaggerations of the feminine stereotype better than the more inconspicuous ways of behaving as a female. However, exaggerations become toned down with time, as I've already mentioned, and the transsexuals wear their femininity with the comfort of an old shoe after they've gotten used to being treated as women always, 24 hours a day, by everyone.

The lesson of this transsexual story is that here you have a transposition of gender identity that has become total. Instead of being secondary as you would have expected it to be, the would-be complement of this person's gender identity has become primary. In other words, it's the masculine schema that is subsidiary here, and the feminine one which is overt and on the surface.

The next set of illustrations are of a female-to-male transsexual (Figures 55–58). You can see the very successful appearance of the man standing in his business suit. I've followed this person since the first hospital registration as a very distressed young woman looking very mannish in severely plain clothes and having a masculine stance and walk. A strict Catholic upbringing made the dilemma of her lesbianism and transsexualism morally untenable, entirely. It was a long, long saga of medical searching and being rejected, and a drama of suicide planned following the final Christmas to be spent with the family, in the old country. A little news item in the local newspaper told of the opening of the gender identity clinic at Johns Hopkins, and so the suicide was postponed forever.

In Figure 57, you see how disappointing an artificial plastic surgical penis is, including all the adjacent scarring of where the skin grafts were taken. I show you this for two reasons: one is to show you that it means a tremendous amount to the person who is obsessed with the idea of being able to stand up to urinate through a penis (still not possible in this case, however); and the other is that we really are not able to solve the problem of creating an artificial penis by surgery with anything like the success of creating an artificial vaginal canal. And I don't think we ever will be able to. That's very bad news for babies born without a penis and assigned

FIG. 55.

FIG. 56.

FIG. 57.

FIG. 58.

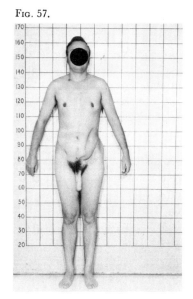

FIGS. 55–58. A female-to-male transsexual after surgical and hormonal masculinization, and with his family.

287

to live as boys. Those who try to get an artificial penis end up with a lump of meat good only for urinating through, and that only if they are lucky. Often the tissues break down and there is a leakage. Also, the artificial urethral canal is not good at resisting the travel inward of infection, so there's a danger of urinary and bladder infection. The worst problem, from the patient's point of view in adulthood, is that a skin-grafted penis has no erectile power. In order for the patient to have sexual intercourse, it needs to be cradled into a cage or shell of a synthetic plastic or rubber penis and held in such a way that the former clitorine tissue, embedded at the root of it, is able to be stimulated. The present patient has been able to solve this problem in his sexual life with his wife. They both are able to have a rather good time sexually, as I have learned independently from each of them, and they both get the satisfaction of climax. Nonetheless, I believe that from the erotic point of view the same result could be obtained with an artificial penis of the strap-on, dildo variety, without the vast amount of time, money, and pain invested in surgery.

Another problem with a plastic-surgical penis which most people simply wouldn't think about is that it has no feelings. Therefore the person has no warning of when it is injured. It is necessary to be continuously careful not to have it rubbing on the clothing and getting ulcerated or otherwise getting squeezed, bruised, or hurt. I suspect that the ultimate answer to an artificial penis will be not an artificial one at all, but the transplanting of a regular penis. That lies in the realm of science fiction. Not only would there be the usual transplant problems of immunological rejection, but the special problems of having to make neural connections with the central nervous system in order to guarantee erection and erotic sensation. Kidney and heart transplants can function without a neural connection, even though there is such a connection in the normal organs.

In Figure 57, you may be able to notice that there is an excellent growth of beard as a result of male sex hormone therapy. You can notice also that the hairline is beginning to recede, which is also a male hormone effect. Anyone who doesn't want to go bald can stop it by being castrated!

In Figure 58, you have a family group. There is a fascinating story here with regard to the female-to-male transsexual as father and also with regard to the gender identity of the partner of the transsexual. I have gotten to know this family well, over the years, through interviews and tests, and I know that this little girl has absolutely no idea whatsoever about her father's genetic status or his surgical status. She behaves toward him in identically the same way as you would expect a little girl to behave toward her father when she dotes on him and is a very feminine little girl. She has no problems about her feminine identity, and she certainly has him twisted around her proverbial little finger. She is a member of the family because her mother and father met one another in the course of the low point in their lives. The father, prior to reassignment, was suicidal and giving up hope of ever being able to achieve the life he believed imperative for him. The mother was in very low spirits because she was pregnant and had lost the father of her baby. The couple found one another as tenants of a cold-water, walk-up tenement, one lonely, snowbound Christmas. Three years later they reunited and decided on marriage. Here is a story of rehabilitation which is the reverse of the falling dominoes, in the sense that three people become mutually supportive—four people, in fact, for an aging parent is also a member of the household. This parent has no knowledge of her son-in-law's medical history and, so far as I know, has not had any reason to suspect it.

The sexual relationship between the husband and wife is not really the relationship of lesbianism as it is traditionally understood. I asked the wife about her feelings concerning the fact that technically she would be considered in a lesbian relationship. She said in so many words that her husband has more understanding of her sexual needs than her child's father ever had. Above all, she believed, when there is a good relationship going, a good affection and a good comradeship in a marriage, there will be little difficulty with a deficit in the erotic relationship per se. In her own marriage she did not feel that she was putting up with any deficit, because she always enjoys their sexual relationship—their copulation—and she always gets a sexual climax, as does her husband. I've decided that this woman has a completely female-differentiated gender identity and that the quality of her relationship with this man is the same as it would be with any other man, except that there's a special factor of tenderness

and understanding that goes on between them that is not present in all relationships. I am most impressed, however, with the
fact that the little girl is able to establish a daughter relationship
with a genetic female as a father and to show no difference from
typical behavior toward a genetic male as a father.

Transpositions of Gender Identity/Role

In talking to you of transsexualism, I have been talking of one
of the manifestations of transposition of gender identity and role.
Table 2 shows in summary form that transposition can be episodic
or chronic, and total, partial, or optional. I want to emphasize
that I'm not talking of the etiology of transposition, but only of its
phenomenology. I'm not concerned whether a transposition takes
place in the wake of a brain tumor later in life, as has been known
to occur. Nor am I concerned whether it happens because of a
change in hormones after puberty or an imbalance of hormones
prenatally. And I'm not concerned whether it might be the exclusive
product of postnatal social experience. All of these possibilities may
be relevant in certain cases. I'm interested here simply in describing
phenomenologically which transpositions have been observed to
take place.

TABLE 2
Transpositions of Gender Identity/Role

	Total	Partial	Optional
Episodic	Transvestism	Bisexualism	Avocational role transposition
Chronic	Transsexualism	Homosexuality	Vocational role transposition

Transvestism of the type that you saw in Figures 40–48 represents
an episodic form of transposition in which each episode is a total
transposition—the person who comes into your office dressed this
week as a woman and next week as a man really does represent
two different personalities. To see how the total personality is split
and divided into those two is a very fascinating and special challenge
in itself. A common observation is that the female is nonaggressive,
whimpering, crying, seductive, and coy—not a very attractive

female stereotype. The male is a rugged, merciless, treacherous stereotype of a male—don't trust him.

Transsexualism, I hardly need to say, is a total and chronic form of transposition. There are only a very rare few transsexuals who ever regret their change. Those who do have most likely been self-willed and impetuous, scorning the 2-year, real-life test. Possibly they are knowingly deceptive in giving biographical details. I've seen one patient (Money & Wolff, 1973) who did make a mistake and who had, in actuality, a dissociative disorder of the typical transvestite type. He had a history of hoodwinking his doctors, particularly his foreign-based surgeon. Indirectly he was trying to commit suicide, and failed.

Transposition that is both partial and episodic manifests itself as the relatively frequently occurring bisexual erotic tendency of either men or women. Bisexualism is socially allowed more openly these days than even 10 years ago. In chronic form, the same type of transposition becomes the obligatory or exclusive form of homosexuality, whether it's lesbianism or male homosexuality. Obligatory homosexuality of the most extreme degree in males manifests itself in highly effeminate behavior; and in females, in the strongly butch type of lesbian behavior.

The far right of Table 2 corresponds to the lower right of Table 1. The issue of much of the current liberation argument is centered here. I mean men's liberation as well as women's. The issue is whether we're going to permit and be happy about changes in the stereotype of what's supposed to be male versus female in careers and pastimes—transpositions, that is to say, in gender-stereotyped vocations and avocations—so as to allow both sexes to join together in the same activity instead of being segregated. It has helped me a lot to see things this way. It seems we're making a storm in a teacup over the right to do a certain kind of work together or to share certain kinds of recreation together, without economic discrimination. There's no implication that men and women will have to forgo the right to have personal, intimate relationships together in love and sex.

With List 2, which is another version of Figure 1, I've nearly finished what I have to say. The list reminds you that when one considers the etiology of the different gender transpositions, one must consider all of the component variables of sex, from chromosomes to assigned sex and gender identity/role. Only then might one understand a particular gender transposition and its origins.

List 2: Component Variables of Sex

1. Chromosomal sex
2. Gonadal sex
3. Hormonal sex: (a) prenatal and (b) pubertal
4. Internal morphologic sex
5. External morphologic sex
6. Assigned sex and rearing
7. Gender identity/role

Now, to bring my paper to a close, I'll show you three illustrations (Figures 59–61) of the case of ablatio penis, already mentioned at the outset. Such cases are rare. I know of three, two of which I have in follow-up care. Both have been reassigned to be rehabilitated as girls. Their importance is that they began life as ordinary boys without congenital defect and without an atypical prenatal hormonal history. They refute the would-be argument of purists who object to conclusions about gender identity based on intersexuality and genital birth defects on the grounds that—here I quote what I once heard—"Money studies only odd and atypical cases, not normal ones."

In Figure 59 you have twins whose embryogenesis and fetal development was normally male. The sex reassignment of the one was made because of an accident. You see (Figure 60) that it was truly a total accident. There is no penis left at all. It was lost as the result of a miscalculation in the use of an electric cautery instead of a blade for circumcision. A burn killed the tissue of the penis, which, unable to heal, withered and dropped off.

The child was sex-reassigned after tremendous agonizing on the part of the parents. There was much hiding of the head in the sand on the part of various professional people, so that the reassignment decision was not formalized until the baby was 17 months old. She is now nearly 9 years old.

It is quite remarkable to see the difference between her and her twin brother now. As you might expect, after what you've heard

FIG. 59. Identical twins, age 6, one reassigned as a girl at age 17 months, following accidental ablatio penis at age 7 months.

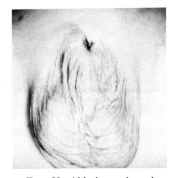

FIG. 60. Ablatio penis, prior to surgical feminization.

FIG. 61. The twin with a history of ablatio penis, age 6, developing behaviorally with a feminine gender identity differentiation, following reassignment.

earlier about prenatal male-hormone influences, the little girl is a tomboy. But the postnatal influences of gender identity differentiation have swung her over in the female direction. I'll draw your attention to pages 118 to 123 in *Man and Woman, Boy and Girl*, should you want to read about the way the mother has made her adjustment to the sex-differential treatment of these two children. It's quite fascinating how she leaves one in no doubt that input from parents is profoundly important in the differentiation of male and female gender identity, respectively, in the two children.

One particularly illuminating example reported by the mother is that the girl has been the dominant twin from the beginning. But, as the mother describes it so beautifully, she asserts her dominance over her brother by being a fussy little mother hen, looking after him. He plays the traditional protective male role, taking up for his sister and fighting on her behalf if she is attacked. Here is evidence that even the stereotypically masculine trait of dominance assertion can have a feminine metamorphosis in the differentiation of the feminine gender identity as compared with the masculine one.

In the last illustration (Figure 61) you have a pretty persuasive example of feminine "body talk." The pose was not instructed. It was her own decision when, in my office I asked her for her photograph. If you look again at Figure 57, you will see that in addition to the behavioral difference, the twins are already slightly different in height and growth rate. They also have a dental difference, some of the boy's teeth, but none of the girl's teeth, being irregularly placed. They are identical twins, but not everything about them is identical. The full extent of their difference will become evident at puberty when the girl feminizes under the influence of exogenous estrogen and the boy masculinizes from endogenous androgen. Then also one will have the manifestation of difference in erotic and romantic imagery and practice. These are the capstone, as it were, completing the edifice of gender identity/role as a durable structure.

REFERENCES

Money, J. Pre-natal hormones and intelligence: A possible relationship. *Impact of Science on Society*, 1971, **21**, 285–290.

Money, J., & Ehrhardt, A. A. *Man and woman, boy and girl: The differentiation and dimorphism of gender identity from conception to maturity.* Baltimore: Johns Hopkins University Press, 1972.

Money, J.; Hampson, J. G.; & Hampson, J. L. An examination of some basic sexual concepts: The evidence of human hermaphroditism. *Bulletin of the Johns Hopkins Hospital,* 1955, **97,** 301–319.

Money, J., & Wolff, G. Sex reassignment: Male to female to male. *Archives of Sexual Behavior,* 1973, **2,** 245–250.

Sherfey, M. J. *The nature and evolution of female sexuality.* New York: Random House, 1972.

Tanner, J. *Growth at adolescence.* Oxford: Blackwell, 1962.

Chronological List
of Contents of the Nebraska
Symposia on Motivation

1953 (Vol. 1)

Brown, J. S. Problems presented by the concept of acquired drive, pp. 1–21.

Harlow, H. F. Motivation as a factor in new responses, pp. 24–49.

Postman, L. J. The experimental analysis of motivational factors in perception, pp. 59–108.

Nowlis, V. The development and modification of motivational systems in personality, pp. 114–138.

Newcomb, T. M. Motivation in social behavior, pp. 139–161.

Mowrer, O. H. Motivation and neurosis, pp. 162–185.

1954 (Vol. 2)

Farber, I. E. Anxiety as a drive state, pp. 1–46.

Atkinson, J. W. Exploration using imaginative thought to assess the strength of human motives, pp. 56–112.

Ritchie, B. F. A logical and experimental analysis of the laws of motivation, pp. 121–176.

Festinger, L. Motivation leading to social behavior, pp. 191–219.

Klein, G. S. Need and regulation, pp. 224–274.

Nissen, H. W. The nature of the drive as innate determinant of behavioral organization, pp. 281–321.

1955 (Vol. 3)

Maslow, A. Deficiency motivation and growth motivation, pp. 1–30.

McClelland, D. C. Some social consequences of achievement motivation, pp. 41–65.

Olds, J. Physiological mechanisms of reward, pp. 73–139.

Peak, H. Attitude and motivation, pp. 149–189.

Young, P. T. The role of hedonic processes in motivation, pp. 193–238.

Rotter, J. B. The role of the psychological situation in determining the direction of human behavior, pp. 245–269.

1956 (Vol. 4)

Beach, F. A. Characteristics of masculine "sex drive," pp. 1–32.
Koch, S. Behavior as "intrinsically" regulated: Work notes towards a pre-theory of phenomena called "motivational," pp. 42–87.
Marx, M. H. Some relations between frustration and drive, pp. 92–130.
Miller, D. R., & Swanson, G. E. The study of conflict, pp. 137–174.
Seward, J. P. A neurological approach to motivation, pp. 180–208.
Solomon, R. L., & Brush, E. S. Experimentally derived conceptions of anxiety and aversion, pp. 212–305.

1957 (Vol. 5)

Morgan, C. T. Physiological mechanisms of motivation, pp. 1–35.
Lindsley, D. B. Psychophysiology and motivation, pp. 44–105.
Rodnick, E. H., & Garmezy, N. An experimental approach to the study of motivation in schizophrenia, pp. 109–184.
Wittenborn, J. R. Inferring the strength of drive, pp. 191–259.
Sears, P. S. Problems in the investigation of achievement and self-esteem motivation, pp. 265–339.
Osgood, C. E. Motivational dynamics of language behavior, pp. 348–424.

1958 (Vol. 6)

Bolles, R. C. The usefulness of the drive concept, pp. 1–33.
Estes, W. K. Stimulus-response theory of drive, pp. 35–69.
Spence, K. W. Behavior theory and selective learning, pp. 73–107.
Littman, R. A. Motives, history, and causes, pp. 114–168.
Eriksen, C. W. Unconscious processes, pp. 169–227.
Malmo, R. B. Measurement of drive: An unsolved problem in psychology, pp. 229–265.

1959 (Vol. 7)

Schneirla, T. C. An evolutionary and developmental theory of biphasic processes underlying approach and withdrawal, pp. 1–42.
Hess, E. The relationship between imprinting and motivation, pp. 44–77.
Cattell, R. B. The dynamic calculus: Concepts and crucial experiments, pp. 84–134.
Levin, H., & Baldwin, A. L. Pride and shame in children, pp. 138–174.
Whiting, J. W. M. Sorcery, sin, and the superego. A cross-cultural study of some mechanisms of social control, pp. 174–195.
Janis, I. L. Motivational factors in the resolution of decisional conflicts, pp. 198–231.

1960 (Vol. 8)

Barker, R. G. Ecology and motivation, pp. 1–49.

Mandler, G. The interruption of behavior, pp. 163–219.
Schachter, S., & Latané, B. Crime, cognition, and the autonomic nervous system, pp. 221–273.

1965 (Vol. 13)

Kendler, H. H. Motivation and behavior, pp. 1–23.
Leeper, R. W. Some needed developments in the motivational theory of emotions, pp. 25–122.
Premack, D. Reinforcement theory, pp. 123–180.
Hunt, J. McV. Intrinsic motivation and its role in psychological development, pp. 189–282.
Campbell, D. T. Ethnocentric and other altruistic motives, pp. 283–311.
Guilford, J. P. Motivation in an informational psychology, pp. 313–332.

1966 (Vol. 14)

Holt, R. R. Measuring libidinal and aggressive motives and their controls by means of the Rorschach test, pp. 1–47.
Burke, C. J. Linear models for Pavlovian conditioning, pp. 49–66.
Masling, J. Role-related behavior of the subject and psychologist and its effects upon psychological data, pp. 67–103.
Dethier, V. G. Insects and the concept of motivation, pp. 105–136.
Helson, H. Some problems in motivation from the point of view of the theory of adaptation level, pp. 137–182.
Malamud, W. The concept of motivation in psychiatric practice, pp. 183–200.

1967 (Vol. 15)

Berlyne, D. E. Arousal and reinforcement, pp. 1–110.
Scott, J. P. The development of social motivation, pp. 111–132.
Katz, I. The socialization of academic motivation in minority group children, pp. 133–191.
Kelley, H. H. Attribution theory in social psychology, pp. 192–238.
Pettigrew, T. F. Social evaluation theory: Convergences and applications, pp. 241–311.

1968 (Vol. 16)

Grossmann, S. P. The physiological basis of specific and nonspecific motivational processes, pp. 1–46.
McClearn, G. E. Genetics and motivation of the mouse, pp. 47–83.
Levine, S. Hormones and conditioning, pp. 85–101.
Heckhausen, H. Achievement motive research: Current problems and some contributions towards a general theory of motivation, pp. 103–174.
Lazarus, R. S. Emotions and adaptation: Conceptual and empirical relations, pp. 175–266.
Aronfreed, J. Aversive control of socialization, pp. 271–320.

1973 (Vol. 21)

Alphabetical List of Contents of the Nebraska Symposia on Motivation by Author

Cook, S. W. Motives in a conceptual analysis of attitude-related behavior. 1969, **17**, 179–231.

Denenberg, V. H. The mother as a motivator. 1970, **18**, 69–93.

Dethier, V. G. Insects and the concept of motivation. 1966, **14**, 105–136.

Deutsch, M. Cooperation and trust: Some theoretical notes. 1962, **10**, 275–319.

Donaldson, M. Preconditions of inference. 1971, **19**, 81–106.

Edwards, A. L. The assessment of human motives by means of personality scales. 1964, **12**, 135–162.

Ekman, P. Universals and cultural differences in facial expressions of emotion. 1971, **19**, 207–284.

Elkind, D. Cognitive growth cycles in mental development. 1971, **19**, 1–32.

Epstein, S. The measurement of drive and conflict in humans: Theory and experiment. 1962, **10**, 127–206.

Eriksen, C. W. Unconscious processes. 1958, **6**, 169–227.

Estes, W. K. Stimulus-response theory of drive. 1958, **6**, 35–69.

Exline, R. Visual interaction: The glances of power and preference. 1971, **19**, 163–206.

Falk, J. L. The behavioral regulation of water-electrolyte balance. 1961, **9**, 1–33.

Farber, I. E. Anxiety as a drive state. 1954, **2**, 1–46.

Festinger, L. Motivation leading to social behavior. 1954, **2**, 191–219.

Flynn, J. P. Patterning mechanisms, patterned reflexes, and attack behavior in cats. 1972, **20**, 125–153.

Gagnon, J. H. Scripts and the coordination of sexual conduct. 1973, **21**, 27–60.

Grossman, S. P. The physiological basis of specific and non-specific motivational processes. 1968, **16**, 1–46.

Guilford, J. P. Motivation in an informational psychology. 1965, **13**, 313–332.

Harlow, H. F. Motivation as a factor in new responses. 1953, **1**, 24–49.

Heckhausen, H. Achievement motive research: Current problems and some contributions towards a general theory of motivation. 1968, **16**, 103–174.

Heider, F. The Gestalt theory of motivation. 1960, **8**, 145–172.

Heilbrun, A. B., Jr. Parent identification and filial sex-role behavior: The importance of biological context. 1973, **21**, 125–194.

Helson, H. Some problems in motivation from the point of view of the theory of adaptation level. 1966, **14**, 137–182.

Hess, E. The relationship between imprinting and motivation. 1959, **7**, 44–77.

Hilgard, E. R. The motivational relevance of hypnosis. 1964, **12**, 1–44.

Holt, R. R. Measuring libidinal and aggressive motives and their controls by means of the Rorschach test. 1966, **14**, 1–47.

Hunt, J. McV. Intrinsic motivation and its role in psychological development. 1965, **13**, 189–282.

Hutchinson, R. R. The environmental causes of aggression. 1972, **20**, 155–181.

Janis, I. L. Motivational factors in the resolution of decisional conflicts. 1959, **7**, 198–231.

Katz, I. The socialization of academic motivation in minority group children. 1967, **15**, 133–191.

Newcomb, T. M. Motivation in social behavior. 1953, 1, 139–161.

Nissen, H. W. The nature of the drive as innate determinant of behavioral organization. 1954, 2, 281–321.

Nowlis, V. The development and modification of motivational systems in personality. 1953, 1, 114–138.

Olds, J. Physiological mechanisms of reward. 1955, 3, 73–139.

Olweus, D. Personality and aggression. 1972, 20, 261–321.

Orne, M. T. Hypnosis, motivation, and the ecological validity of the psychological experiment. 1970, 18, 187–265.

Osgood, C. E. Motivational dynamics of language behavior. 1957, 5, 348–424.

Peak, H. Attitude and motivation. 1955, 3, 149–189.

Pettigrew, T. F. Social evaluation theory: Convergences and applications. 1967, 15, 241–311.

Pfaffman, C. The sensory and motivating properties of the sense of taste. 1961, 9, 71–108.

Postman, L. J. The experimental analysis of motivational factors in perception. 1953, 1, 59–108.

Premack, D. Reinforcement theory. 1965, 13, 123–180.

Pribram, K. H. Reinforcement revisited: A structural view. 1963, 11, 113–159.

Rapaport, D. On the psychoanalytic theory of motivation. 1960, 8, 173–247.

Ritchie, B. F. A logical and experimental analysis of the laws of motivation. 1954, 2, 121–176.

Rodnick, E. H., & Garmezy, N. An experimental approach to the study of motivation in schizophrenia. 1957, 5, 109–184.

Rogers, C. R. Actualizing tendency in relation to "motives" and to consciousness. 1963, 11, 1–24.

Rosenberg, B. G., & Sutton-Smith, B. Family structure and sex-role variations. 1973, 21, 195–220.

Rotter, J. B. The role of the psychological situation in determining the direction of human behavior. 1955, 3, 245–269.

Sarason, S. B. The contents of human problem solving. 1961, 9, 147–174.

Schachter, S., & Latané, B. Crime, cognition, and the autonomic nervous system. 1964, 12, 221–273.

Schneirla, T. C. An evolutionary and developmental theory of biphasic processes underlying approach and withdrawal. 1959, 7, 1–42.

Scott, J. P. The development of social motivation. 1967, 15, 111–132.

Sears, P. S. Problems in the investigation of achievement and self-esteem motivation. 1957, 5, 265–339.

Sears, R. R. Dependency motivation. 1963, 11, 25–64.

Seward, J. P. A neurological approach to motivation. 1956, 4, 180–208.

Simon, W. The social, the erotic, and the sensual: The complexities of sexual scripts. 1973, 21, 61–82.

Solomon, R. L., & Brush, E. S. Experimentally derived conceptions of anxiety and aversion. 1956, 4, 212–305.

Spence, K. W. Behavior theory and selective learning. 1958, 6, 73–107.

Subject Index

Author Index